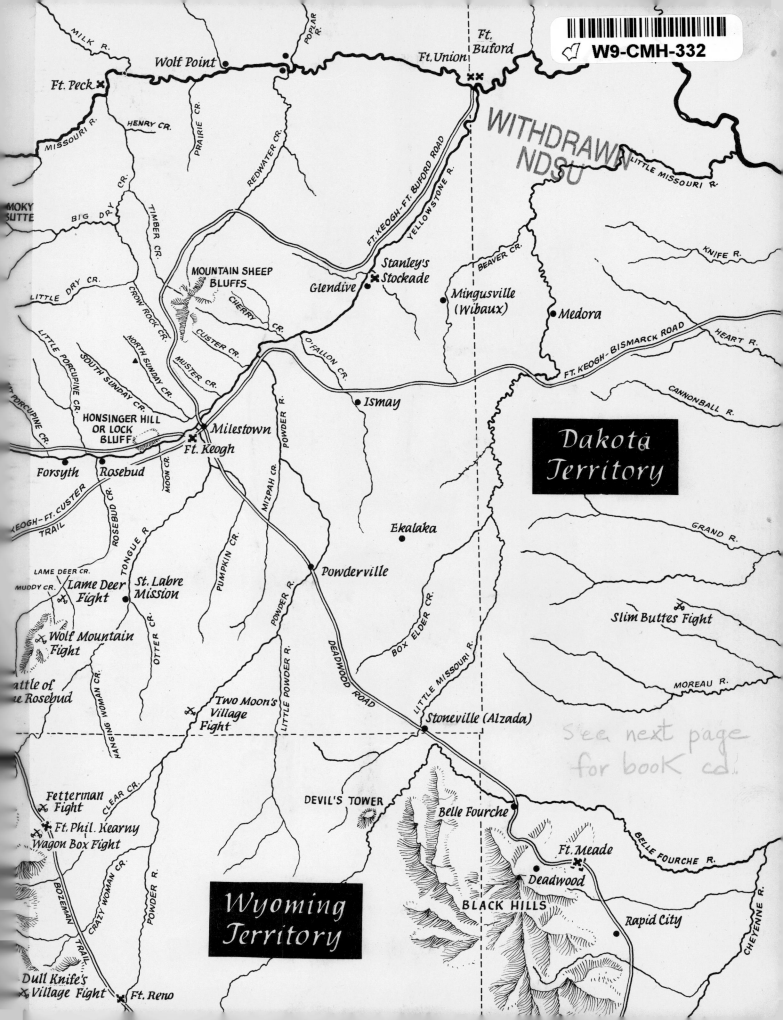

MILK R.

Wolf Point

POPLAR R.

Ft. Union

Ft. Buford

Ft. Peck

MISSOURI R.

HENRY CR.

PRAIRIE CR.

REDWATER CR.

LITTLE MISSOURI R.

KNIFE R.

SMOKY BUTTE

BIG DRY CR.

TIMBER CR.

MOUNTAIN SHEEP BLUFFS

FT. KEOGH-FT. BUFORD ROAD

YELLOWSTONE R.

Stanley's Stockade

Glendive

BEAVER CR.

Mingusville (Wibaux)

Medora

LITTLE DRY CR.

LITTLE DRY CR.

CROW ROCK CR.

NORTH SUNDAY CR.

CHERRY CR.

CUSTER CR.

MUSTER CR.

O'FALLON CR.

FT. KEOGH-BISMARCK ROAD

HEART R.

CANNONBALL R.

PORCUPINE CR.

LITTLE PORCUPINE CR.

SOUTH SUNDAY CR.

Ismay

Dakota Territory

HONSINGER HILL OR LOCK BLUFF

Milestown
Ft. Keogh

POWDER R.

MIZPAH CR.

Forsyth

Rosebud

MOON CR.

Ekalaka

GRAND R.

KEOGH-FT. CUSTER TRAIL

ROSEBUD CR.

TONGUE R.

PUMPKIN CR.

Powderville

POWDER R.

BOX ELDER CR.

LITTLE MISSOURI R.

Slim Buttes Fight

LAME DEER CR.

MUDDY CR.

Lame Deer Fight

St. Labre Mission

OTTER CR.

DEADWOOD ROAD

MOREAU R.

Wolf Mountain Fight

LITTLE POWDER R.

attle of e Rosebud

HANGING WOMAN CR.

Two Moon's Village Fight

Stoneville (Alzada)

See next page for book cd.

Fetterman Fight

CLEAR CR.

DEVIL'S TOWER

Belle Fourche

BELLE FOURCHE R.

Ft. Phil. Kearny
Wagon Box Fight

CRAZY WOMAN CR.

POWDER R.

Ft. Meade

Deadwood

BOZEMAN TRAIL

Wyoming Territory

BLACK HILLS

Rapid City

CHEYENNE R.

Dull Knife's Village Fight

Ft. Reno

THE FRONTIER YEARS

©L.A.Huffman   (1926)   1854–1931

by Mark H. Brown

and W. R. Felton

THE FRONTIER YEARS

L. A. HUFFMAN, Photographer of the Plains

HENRY HOLT AND COMPANY · NEW YORK

DEDICATED to those friends of L. A. Huffman who loved their Montana homeland better than life itself—Little Wolf, Dull Knife, and their people

CONTENTS

PROLOGUE

These are the scars of an old trail cut in the virgin sod of a Western prairie. Before they were blotted out by the plow, such marks were to be seen crisscrossing every state in the West. Some were cut by the hoofs of long lines of buffalo filing from the open prairie to water, others were worn by the trail herds from Texas and Oregon, and still others were ground out by the wheels of heavily loaded wagons. Most of these marks are uninteresting to look at, yet they can provoke, in the mind of a pioneer who had traveled along them, nostalgic memories of yesterday. Forever lost, however, are the thoughts which were in the mind of the pioneer photographer who took this photograph.

This picture shows part of the frontier highway which linked Fort Keogh, Montana, to Bismarck, North Dakota, in the late 1870's and early 1880's. Along its 300-odd miles—in blistering heat, stinging cold, sticky mud, choking dust, and driving snow—rolled the wagon trains of the freighters, stagecoaches, buckboards of the mail-carriers, wagons of the hide-hunters and ranchers, and many other vehicles. And those who passed this way were a colorful procession. There were bull-whackers and mule-skinners with long lash and vivid profanity, stagecoach drivers proud of their skill with reins and whip, cavalry and infantry, merchants, brides on their way to the task of making a home of a rough log cabin, prostitutes, gamblers, "soldiers of fortune" far from their native land, outlaws, cowboys, and, at rare intervals, a doctor making a lonely trip of 30 or 50 or 80 miles behind a pair of broncs that had to be tied to a post before they could be hitched.

Memories of all of these must have passed through the mind of the man who took this picture. Perhaps, in his imagination, he also saw the Seventh Cavalry on their way to that sagebrush-covered ridge along the Little Big Horn River from which almost half of them never returned. And no doubt he remembered vividly a bitter cold day in December years before, when, in a mail-carrier's buckboard with an outlaw for a fellow passenger, he, too, traveled along this trail.

While the written word has done much to preserve history, pictures are necessary to supplement the printed page. No other section of the American frontier has been so richly endowed with a pictorial record of its past as has the area encompassed by the headwaters of the Missouri River and its tributary, the Yellowstone. For almost a century, beginning in the 1830's, artists with pencil and brush added to this record. Although paintings and drawings often provide a very valuable record, when pictures are considered from the standpoint of exactness the work of the photographer must come first. Only the camera can make a precise record of a scene or subject.

Several photographers have worked on this frontier. In the 1870's William H. Jackson, W. H. Illingworth, S. J. Morrow, and D. F. Barry made visits to this area and gathered an assortment of pictures. Then, in the evening of December 11, 1878, a new post photographer arrived at Fort Keogh, Montana Territory. He was L. A. Huffman, a young man of pioneer stock, and he came to stay. When he died in 1931, he left a priceless collection of pictures of Indians in the last days of buffalo-skin tepees, hide-hunters, and the buffalo, the days of the open range when men carried the law on their hips, the lonely life of the sheepherder, the growth of the range towns, the coming of the railroads, and the final infiltration of the "plow man."

On the pages which follow are reproduced a part of what Huffman regarded as the best of his "gatherings." These are the pictures of the people whose work and play etched these ruts in the prairie sod. Thanks to Huffman's work, it is possible to turn back the clock of time to the day when

'Twas good to live when all the sod
  Without no fence or fuss,
Belonged in partnership to God
  The Gover'ment and us.
With skyline bounds from east to west
  And room to go and come,
I loved my fellow man the best
  When he was scattered some.[1]

There was a sunny, savage land
    Beneath the eagle's wings
And there, across the thorns and sand,
    Wild rovers rode as kings.[1]
                    Badger Clark

MONTANA—1860 to 1878

The last frontier—that vast stretch of open country in the western Dakotas, eastern Montana, and northern Wyoming which was the home of the Crows, Sioux, Northern Cheyennes, Blackfeet, and the last great herds of buffalo—had a fascination for adventurous men. True, there were furs to be had for the trapping, grains of gold among the sands of some of the streams in adjacent mountains, and wide ranges on which to raise cattle. But there was something more—the land was open and wild, and its freedom and dangers had a strong attraction for those bred in the restless tradition of the frontier.

It is not strange that this land should have attracted L. A. Huffman. His forefathers were frontiersmen when war parties of Shawnees and Delawares, silently and in single file, threaded their way through the forests of Ohio and West Virginia, and when emigrants and their belongings floated down the Ohio River in flatboats to the settlements farther west. When an old man, Huffman wrote that "Tales of these days told me by my grandfathers kindled in my boyish heart the desire to push beyond the horizon." However, when he came to Montana Territory the wild, free life of the early frontier was drawing to a close, and it fell his lot to record only the final days of this period. And because his story is not complete within itself, the thread of the history of the preceding years has been outlined here.

This was, and still is, a magnificent country, its broad expanses of brown prairie broken here and there by an isolated butte, a range of rugged, pine-topped hills, or rough breaks along the streams. Mountains, dark with pine, rose sharply from the plain. Etched deeply into the expanses of prairie were the valleys

2. "Corraled for the Noon Change."

of the Missouri, the Yellowstone, and their tributaries. These were bordered here and there by areas of rugged badlands, grim and forbidding to the traveler but with a certain eerie beauty in the softly blended blues, grays, and yellowish-browns of the shales and sandstones. And where the dull red scoria occurred, it is not difficult to understand why General Sully remarked as he stood on the eastern escarpment of those badlands along the Little Missouri, "There is Hell with the fires out." It was a magnificent country, but now it is fenced and the romance and the wildlife that were once a part of it are gone. Only the prairies and the mountains and the memories remain.

Plains and mountains constituted only a part of the picture. There were streams of sweet, life-sustaining water, and sluggish streams and pools bitter and deadly with alkali. Winter's numbing cold threatened and took life, and so did the shimmering heat of summer. And the wind, unobstructed in its course, blew for days on end, an endless tugging at everything, movable and immovable. In the spring when there was rain, the prairies were green and the frogs croaked day and night, and even the barren badlands were decked with yellow daisies, deep mauve hyacinthine blossoms, the carmine of clustering vetches, and the white of Mariposa lilies; but for the rest of the year plant life was almost dormant. However, there was something more about the country than that which met the eye. The great spaces forced themselves upon those who traveled or lived on them, and sometimes demanded that they must be felt as well as seen. Perhaps it was the ease with which one could see great distances, perhaps it was the clear, blue sky overhead or the stars seemingly so close and large at night, perhaps it was the ceaseless wind, perhaps it was the mysterious blue haze on the distant hills—one thing was certain, once one had seen and felt this country, one never forgot.

Across this vast stage moved many colorful individuals to play their bits in a frontier drama which lasted for almost a century. These varied as to race, background, morals, and occupation but they all had one imagination-capturing quality—their daily lives were rarely characterized by colorless mediocrity. Some were good and some were bad, but those who were inefficient were not likely to be blessed with long life, for the frontier was no place for amateurs, honest or dishonest, moral or immoral. And fate, fickle as always, rewarded some with fame—sometimes earned, sometimes unearned—others with fleeting recognition that lasted for a generation, and many with a nameless and forgotten grave.

Even when Huffman came to Fort Keogh part of the history of this prairie frontier lived only in the memories of old-timers. To the westward beside the Yellowstone River, "Pompys Tower" stood as a reminder of William Clark and his venturesome companions as did, also, Buffalo Rapids to the eastward. However, of the little log trading posts which once dotted the valley of the Yellowstone not even a mark on the prairie sod remained to show where they stood. Dead for many years in forgotten graves were most of those to whom a horse, a Hawken rifle, a squaw, and a few beaver traps represented the essentials necessary for a way of life. Dead also was Father Pierre—Jean De Smet, the fearless priest whose doings left a lasting impression. But tales of the adventures of these days were still related beside campfires; and there were still scars from the days when alcohol was used to debauch and swindle the Indian, and from the scourge of smallpox brought by the steamboat *St. Peters* and her infected cargo in 1837.

3.   "Mandan Earth Lodge. Lewis and Clark Trail, west bank Big Missouri."

4. "One of the Last of the Mandans, Nov. 20, 1902."

However, it was not necessary to recall the days of Lewis and Clark and the fur trade to find stories of stirring adventure, for many of Huffman's associates had had colorful experiences of their own. When the fur trade began to lose its importance as a major enterprise, gold-mining came into prominence in the mountain valleys near the headwaters of the Missouri. A French half-breed discovered gold in 1852, but it was not until five years later when a group of unsuccessful miners returning to the States from California turned north to prospect that an effort was made to exploit this knowledge. In 1861, after considerable prospecting, these men found gold in paying quantities, and in June, 1862, the fabulously rich strike in Alder Gulch was revealed. Thousands of fortune-seekers flocked into this 12-mile-long valley and by the end of the year the sands of this little stream and the alder-covered flats adjacent to it had yielded an estimated $10,000,000 in dust and nuggets.

Included in the horde who flocked to these diggings were industrious and upright citizens, parasites as gamblers and prostitutes, and some of the toughest thugs the frontier ever knew. Three towns, Nevada and Virginia City in Alder Gulch and Bannock on Grasshopper Creek, mushroomed. Life in these towns moved at a fantastic pace, and in Virginia City every third building was a saloon and houses of ill fame were almost as numerous. However, placer-mining was as transitory an occupation as was the trapping of beaver from these same streams 20 or 30 years before. When the gold was gone, the life it supported also vanished.

5. Leggins, a Mandan Indian.

One facet of this life—the vigilantes—did leave a lasting impression, however, and set a pattern—in more ways than one—for action on future occasions.

The primitive law enforcement of miners' courts broke down when honest men did not dare express their opinions to their neighbors; and it took a determined effort on the part of a small, well-organized group to break the web of fear spun by the gang of road agents, stool pigeons, and their helpers captained by the often-genial, well-groomed gambler, Henry Plummer. Among these vigilantes were several who later became good friends of Huffman. One of these was Granville Stuart who, with his brother James, is credited with setting the first sluice to wash gold in Montana. Granville was running a blacksmith shop in Virginia City when the vigilantes put an effective stop to the activities of the "Innocents," as the outlaws called themselves. Twenty years later when he assumed command of the vigilantes who waged war on the cattle rustlers in eastern Montana, Stuart put to effective use the procedures he learned here.

Another whom Huffman knew was John X. Biedler, or "X" as he was usually called. "X" ran a saloon for a time in Milestown, the frontier village which grew into Miles City, but he spent most of his later years as an officer of the law. He was a very efficient man in a cheerful sort of way and was well known for his wit and quick thinking in tight spots. It was he who lent something more than moral support to Colonel Wilbur Saunders, the prosecutor at the crucial trial of George Ives, by patrolling the edges of the restless throng at that open-air court with a double-barreled shotgun on his shoulder.[2] He also officiated as adjuster of the ropes for the five who were hanged at one time from the ridgepole of an unfinished cabin in Virginia City.

The activity in the gold fields emphasized one of the disadvantages of Montana—inaccessibility. The road which Lieutenant John Mullen, at the direction of Congress, surveyed and built between the heads of navigation on the Missouri and Columbia rivers during the years of 1859–1862 helped to lessen the problem. However, it did not eliminate the long miles between Fort Benton and the lower river ports or the treacherous sand bars and snags which menaced steamboat navigation. The other means of access was by road to Fort Hall, but freight over this route had to be twice-hauled over the continental divide. In the winter of 1862–1863, John Bozeman and his partner laid out the obvious short cut to the Overland Trail by the way of the eastern edge of the Big Horn Mountains—but the Sioux would not tolerate a wagon road through their choice hunting grounds. The closing of this road, hazardous as it had been, by the treaty of 1868 caused considerable grumbling at the northern terminus; and, of course, it was the breaking of this treaty which paved the way for the last war with the Sioux.

There were other developments during this decade of the 1860's. Cattle and sheep were trailed to the mining camps to be killed for meat, thus starting the livestock industry on the plains adjacent to the mountains. The end of the Civil War brought a flood of restless men, many of them Confederate soldiers seeking a new stake for themselves. Fort Union, a symbol of the power of the American Fur Company for 39 years, was abandoned in 1868. Small trading posts sprang up here and there over the country but the days of the old-time beaver trapper were gone. The Territory of Montana stood on the threshold of a new era, and the old life tottered on feeble legs.

The early 1870's brought hopes that the problem of transportation would soon be solved. While the track-laying parties were pushing across the Dakota prairies to Bismarck, the Northern Pacific Railroad began surveys in the Yellowstone Valley. The Sioux and Cheyennes forced the party working in the upper Yellowstone Valley to abandon its work in 1872; and the following year the surveying party went out from Bismarck with a strong military escort under the command of General David Stanley. Included in these troops was part of the Seventh Cavalry under (then) Lieutenant Colonel George A. Custer.[3] While Custer's men were in the vicinity of Lock Bluff, a few miles above the present location of Miles City, Rain-in-the-Face killed the veterinary surgeon and the regimental sutler, thus beginning an incident which lasted three years and ended in a myth which has been perpetuated to the present day.

Custer's report of finding gold on French Creek while making an armed reconnaissance of the Black Hills sent a horde of miners into this forbidden area. The government made a feeble effort to eject the illegal entrants, the Sioux refused to sell, and in 1875 General Sheridan, foreseeing the inevitable, sent a small party from Fort Abraham Lincoln to make a reconnaissance of the Yellowstone Valley. This survey was made by water and Grant Marsh, the able shallow-water pilot, took the lightly loaded *Josephine* to Hell Roaring Rapids, a record 483 miles above the mouth of the river.

Ten days after Marsh set this record, Major F. D. Pease [4] and two partners,

6. "Snake Whistle, a young Cheyenne warrior, 1879."

having conceived the idea that a trading post at the mouth of the Big Horn would prove profitable, launched three loaded flatboats on the swift current of the upper Yellowstone. Pease and this party of 25 reached the broad bench opposite the mouth of the Big Horn after swamping one boat and upsetting another, fortunately without serious loss, and built a stockaded post about 100 feet square. Although the Crows were friendly, the Sioux maintained a hostile vigil that made life uncertain for those who lived at the post. In March of the following year a party of soldiers and civilians came down from Fort Ellis, and although "none of those at the stockade but the traders wished to leave . . . all were forced to go." [5]

As Major Pease's venture was breaking up, General Crook's troops were marching north from Fort Fetterman to fight the first engagement in Sitting Bull's war—a war which was to provide many fascinating human-interest details, and an exhibition of childish planning in the War Department. The grand strategy envisioned Crook marching northward from Fort Fetterman, Terry coming in from Fort Abraham Lincoln, and Gibbon bringing his troops down

7.   "Young Spotted Eagle."

from Fort Ellis and Fort Shaw. These three forces were to converge on the prairie stronghold of the Sioux and crush the hostiles between them. What the War Department generals overlooked was that the principles of war operate regardless of whether the foe is civilized or uncivilized. Specifically, the cardinal rule which was ignored in this campaign Napoleon set down as his Fourth Maxim of War:

> When one marches to the conquest of a country with two or three armies, each of which has its separate line of operation up to a certain point, it is a principle that the union of these various bodies must never be made near the enemy, because the enemy, by concentrating his forces, may not only prevent their junction but *may beat them separately.*

The contemplated maneuver could not be properly coordinated, and the uneducated savages unwittingly exploited their opportunity to an extent sufficient to almost nullify the efforts of the troops.

The various movements of the columns in the field, almost invariably presented in part or in a piecemeal manner in popular accounts, were: Crook's troops marched northward early in March, fought an abortive action against Two Moon's winter camp,[6] and then had to return to their base of supplies and refit. As Crook was withdrawing, Gibbon came down the north bank of the Yellowstone as far as Fort Pease where dispatches reached him directing that he not advance farther until Terry and Crook could get started—a "pleasant" situation in the middle of a hostile country! Several weeks later Terry and Gibbon finally united their troops. As these two generals were planning a pincers movement against the Sioux camp—about which they had practically no concrete intelligence—Crazy Horse hit Crook's column on the Rosebud and forced the troops to turn back to their temporary supply base at the foot of the Big Horns. There they marked time for over a month until reinforced by Merritt's men. The hostiles, flushed by this victory, inflicted a disastrous defeat on Custer a few days later—who also made the error of attempting a maneuver with divided forces, the movements of which he could not coordinate. Then they scattered like a covey of quail before the column of Terry and Gibbon.

Finally, in August all the troops united in the valley of the Yellowstone. With supplies short, clothing worn, and Crow and Shoshone scouts restless to return home, the force broke up. Some of the troops returned to their home bases; Terry left Miles on the Yellowstone to establish the Tongue River Cantonment and to chase some of the scattered bands of hostiles; and Crook's troops went eastward and then southward to Deadwood in one of the most grueling marches ever made by troops in the West. All that had been accomplished was to keep the hostiles stirred up and not permit them to spend the summer in peace.

But the constant pressure on the Indians paid off the following winter. Crook's column, reformed around Mackenzie, and the Fourth Cavalry fresh from the southwest, together with a large force of Indian scouts, destroyed Dull Knife's winter camp one bitterly cold November morning, and forced the Cheyennes and some of the Sioux to recognize the handwriting on the wall. Most of them surrendered early the next spring—all but Sitting Bull and his immediate followers. This stouthearted patriot slipped across the line into Canada, defeated but still free and defiant.

In contrast to the drab military results, the human-interest angles of this campaign were many and colorful: Crook's troopers, on the first winter campaign, living on the bleak plains without shelter in weather so cold that loaves of bread at the campfire were often thawed at one end and "hard as flint and cold as charity" on the other; Bourke, Crook's aide, watching with enthusiastic admiration the precise drilling of the Shoshone scouts under an ex-Confederate cavalryman; Gibbon's men idling at Fort Pease while Two Moon and some of his warriors stole the ponies of the Crow scouts out from under their very noses—a most humiliating thing to the cleverest horse thieves on the plains; Matt Carroll, the Diamond R wagon boss, pushing his wagon train at the marching speed of cavalry in the wake of Terry's troops; Little Face, the Crow scout, relating in a "choking voice" the first news of Custer's defeat to Lieutenant Bradley, while his companions sitting on the ground nearby wept and chanted a "dreadful mourning song"—and Bradley reporting the grim story to Terry who sat on his horse "silent and thoughtful, biting his lower lip" while other members of his staff sneered at the story; and Marsh driving the *Far West* 710 miles in a record 54 hours to bring the wounded—and the story—to Bismarck, only to find that "moccasin telegraph" had already brought word of the disaster.

And the color continued to the end of the campaign: Crook's troopers laboriously plodding through the gumbo mud to Deadwood—often without wood for fires, drenched almost daily by cold rains, boots shrunk on their swollen feet, and almost nothing to eat but the leathery, nauseating meat of exhausted horses and mules; the deadly tribal hatreds within Crook's force of Indian scouts before

8. "Scorched Lightning. Mininconjoux Sioux in [grizzly] bear necklace."

he moved out against Dull Knife—the North Brothers' Pawnees looking with covetous eyes at the scalp locks of Lieutenant Clark's Sioux and Cheyennes; and one of the bravest of the Sioux scouts coming into Bourke's tent the night after the troops had destroyed Dull Knife's camp and, with tears in his eyes, lamenting, "Cheyenne papoose heap hung'y." No other campaign in the West produced such a varied array of "color."

This war also saw some famous scouts in action. The most valuable was Crook's favorite, Frank Grouard, son of a Frenchman and a South Pacific islander. The Hunkpapa and Oglala warriors, among whom this dark-complexioned mixed blood spent five years as a captive, believed as long as they lived that he was part Sioux and laughed at anyone who tried to tell them differently.[7] William F. "Buffalo Bill" Cody, the genial, likable plainsman with a decided flair for self-aggrandizement—sometimes at the expense of fact—served in a minor capacity under Merritt. Custer's favorite, soft-spoken "Lonesome Charley" Reynolds, on whose shoulders rested a mantle of mystery, died in the initial clash in the Battle of the Little Big Horn. Frank North, who with his brother Luther North led a formidable band of Pawnee scouts, was probably the best revolver shot in that part of the West, not excepting the legendary James "Wild Bill" Hickok.[8] Luther S. "Yellowstone" Kelly, engaged by Miles when the latter built the Tongue River Cantonment, served during the latter part of the campaign and was regarded as a very valuable scout. And although not a plainsman, Captain Grant Marsh had a niche of his own—he had no peer on the upper Missouri as a steamboat pilot.

The summer and fall of 1877 saw the strangest of all the Indian wars fought. Greedy settlers in western Idaho goaded the intelligent, friendly, honest Nez

9. "Spotted Eagle's Hostile Sioux Village."

Perce until they went on the warpath. Chief Joseph, realizing his people could no longer remain in their homeland, led them eastward across the rugged Coeur d'Alenes, southward and eastward across the Yellowstone National Park, and then northward in one last desperate push for freedom beyond the Canadian border. When Miles surrounded him in the Bear Paw Mountains he thought he was safely across the border. Joseph had done the unprecedented by fighting a war, for the most part, according to the white man's code and, although untrained in the art of war, he demonstrated conclusively that he was a fine general. His 2000-mile retreat, encumbered by all his people and their impedimenta, was an achievement of which any military man could have been proud.

This—very briefly—is the story of the frontier to which Huffman came. Even as he arrived, Little Wolf and Dull Knife were leading part of the homesick Northern Cheyennes in a courageous struggle to escape from the reservation in Indian Territory to their Montana homeland. At Fort Keogh he met scouts and soldiers who had seen action against the Sioux and the Nez Perce. Among these were Lieutenant W. P. Clark who had starved with Crook and who had charged with Mackenzie into Dull Knife's camp; Lieutenant Sibley had been in charge of a small party which played a desperate game of hide-and-seek with a band of Sioux in the Big Horns after the Battle of the Rosebud; and Lieutenant Godfrey had ridden with Custer and had been wounded in Joseph's last stand. Among the scouts were "Yellowstone" Kelly, Johnny "Big Leggins" Bruguier[9] who, like Grouard, had lived with Sitting Bull, "Liver-Eating" Johnson, Joe Culbertson, and the cripple George Boyd whose club feet left a trail—so one story goes —that confused a Sioux hunting party and saved his life.[10]

In the nearby camps were Hump and his Minniconjou, Two Moon and part of the Cheyennes, and important men like Fire Wolf, Spotted Bear, and Brave Wolf whose stories should have been recorded. On the streets of Milestown and in his little studio he met Granville Stuart, "X" Biedler, Major Pease and his associates, Captain Marsh, Calamity Jane, Jim Pym, and many others to whom fate has not been so kind. It must have been with thoughts of these in mind that a Montana poet wrote:

> O dimming trails of other days,
> Your lure, your glamour, and your ways
> Will last while those who knew you live.
> And, fading, to the past will give,
> To guard and to forever hold,
> A wealth of stories never told.[11]

Kind fate had it I should be Post Photographer with the Army during the Indian campaigns close following the annihilation of Custer's command. This Yellowstone–Big Horn country was then unpenned of wire, and unspoiled by railway, dam or ditch. Eastman had not yet made the Kodak, but thanks be, there was the old wet plate, the collodion bottle and bath. I made photographs. With crude home-made cameras, from saddle and in log shack, I saved something. Yes, it was worthwhile, despite the attendant and ungodly smells of the old process.

Round about us the army of buffalo hunters—red men and white—were waging the final war of extermination upon the last great herds of American bison seen upon this continent. Then came the cattleman, the "trail boss" with his army of cowboys, and the great cattle roundups. Then the army of railroad builders. That—the railway—was the fatal coming. One looked about and said, "This is the last West." It was not so. There *was* no more West after that. It was a dream and a forgetting, a chapter forever closed.

L. A. Huffman

L. A. HUFFMAN, FRONTIER PHOTOGRAPHER

Few pioneers left a complete record of their lives and Huffman was no exception. His pictures and fragmentary manuscripts[1] recorded bits of the lives of those among whom he lived; but his own personal experiences, for the most part, have been handed down by word of mouth, and his quiet modesty, even with his own family, has undoubtedly left many interesting experiences untold. This brief sketch, pieced together from various scattered bits, provides a general picture of the man, his problems, his equipment, and his personality, all of which are reflected in various ways in his photographs.

Laton Alton Huffman was born October 31, 1854, on a frontier farm near Castalia, Iowa. His father, Perrin Cuppy Huffman, was the grandson of a German emigrant; his mother's maiden name was Chastina M. Baird. Laton had no brothers and only one sister, Ardelle—or Dell as he usually called her. His forebears were pioneers along the Ohio River when the area below Fort Pitt was called the Northwest Frontier. Some of them[2] scouted with Samuel Brady, well-known frontier leader of the times, and fought the Shawnees and Delawares alongside the Zanes, Wetzels, Millers, and others of that resourceful breed who put their faith in God—and a long-barreled flintlock rifle.

Huffman's desire to push westward came from his heritage, from the tales of adventure told him by his "uncles, sire, and grandsires—pioneers all," and from his early surroundings. Of his several boyhood homes in northeastern Iowa, the one he remembered best lay beside the military road which connected Fort Crawford and Fort Atkinson.[3] Three Indian treaties were negotiated at Fort Crawford; Black Hawk, in the twilight of both his years and his fame, had finally been defeated nearby; and the nearby village of Prairie du Chien was a very important fur-trading center. Huffman noted later that the many legends of this area were a strong influence on his young mind.

Of his childhood, Huffman wrote:

> My early life was spent on the prairies of Iowa where I was born. I loved the open; I loved horses. I ranged on Saturdays—and maybe Sundays too—the nearby woods and fields and later, in the saddle, the remote and unclaimed prairies where the streaks made yellow by Indian head and wild sunflower [4] marked the deserted trails that the departed red men and the wild things had worn deep in the black soils and across the "blue stem" swales of Winneshiek and Chickasaw [counties] while journeying toward the hunting grounds of the Missouri and the Little and Big Sioux Rivers.[5] My love of books came only when school days were far in the past. The first rude school my boyhood knew was by a brook. Memory serves me not as to who taught or what; but the cool shade beneath the pole bridge nearby, the swimming place . . . , and the spot just around the bend where we used to dig in the mounds [6] for mica and arrowheads are vivid clear. And the last school was two stories and more pretentious but the site was even worse. It overlooked woods that beckoned and stretches of prairie where the native grasses rippled in the breeze.[7]

The area where he spent his boyhood had much natural beauty—rolling hills with forests of hardwoods, clear, spring-fed streams, bits of prairie on the narrow divides between the drainageways, and rugged outcrops of gray limestone at the crests of the steeper hills. In the fall the countryside blazed with the scarlet of patches of sumac, the gold of the quaking aspen, cottonwood, and birch, the deep reds and browns of the oaks and maples, and the whole touched here and there by the dark green of scattered cedars along the limestone outcrops. No doubt Huffman was impressed by the beauty of his surroundings, and the small game which abounded provided a fascinating attraction for boys such as he with a love for the open. Many years later, after having experienced the thrills of hunting almost every species of big game ranging in the West, he recalled that the "impression most indelible of all" came when he was eight years old. His parents were moving to a new farm and as he jolted along in a wagon piled high with household belongings:

> Squirrels chattered at us from the low hanging white oak and walnut boughs at every turn. Pheasants [8] rose with a frightening whirr and at one place four or five were surprised "dusting" in a sunny stretch and father stopped the team only a wagon length from them so that we might get a good look at them. Instead of taking wing they shook the dust from their bodies and strutted along the road flirting their tails at each step and pertly turning their heads first this way and then that to watch our movements and finally disappearing among the wild thorn apple and cherry trees that grew everywhere at the roadside.
>
> One stretch of road lay along a high ridge where the view was less obstructed by undergrowth and the great oaks, elms and maples with now and then butternut and walnut laden with green nuts stood wider apart and gave more extended views. Here two grey wolves came into view and at a respectful distance followed stealthily, occasionally sitting down dog fashion at the roadside until a turn hid them from view only to appear again a moment later to repeat the performance. . . .[9]

No doubt he went hunting as soon as his parents allowed it and among the stories of his hunting experiences none shows keener pleasure than the account of his pursuit of a partridge.

> Our home was then at the edge of Teabouts village. . . . At our very back door were the grand old oak and maple forests in which I spent my happiest boyhood days with Bert, Dave and George and Sauk, the black-tipped yaller pup. One November day George and I were permitted to go partridge hunting in the Cutler woods, George armed with his bow and I with a withy hickory stick a yard long for twisting rabbits out of hollow logs. There was an inch of new snow. Tracks of partridges, bevys of quail, and rabbits were everywhere. So was Sauk, stirring them up and at length treeing a partridge at which George expended in rapid succession his six arrows without other effect than to increase Sauk's uproarious barking. The cock sat immovable not thirty feet above our heads on the branch of a thorn apple bush. I bethought me of the hickory club, wondered if I might not make a lucky cast, and sent the little hickory wand whirling at the saucy bird with all my strength; and down he came with a broken neck. That was a great moment, and [provided] a proud homecoming for two lads.

"As a lad of thirteen," Huffman wrote, "I was assuming responsibilities and earning my first small but real wages 'riding line' keeping the [sod]breakers' oxen and Mostler's cattle off his own and his widely scattered neighbors sod crops and hay reservations lying far out on the unfenced lands. . . ." Mostler, who had hired the boy, was farming on the undulating prairie of Chickasaw County just to the west of the rolling timbered country where Huffman's father farmed; and here the incident occurred that crystallized his boyhood yearnings for the frontier. He was asked to carry a message to some land surveyors who were working 30 or 40 miles away out on the prairie.

> Hastily drawing on the back of a letter I was to carry a rude map with a cross or two indicating where I *might* find shelter and food, and possibly pick up fresh news of the camp I was seeking, and giving me some parting words of advice and caution about the trails and the care of his pride, the high strung and beautiful bay mare, my employer bade me set out on my first long cross-country ride. Never can I forget the feelings born in my bosom that day. Once the mare with her long swinging strides had carried me far out upon that billowing plain, fire swept the fall before, now carpeted afresh with the waving grasses of green, dotted with "island" groves [10] just outside the zone of the settler, and still unblemished by his black patches of newly turned sod. Just the wide sweep of sky and soft yielding turf and dim trails suggesting the teeming wild life so late it had known. Here a shriveled horn, there a fragment of white bleaching bone.
>
> Evening approached and the last slanting beams faded from hill and vale. How my horizon had widened in those few fleeting hours; how much vaster the world seemed than ever before. I was to spend my first night alone on the prairies. Thirty years and more have mingled with the current of time, yet undimmed remains the picture of the little spring with its sheltering copse of hazel, summach and haw where we rested. The mare grazed while I, with relish known only to a boy, ate my allowance of bread and cold meat, drank again at the spring, arranged and re-arranged saddle and blanket to serve as a couch, watched the stars come out, patted and leant a long time on the mare's

neck and wondered what she saw with her long, far away listing gaze into the depths of that gathering night. What an age it seemed that I lay there, wide eyed, alert to every sound of rustling twig and chirping insect before oblivion came for a brief space. Then, of a sudden, there was the glowing east, the new day. The mare at her tether was listening and looking intently at some dim moving object afar on the plain. A horseman was approaching and his beast sent a whinnying hail. The mare echoed it back. Now enter the hero of my boyish dreams, the plainsman, the first of his kind my eyes had ever beheld. There he was riding the wild dappled mustang that Catlin has painted, the wide pommeled, tapiderod,[11] Mexican-bespangled saddle with silver trappings, the rifle asling [12] and the coiled rawhide lasso braided from the skin of the bison, the jingling spur and sombrero, the jacket and leggins of deerskin with the dangling fringes that shook round his shoulders and moccasined feet as he rode, Mustang Ben, with the great tawny beard, big reassuring voice was dismounting before me and offering "Good Morning" and the grasp of his hard, hairy hand. Tales of his adventures and prowess in bringing bands of wild horses for barter out of the border of the buffalo and Indian land had fired my imagination long before.

Everything dates from that chance meeting. Ben and his wild riders and herd of mustangs were going my way to sell ponies to the surveyors. For two blissful days I lived the wild life to the full, saw the vaquero do his wonders, heard his tales of the chase, came quite under the spell from which, while life is vouchsafed me, I may never emerge even though that wild life with its actors, stage settings and charm passed like a tale that is told to the realm of the dreamer, the wordsmith, the painter.

During the next 11 years Huffman made "devious wanderings seeking a livelihood—but adventure more." His father moved the family to Waukon, Iowa, in 1865 where he opened a photographic studio. Farm work in these times required both brawn and endurance, for the labor was heavy and the hours were often from daylight to dark; and since both father and son were of slight build it is not strange that the father sought a new occupation. Laton, though slight of build, turned to the farm for employment from time to time even though he "detested the pig-sty and dairy" and preferred the open with a horse between his knees. In his search for employment he wandered north to Fargo and the Devils Lake country in North Dakota where he worked at various tasks ranging from standing in line for would-be homesteaders at claim offices to working with a railroad surveying party.

Apparently he saved at least part of his wages, for he later returned home to work in his father's shop until he had learned the techniques of photography, and then, when about 21, he opened a studio of his own at Postville, a nearby village. Here he fell in love with a red-haired schoolteacher somewhat his senior, and when she gave her more serious affections to an older man, he "pulled his stakes." Broke—he turned northward again in the spring of 1878 and found employment in the photographic shop of Frank Jay Haynes [13] at Moorhead, Minnesota. Haynes took a liking to the young photographer and took him to live in his home: at night the two would often sit on a bench outside the little studio and talk. Both saw new developments coming to the frontier, but neither could guess just what they would be nor how big they would become. The feeling that he stood on the threshold of change made Huffman restless and, when the urge could no longer be denied, he drew his pay and returned home for a short visit. Then he set out southwestward where

> . . . the fall of 1878 found me between the Smoky Hill and Solomon [rivers] in Kansas, and near the track of Little Wolf's Cheyennes, then on their war tour that ravaged that section. And memory serves me well, too, about a night when our train was held up, and the few scattering settlers near brought their flocks and families to our common camp; and, too, I still recollect the recounting of the murder of the Cooper families there related by the campfire and the despair I read upon the womens' faces, and the fear and resolution, too, upon the faces of the men, and the next morning, and our separation after the news had come that the Cheyennes had pushed on to the north.[14]

This was during the last week of September. Here he almost met two men who later became his friends. One of these was Little Wolf, who might have attempted to lift his scalp had the opportunity presented itself, and the other was Hyram "Hi" Bickerdyke,[15] one of the scouts with the Fourth Cavalry and Nineteenth Infantry then on the trail of the hostiles.[16]

Huffman's stay in Kansas was short and why he left is not known. At any rate, he soon retraced his steps by the way of St. Paul to Moorhead, and, after working on a farm until he had accumulated a few dollars, he then headed for the Territory of Montana. With him he bore a letter of recommendation from Senator William B. Allison, a friend of his father, to Colonel Nelson A. Miles, the commandant of Fort Keogh. There is a story that Huffman had learned, while visiting a dealer in photographic supplies at St. Paul, that the post photographer at Fort Keogh had been dismissed, that no successor had been appointed, and that he felt that this was his opportunity. One thing is certain: the hope of getting this position led him at the age of 24 to the prairies of Montana.

In 1878 Bismarck, North Dakota, was the last outpost of civilization before one jumped off for the frontier posts along the Yellowstone—if, indeed, this tough little terminal town where whisky and lead were the two common causes of death could be called civilized. When Huffman arrived, General Rosser was engaged in building the "ice bridge" across the Missouri, an important innovation which allowed the Northern Pacific Railroad to move supplies and equipment across the frozen river before the conventional bridge was constructed.[17] Huffman, however, was not interested in either Bismarck or railroad construction.

Only two things appear to have made an impression on the slender photographer. One was that at Fort Abraham Lincoln were stationed the survivors of the Battle of the Little Big Horn two years before, among them the clay-bank sorrel horse which had been ridden by Captain Miles Keogh on that fateful Sunday. Here the realization came to him that at last he stood on the threshold of the land of the buffalo, Indian, soldier, trapper, and fur-trader. Another impression was of a dominant feature of the society which he was about to enter. On the hills across the river, Huffman noted a Diamond R bull train.[18] These slow-rolling wagons brought food, clothing, equipment, and, of course, liquid goods to the isolated settlements and army posts; and they were then as indispensable as the railway train is today. Huffman recalled that the wagons were painted blue and that "you could hear the snow squealing under the bulls' feet, and see their

ribs. . . . The wind was howling around, and it was twenty below zero." Milestown and Fort Keogh were more than 300 miles away, a trip that took 72 hours
in a light buckboard. What that distance meant in terms of hardship and toil to
a bull-whacker is not known; few bull-whackers were the sort who kept a journal
for posterity!

Huffman's memories of the discomforts he suffered during the trip from
Bismarck to Fort Keogh were still vivid when he was an old man. The journey
was made in a buckboard of the "Star Route," one of the facilities supported by
Congress for carrying the mail; and the route "paralleled the then being graded
line of the Northern Pacific Railway." The buckboards in use had two seats with
a space behind for mail sacks and were entirely open to the weather. The country
through which the route ran was harassed by the Sioux, and the trip was made
every other day by "three 'swing' drives between Bismarck and the mouth of
Powder River on the Yellowstone." There were "six, possibly seven stations"
where horses were changed, and of these Huffman later recalled the names Tobacco Garden, Plowed Ground, and O'Fallon Creek. At Tobacco Garden he had
to lay over.

Two things which would effectively shield the traveler from the cold in
this country were a buffalo robe and a fur overcoat made from a buffalo hide.
Huffman had neither, nor did he have a blanket or even a reasonably heavy overcoat. Only one who has attempted such a journey in an open vehicle, inadequately
clothed, when temperatures were 20 below zero during the day, and something
lower at night, can understand what torture this trip must have been. Huffman
was the only passenger at the start, but that night after they were well out of
Bismarck an outlaw stopped the vehicle and climbed in.

[The] outlaw, Charlie Northrup, [was] the hardest fighter I ever knew,
the bigger his opponent, the better he liked it. Northrup was fearful that he
was under suspicion for complicity in the disappearance of [some] government mules. He wore long boots no overshoes, [and] carried a revolver. . . .
As we drew near the place where we found the dead carcass of a buffalo, the
first I ever saw, I was completely worn out and had had little sleep for some
days. Charlie was watching, and said, "Kid, if anything happens you make
your getaway. They will never get me." [19]
My father had given me, when I left him, a pair of very thin Alfred Dodge
felt shoes. Charlie said, "Kid, I believe your feet are freezing." I put on the felt
shoes and saved my feet. We drove up to a little stage station—they could
not build them very large.[20] [On going through the door] I cut my head on the
door frame. Inside was Oscar Brackett, one of the foremost hunters in the
country. He looked at me and said, "you are all in. How did you hurt your
head?" Charlie told him something about my being an allright kid, and said,
"I will take his baggage through to Fort Keogh." I had $20.00 in my pocket.
Oscar took good care of me for two days, and the next day, after a long sleep
and a bellyful of Buffalo meat I heard the squealing [of the wheels] of a wagon
train [on the snow].

Huffman, still wearing his felt shoes, went out to look the wagon train over.
When Fort Keogh was built shutters for the windows had been shipped from the
"states." These were stored at Fort Abraham Lincoln and the only time anyone

10. "Main Street, Miles City 1879."

L. A. HUFFMAN, FRONTIER PHOTOGRAPHER   33 🦢

11.   "Ye Studio—La Atelier 18 x 40. 3 rooms."

became greatly interested in them was each year shortly before Christmas. This interest then reached the point where it seemed necessary to send a wagon train for some shutters, which train always brought back—along with a few shutters —fresh provisions, liquors, and other necessities for a Merry Christmas at the post. It was a "window-shutter" train which Huffman saw. Lieutenant Oscar Long was in charge, and "Yellowstone" Kelly was one of the party. Kelly took a kindly interest in the tenderfoot, inquired about his plans, and asked him if he did not have any boots. Later they were to travel and starve together—the acid test of a man on the frontier—and became fast friends.

The food at Brackett's stage station may have been chiefly buffalo meat, or buff as it was called, and the bed but a crude bunk filled with wild hay and covered with a few buffalo robes, but sleep and warm food soon restored the traveler and when he left by the next buckboard he had made the acquaintance of Long, Brackett, and Kelly, three men who were to become his lifelong friends. The remainder of the trip was uneventful and the stage arrived at its destination in the evening. Unfortunately, Huffman never recorded his feelings when that tired team of broncos trotted down the one and only street of Milestown past the dim, yellow lights from frosted windows of saloons and dance halls and on to Fort Keogh two miles beyond.

Many years later, after a winter evening spent reminiscing with General Miles and a half dozen other old-timers, Huffman wrote:

It . . . rained and snowed by turns . . . and I was reminded of the 11th of December 1878 when I alighted from the Star Route buckboard near the General's quarters at Fort Keogh. For an hour after getting the kinks from the 300 mile stage ride out of my system I wondered how I would make myself known on a stormy night like that in my horse fighting clothes [21] and no others at hand. I recall that the Officer of the Day, long since passed away, kindly informed me that the general was out on a campaign [22] but from where we stood he pointed [out] the window through which I saw Mrs. Miles. . . . I bore a letter from a Senator . . . addressed to General Miles. I handed it to Mrs. Miles. . . . I recall with great pleasure that she glanced at it and talked with me for half an hour in the most kindly way and [was always friendly] during my two year residence at that post.[23]

In due time Huffman found his former fellow traveler, the outlaw Northrup, asleep on the floor back of the bar in a saloon, his head pillowed on the carpetbag which contained all of Huffman's possessions and which he had trusted to "Charlie" for safe delivery. The adjutant at the post stretched his authority and allowed Huffman to move into the shack occupied by the former post photographer. The walls of this three-room building were constructed stockade-fashion of cottonwood logs placed upright, and the roof was covered with dirt. What it lacked in careful construction it made up in size, as it was 18 by 40 feet, which was ample for a studio and bachelor quarters. Thus, unofficially for the time being, Huffman became the new post photographer.

This was a civilian position and, as such, carried no remuneration other than the occupation of this rude building for a studio and quarters, the privileges of the officers' club, and the opportunity to engage in a business enterprise. Huffman's income was to consist of the profits—if any—from the sale of his pictures. As his predecessor had gone broke, one suspects there were reasons other than natural interest why Huffman, during his first years in Montana, acted as a guide for hunting parties, himself hunted buffalo for hides, and started a small cattle ranch. However, the financial difficulties of the preceding photographer gave Huffman a convenient opportunity to acquire his initial equipment and supplies. These had been put up as collateral for a loan on which the debtor had defaulted, and Laton was able to secure them—no doubt to the great relief of the interim owner.

After settling himself in his new quarters, Huffman set about securing a horse and an outfit for living in the open—doubtless an easy task for anyone with a quasi-military status stationed at a frontier post. Then he closed up the studio and headed out into the country north of the Yellowstone River. With the exception of the region where he later had his ranch on a tributary of the Rosebud River, this great stretch of open country into which he made his first trip held first place in his affections from this day until he died. He referred to it as "The Big Open" and described it as

. . . the great flat-iron shaped country lying between the Yellowstone and the Missouri, its eastern point at their junction . . . its base, the broad end, bounded by the Musselshell and the Great Porcupine, stretching in unbroken wilderness 200 miles in length east and west and a hundred and twenty miles broad at the widest . . . studded with a myriad round buttes, scored by its thousands of dry creeks, narrow wooded streams of sweet water, treeless streams fed by springs so bitter of alkali that beast must be sore athurst to drink, wide basins thick covered with sage—where then countless bands of antelope fed and . . . in winter . . . pawed the snow for the succulent cacti —wide rolling far reaching smooth bunch-grass covered plains . . . extending to the belt of the pine-topped hills of its far northern rim where vast tracts of badlands, deep scarred and forbidding reach down to the dense, almost impassable thickets of diamond willow and thorny buffalo berry thickets that fringe the Missouri . . .

On this first trip he went northwest to the vicinity of Smoky Butte [24] and, after wandering around for a few days, fell in with a party of hide-hunters, headed by "Doc" Zahl, which was camped on Redwater Creek. Then he returned to the post and made a second trip into the area carrying his photographic equipment. It was on this second trip that he made his first picture of wild buffalo and hide-hunters.

Later Huffman looked back at the years of 1879, 1880, and 1881 as those he enjoyed most of all. He believed that "there *was* no more West" after the coming of the railroad,[25] but his own pictures show that this was not strictly true, particularly in remote areas. During these early years Huffman hunted buffalo for hides and meat, scouted for lariat Indians with "Yellowstone" Kelly, sought timber for the government sawmills, and served as a guide for Eastern sportsmen out for big game.

One for whom he guided and photographed was George O. Shields, a sports writer for *The American Field*,[26] who provided him with considerable indirect publicity. On February 1, 1881, Huffman wrote his father:

Have you noticed the Holiday No of "American Field" Illustrated with my views. . . . I think I have been personally and by letter had 40 propositions to go [hunting] during the summer coming. I dont allow myself to plan . . . trips anymore but my business will require me to take in some locality for new negatives during the summer.

The "new negatives" were needed to make scenic views, the sale of which formed a considerable part of his business. Of these, pictures of the Yellowstone National Park became, a year later, a very important part as his catalogue for 1883 indicates. A trip to the park was a fair-sized undertaking, involving at least 750 miles of travel with pack horses. "Well I have not yet been to stinking water [27] and the national Park," he wrote his father on July 10, 1882, "but am daily expecting a date from Col Clough or Capt Huggins. If I dont soon get it I am going to cinch up and light out alone."

This particular trip, which he evidently had to make with a single companion, is one of the few cases where a record exists of his travels for pictures. On his return he wrote his father: [28]

Yours of the 1st inst just at hand this PM. I wrote to Dell [29] from "Mammoth Springs" about 15 of Aug and it seems you have not heard of me since my departure. Those 56 days are among the best of all my wanderings. To repeat what has so oft been said of the "wonderland" or to try to expatiate on what one can see there is folly. I had the honor to meet John McCullough [30] and "punished several hours" with him and others of Phils [31] party   I made a raft of logs and taking the faithful Kennedy [32] and my new 76 outfit on board

12. "General Sheridan and Party. Old Faithful in action." (1882)

after a long hard pull—or pole—rather—crossed the Yellowstone above the falls—went down on foot 6 miles and back securing views that no other feller got   My view of both falls and Grand Canyon will in consequence not be the old stereotyped kind as you shall see. But the getting back again. the raft went down easy but to plunge into cold water all exhausted from a long tramp and drag the craft up stream to a safe point to start in for camp was something more interesting. the banks are perpindicular and the bottom full of boulders. but I made it safely and was warmly congratulated by several spectators who seemed to think my escaping being dashed to pieces wonderful— . . .

Specimens—no I did not bring back an ounce of anything except an old rusty pistol and medicine sack from beside the skeleton of some unfortunate Nez Perce—Theres an old battlefield and log fort on the south side of Clark Fork canyon [33] away up on the side of the mountain where no one ever finds his way except some crazy Photog—I was led to it by a wounded elk and while butchering him for his tenderloin accidentally made the discovery

One wants to carry specimens from a hundred places—but let me say to you that in swimming rivers, cutting out trails unpacking animals and carrying your plunder where a horse gives up makes one lose his grip on specimens— by a large Majority—

The pictures of the Yellowstone Park which Huffman took on this trip were

L. A. HUFFMAN, FRONTIER PHOTOGRAPHER   37 &

popular with the buying public. Of particular interest, however, are the comments of Huffman's father who gave them a critical—and professional—examination. On November 26, 1882, the father wrote:

> We recd the stereos and thank you heartily for the kindness and hope to be able to repay you. You marked one of the Great Canyon of the Y[ellowstone] as a failure. want of foreground. let me tell you that is the grandest view of the Bunch. I have seen many of the same views but not from that same point exactly. but yours gives the best distant view of the falls and the finest Idea of the wonderful depth & grandeur of the Canyon. I have Crissmans [34] work at hand to compare. Your work is all better except the Instantaneous of Old F[aithful] in action. Criss told me he spent 8 days in getting that picture to his satisfaction. but he got it. Your views "a whole Jag of Geysers," is grand. I expect if I live, to come and see you (in that new house with a W[ife]) and the Y. park next season

As Huffman sold some of his "wonderland" pictures the following summer to two very critical buyers, his father's enthusiasm would seem to have been something more than paternal pride.

While Huffman made no mention of it in his letter, he made an extensive detour before returning to Miles City from his trip to the National Park. One morning, while winding along a lonely game trail in the valley of Clark Fork, he met George Shields and five others on a hunting trip. As Shields insisted that Huffman's services were indispensable to him, he cut four horses out of his string and turned back with Shields, while his companion took the remainder of the horses back to Milestown. Shields left a complete narrative of this trip in his book of hunting stories; [35] and some of the photographs Huffman made on this trip are reproduced in another chapter.

One other early activity in which he engaged is of particular interest. October, 1880, found him and his partner, Eugene Lamphere [36] building a cabin, making hay, and preparing to winter some stock in the valley of Lame Deer Creek where the village of Lame Deer is now located. Thus he became the first rancher in the valley of the Rosebud. His brand was the Hl, sometimes called the H half H, but properly known as the H Lazy L—the H representing Huffman and the L, Lamphere. Later he sold the brand when the area became part of the reservation for the Northern Cheyennes, but he always referred with pride to the days when he had a brand and repped at the roundups.

Huffman accepted risks as part of his work in securing his pictures, and there was only one adventure which he recalled in later life as having cost him some extremely anxious moments. In 1880, while hunting alone in the badlands of the big Missouri, he noticed on the top of a nearby butte a small, gray object that kept appearing and disappearing. The movements appeared to be signals of some kind, and, as trouble with small raiding parties of Sioux from across the Canadian line was no rarity, Huffman was worried. However, after watching for a time he decided to investigate. The object proved to be a badly worn warrior's drum—a disc of rawhide stretched over a hoop—swinging from the tip of a piece of a lodgepole erected beside a cairn of stones marking a grave. For once Huffman turned grave-robber and carried the drum home.

His studio often attracted interesting visitors day in day out and it acted

13. "Grand Canon from Eagle Nest, 1882."

as a magnet to a group, both red and white, who loafed there whenever there was an excuse. Huffman jotted down brief descriptions of some of these early days at the fort:

> . . . in that shack of mine on a good many occasions, Colonel Ilges [37] and Two Moon and I foregathered for a smoke and a chat. Sometimes we had an interpreter and sometimes not, but it became apparent to me very soon that Colonel Ilges and Two Moon were [very good friends] . . . the kind Two Moon and I were destined to be.

> And there lived among the Cheyennes during these days Spotted Bear, an old and wrinkled man [who] used to visit my shack often and I remember that one day he was at my door when Clark and John Brughier [38] rode up and joined us. Clark joked "Old Spot" [and] asked Brughier to ask the old man if it was true

L. A. HUFFMAN, FRONTIER PHOTOGRAPHER   *39*

14. "Lame Deer Cheyenne Agency of today. Site of the first home of the Huffman Pictures, the H lazy L cow camp."

15. "Spotted Bear, Hunkapapa Sioux—In my old studio at Fort Keogh, 1878. Scout at Fort Keogh, Montana Territory 1879."

that he sat down on the hill and cried the day that Custer fell.[39]

Captain Clark had a great admiration for Little Wolf and Little Wolf for Clark, the dashing cavalryman, who was adept in sign language. . . . And in my studio Clark and Little Wolf in those days conspired together to not only translate the sign language, but to photograph the living Indian in the various attitudes. But that, with many another dream of Clark's and mine . . . is passed away. The Indians didn't take kindly to it, and we couldn't make it go.[40]

"Yellowstone" Kelly, whom Huffman met at the Tobacco Gardens stage station, also became a frequent visitor. Kelly was an unassuming man and differed from many of the frontiersmen of that time in that he did not care for

16.   The studio built of lumber from the *F. Y. Batchelor*.

liquor and gambling and carousing. Often, upon returning from a scout, he would lie down on a pile of buffalo robes in the corner of the studio to sleep. He liked to read, particularly history, and to discuss the things he had read; and he did considerable of both in Huffman's office.

There is no definite record of when Huffman gave up his position at Fort Keogh and moved to Miles City. On February 6, 1880, he wrote to his father, "Am strongly urged to open a studio at Miles City the coming summer—Will think about it"; and another letter dated a year later indicated that he had moved into Milestown.

Over the years he owned a number of studios, and one of these was an unusual structure. *The F. Y. Batchelor* [41] was one of the steamboats engaged in carrying buffalo hides down the river in the early 1880's. When this business was at its peak, every hide that could be put on was piled aboard these steamboats, and in order to increase the capacity of this boat the staterooms back of the pilothouse were torn out. Huffman bought this salvage lumber and from it built a studio. As some of the lumber was cut on the bias to conform with the contours of the boat, it required some ingenuity and unorthodox construction to erect a building from it. Another studio burned, and with it went some choice negatives, including the pictures of the evacuation of the Sioux from their prisoner-of-war camps around Fort Keogh to the Standing Rock Agency. Huffman always spoke of this loss with deep regret, and no doubt this accounts for some of the gaps in subject matter which become obvious when the collection is studied.

Huffman's early pictures were made with a stereographic camera which used a five-by-eight-inch glass negative.[42] As previously noted, a considerable part of his income came from the sale of scenic pictures; and one very common form in which such pictures were sold was cards for the stereoscopes which were common items of equipment in the parlors of those days. Huffman's papers contain only one description of his early cameras, and, unfortunately, one important page of this manuscript is missing. In writing of a trip with an unpredictable pack horse, Crackers, he noted:

    . . . dry plates—almost the earliest known and a 5 x 8 camera, a primitive thing with a home made tripod constructed almost without metal, the leg hinges and head cut from thick green buffalo hide which when dry was hard as horn that old Crackers could not "fix" when he'd roll trying to relieve himself of his load, as he did the polished brass and nickel tipped contrivance which once we set out with.

Sometime in 1884 or 1885, Huffman changed to a conventional single-lens camera using a glass plate six and a half by eight and a half inches, and this equipment he used almost exclusively from this time on. He once remarked that this camera was a homemade affair weighing about 50 pounds. As the camera sometimes got rough use when carried into the field, strength was a necessary requisite. In one short diary of a trip with a roundup, Huffman described a night when a storm blew every tent flat but his little tepee, mixed the herds of cattle, and caused everyone much trouble. The final entry for the day was, "The 6^28^2 camera is badly smashed. Its glue and nails for the forenoon."

Huffman's letters to his father contain many illuminating references to the difficulties caused by slow shutters, slow film, and lack of uniformity in materials. The problem of stopping motion was one with which Huffman apparently did considerable experimenting as these three extracts from letters written in 1885 show:

> I send you another picture of Bessie [43] made with the Perry shutter as quick as it can be worked—Pyro and soda developer.[44] I am making daily experiments now and find I am able to take passing horses at a lively trot square across the line of fire—bits of snow in the air—spokes well defined—some blur on top of wheel but sharp in the main—men walking are no trick—the interesting part is I get negatives that are amply strong for printing—will send you proofs sometime— [45]

On April 5, twelve weeks later, he continued, "I am making all my outside work instantaneous now sun or no sun and with wide open lens—" Two months later, he again returned to the subject, this time in a definitely jubilant mood:

> I just returned a few days ago from a 12 days ride with the Powder River Roundup—I shall soon show you what can be done from the saddle without ground glass or tripod—Please notice when you get the specimens that they were made with the lens wide open and many of the best exposed when my horse was in motion— [46]

These comments should be kept in mind in studying many of Huffman's pictures, particularly the range pictures. The lack of definition, sometimes called fuzziness, which may be noted at the edges of some of the pictures was caused by using the widest possible lens opening. This, of course, was necessary because of the "instantaneous" shutter speed, and the slowness of the film. That he shot from horseback is obvious when the perspective is noted, particularly with pictures showing action at the roundup herds; and to have manipulated a 50-pound glass-plate camera and the necessary plate holders and dark slides from the back of an unpredictable bronc was no small achievement.

Not only were his early cameras crude affairs, but the film, or rather plates,

17.   "Early day roundup at work, Powder River, 1886."

and developers were additional handicaps. His early pictures were made using wet plates which compelled the photographer to carry a portable darkroom, usually a small tent. To make a wet plate, a glass plate was first coated with collodion to which a soluble iodide had been added. After being sensitized by immersion in a bath of silver nitrate, the plate was loaded in the camera and exposed while still wet. It then had to be developed before it dried or the picture would be lost. The speed of such plates was very slow, and exposures were measured in fractions of a minute instead of fractions of a second. Also, it took skill to coat the plates properly, and uniform performance could not be depended upon. Two results of this slow speed will be noted in the old pictures—first, that any motion resulted in a blur, and secondly, that all cloud detail burned out and was lost.

To have worked with solutions in a portable tent on the plains in the winter must have been difficult indeed. Some idea of these difficulties may be read between the lines in a letter to his father dated February 1, 1881:

> I made some good views of Buff and sheep on my last trip—Just finished the titles ready for printing today   it was so intensely cold and stormy that I lost some [of the] best opportunities while among the Missouri badlands near Poplar River.

It is no wonder that Huffman was proud of his early pictures, and, considering these difficulties, neither is it surprising that he was alert for any changes in procedure which would make his laborious work with wet plates unnecessary. In the fall of 1881 Huffman guided and photographed for George O. Shields on a trip to the Big Horn Mountains. In Shields' book definite mention is made of the use of dry plates on this trip, and a humorous story is told of one of the several perils which beset the way of a frontier photographer.

While the party was fording the Little Big Horn River, Nig, "a large black mule, who was always disposed to be willful and contrary," deliberately waded toward a deep hole near the ford. As this pack mule's load consisted chiefly of Huffman's photographic outfit—"camera, dry plates, dark tent, etc. . . . . valued at three hundred dollars"—Huffman became "frantic." After Huffman, Shields, and the packer had showered him with sticks, stones, and profanity, Nig turned and brought his burden safely to land.

> We took his load off, opened it, and found that though the lower corners of both boxes were wet, the moisture had not reached their contents. We congratulated Huffman on the fact that his dry goods were still dry—that his stock had not been watered—so to speak—and went on our way rejoicing.[47]

Apparently Huffman continued to use dry plates for studio work after the fall of 1881, for he wrote his father about a year later:

> I can now double discount any wet plate that was ever invented   no spots no blemishes—all clean sharp expressions   pose etc greatly improved by the lessened exposure—I would not take back the Cyanide slop Profanity—cloudy day trouble Failures with kids etc etc if dry plates cost double the present

CATALOGUE

1883.

HUFFMAN'S
Latest Yellowstone National Park Views.
INDIAN PORTRAITS.
Miscellaneous Montana Views and the

ONLY CHOICE HUNTING SCENES PUBLISHED.

L. A. HUFFMAN, Photo and Publisher,   **MILES CITY, MONTANA.**

INDIAN PORTRAITS, CABINET SIZES.

1. "Eta-ma-gozua," or "Rain-in-the-face."
2. "Scorched Lightning," Assinaboine Sioux.
3. Sioux Chieftain, "Spotted Eagle."
4. Young "Spotted Eagle."
5. Princess "Dull Knife," Cheyenne Maiden.
6. "Red Bead" Blackfoot Runner.
7. "Rain-in-the-face," Uncappapa Sioux who killed Custer.
8. Mrs. "Rain-in-the-face."
9. "Lone Wolf," Crow Scout.
10. "Pretty Eyes," Cheyenne Maiden.
11. "Two Moon's Children," Cheyennes.
12. "White Magpie," Teton Orator.
13. "Chief Joseph," Nez Perce.
14. "High Bear," Ogallalla.
15. Sioux Chief "Hump," and favorite wives.
16. "Man-on-the-hill" and wife.
17. Cheyenne Maid, "Medicine Walk."
18. Spotted Elk, Head Warrior, Minneconjoux Sioux.
19. Daughters of "Dull Knife," Cheyennes.
20. "Tall Bear," Minneconjoux Medicine Man.
39. Group of Cheyenne Girls.
21. Wenopa," or Two Moon, Chief of Cheyennes.
38. Sioux Urchins.
22. "Wolf Voice," Gros Ventre warrior.
38. Sioux Woman and Pappoose.
370. "Big Bull," Crow Chief.
275. "Red Armed Panther," Cheyenne.
56. "White Bull," Sioux.
170. "Spotted Fawn," Cheyenne Maiden.
171. "Pretty Nose," Cheyenne Maiden.

INDIAN VIEWS, STEROSCOPIC.

177. Advance of Civilization, Wigwam and Locomotive.
25. Sioux Village on the Yellowstone.
30. "Rain-in-the-face" at Home.
35. "Spotted Bear," Sioux Scout.
50. Sioux Scouts.
33. Sioux Camp Tongue River.
51. Young Teton Sioux.
24. Cheyenne Scouts.
28. Sioux Chief "Hump," and Head Warriors.
52. Yanktonais Camp, Tongue Valley, M. T.
194. "A Sioux Warrior's Grave," Buffalo Range, M.
29. "Rain-in-the-face's Camp."
34. Spotted Elk, Head Warrior, Minneconjoux Sioux.
55. Mother and Daughters, Sioux.
23. "Crow Maiden of Sixteen," Semi-nude.
26. "A Good Indian," Stiff.
37. Sweat Lodge, Sioux Village.

HUNTING SCENES.

196. A House of Buffalo Hides.
187. Camping on Northern Buffalo Range, winter.
195. Camp Emmett.
191. A Monster Buffalo Bull.
192. Taking the Monster's Robe.
193. After the Chase. Buffalo Bulls.
188. Five Minutes work, Nine Buffalo Cows.
189. Taking the Tongues.
71. A Mule Deer.

HUNTING SCENES—Continued.

58. Our Hunting Camp on Little Horn.
72. Our Outfit, Big Horn, 1881.
64. My First Bear.
69. His First Grizzly.
70. Skinning the Grizzly.
74. Our First Elk.
357. A Few Antelope.
358. Our Hunting Party, Clark's Fork Mountains.
359. "Ow's These for Helk'Orns."
347. Slain Monarch of the Mountains.
351. Elk Cow and Yearling.
356. "Here's Meat Thar'll Put Luther in Ye."
353. Successful After a Weary Climb.
355. Uncle Ed. Tells Me How He Got 'Em.
349. Glory Enough for a Day—Elk and Bears.
260. Mountain Sheep.

FORT KEOGH, M. T.

125. Bird's Eye View of Ft. Keogh.
114. Heart Arch, Bad Lands near Keogh.
123. Cheyenne Bluff, above Keogh.
129. Commanding Officers Res. Keogh.
127. Officers' Quarters, Keogh.
128. Barracks, Keogh.

MILES CITY.

161. East on Main Street, Miles City, M. T., 1881.
162. West " " " "
165. Freighting Outfit " " "
165. Park Av. Looking North " 1882.
   Miles City from Inter Ocean Hotel.
   Inter Ocean Hotel.
167. West Main Street.
162. Main Street During March Flood, 1881.

Glendive and Vicinity.

145. Glendive from East.
148. " West.
118. Glendive in 1881.
363. Depot and Merrill House, Glendive.
147. Eagle Butte Cut.
152. Eagle Butte.
143. Bad Lands near Eagle Butte.
144. Toll Road " "
154. Old Government Trail, Bad Lands.
141. Eagle Butte Toll Road.
146. Cedar Bluff Side Cut.

CUSTER'S BATTLE FIELD.

91. Where Custer Fell.
Grave of Lieut. Sturgis.
93. " Col. Keogh.
" Lieut. Crittenden.
99. Monument on Custer's Hill.

Miscellaneous Views.

209. Terry's Landing.
217. Pompey's Pillar.
214. Guys Bluffs from West.
218. Coulson, M. T., from Bluffs.
221. Street View, Billings, 1882.
361. Testing Bismarck Bridge Oct. 21, 1882.
81. Black Canon, Big Horn.
82. Leaning Tower, Black Canon.

YELLOWSTONE NATIONAL PARK.

250. Liberty Cap Mammoth Hot Springs.
252. Specimen Falls " "
254. Terraces " "
256. North from Terraces " "
258. "The Squash" " "
259. Toward Headquarters " "
261. Beautiful Terraces " "
262. Devils Thumb " "
263. Canon of West Gardiner, near Mammoth Hot Springs.
264. Falls " "
266. Canon and Falls of Middle Gardiner.
267. Gibbon Boiling Spring.
268. Roadside Geyser.
269. North from Fountain Geyser, Lower Basin.
270. Fountain Geyser in Action.
271. Paint Pot, Lower Basin.
272. Firehole at Hell's Half Acre.
274. Phil Sheridan in Action Three Miles Distant.
275. Gen. Sheridan and Party—Old Faithful in
277. Gen. Sheridan's Headquarters, Upper Basin.
278. " Pack Train in Camp Upper Basin.
279. Old Faithful in Action.
291. " Getting Ready for Business.
283. Boiling Pool Banks of Firehole River.
294. Tower Castle Geyser from Bee Hive.
295. Giant Geyser Cone, Upper Basin.
296. Giant Geyser in Action.
297. Near View of Giant's Cone.
298. Crater of the Splendid.
299. Splendid from Grotto.
300. Grotto Geyser Cone, Upper Basin.
301. Beautiful Grotto " "
304. Castle Geyser Cone " "
306. Bee Hive Geyser Cone " "
307. Yellowstone Canon near Tower Falls.
309. Tower Falls.
310. " "
311. Jack Baronett's Bridge from South.
312. " " " North.
313. General View of Upper Basin—Morning.
315. Grand Canon of the Yellowstone.
316. " " "
317. " " "
318. Down Grand Canon from Lower Falls.
322. Over the Bank of Lower Falls.
325. Lower Falls, 365 Feet High.
326. Lower Falls, Two Miles Distant.
329. A Glimpse of Lower Falls.
330. Canon and Falls from "Eagle Nest."
321. Upper Falls from Bridle Path.
333. Cascade near Lower Falls.
334. Camping Point Above the Falls.
335. Soda Butte.
336. Soda Butte and Soda Springs.
337. Soda Butte Valley.
338. Soda Butte Creek and Grand Mountain.
339. Soda Butte Creek near Cook City.
341. Soda Butte Creek and Specimen Mountain.
343. Antelope Camp, Bennett's Creek Clark's Fork.

Price per dozen, post paid.................................. $.
Price per gross, post paid................................. $.

price—no baths to keep up inexpensive developer no glass or collodions to buy makes them *as cheap* as wet.[48]

And shortly after he wrote, "I use *nothing* now but 'Eastmans Instantaneous' indoors and out." [49] However, after the newness of the new type of plates palled slightly, Huffman went back to the use of wet plates for certain types of work. Three years later he wrote:

> I now use wet plates to good saving advantage on all adult sitters who come when the light is strong so that I can work in 5 to 12 seconds   I think the work is equal in all respects for cabs [50] and cards and does not bar the use of the dry on everything larger than babies &c &c. I count a saving the past month of $50.00. Glass costs nothing—I have a years stock always ready to clean—its a good way to utilize failures from either process—collodions that I use are all 4 to 6 years old and sound and true—fact is they are some the stage co failed to deliver to me when I first came here. . . . One must make tintypes. that is we small fry must so one must keep a bath and when at leisure we can snatch the face of the cowpunch at a cost of ½ cent saving 12 cents each time   it does not prevent resorting to the dry when crowded for time [51]

The above statement regarding the reuse of glass is very interesting, for one of the striking things about the Huffman negative collection is the complete lack of portrait negatives. The few pictures of early settlers which are included in this collection have been reproduced from cabinet photographs which were among the miscellaneous odds and ends in the studio at the time of Huffman's death. It would appear that Huffman attached no value to such material other than the value of the glass involved, and that he made a practice of cleaning up certain of his old plates and reusing the glass. This practice has undoubtedly resulted in the loss of many interesting photographs of early ranchers, gamblers, trappers, freighters, merchants, soldiers, and—probably—"ladies" whose profession was recognized but not considered socially acceptable.

Huffman's letters to his father contain some mention of the "view" business which he did in these early days. After the railroad reached Miles City in the fall of 1881, there was considerable tourist trade with parties going to the Yellowstone National Park or going hunting; and Huffman's trade consisted, for the most part, of sales to these people and to Eastern dealers. The copy of his catalogue for 1883 reproduced here gives a very concrete idea of what items sold readily, and it will be noted that Indian and Yellowstone Park views composed a major part of the offering. "My layout," he wrote on December 3, 1882, "is about 300 good prime negatives of the staying kind." A few of these negatives were not of his own taking, and he commented on July 4, 1883, "I must close and varnish up my negatives   bought four more nice lots last week making now 10 some of which have increased to quite a handsome figure compared with their cost." Included among these negatives, no doubt, were those of the Little Big Horn Battlefield taken—probably—by S. J. Morrow, the photographer who accompanied the burial party which visited the battlefield a year after the battle and properly buried what remained of the bodies of Custer's men.

Although he saw his pictures go to many buyers, some of them in Europe,

19.   "Where Custer Fell."

one sale gave him unusual pleasure and provided a very interesting contact. In a letter telling his father of the visits of Henry Ward Beecher, senators, representatives, and governors, he noted:

> On Friday morning two very plain men stopped in to look at views—the younger mentioned Crissman & Jackson [52] then introduced Dr. F. V. Hayden We spent the entire forenoon in discussing the Park and Big H[orn]   Dr Hayden is a man 53 and one of the most interesting men in conversation—he showed his appreciation of the views as did Dr Peale [53] by buying it. They were here 3 days and we had some pleasant strolls and no one knew until they left not even the newspapers or Hotels that they were other than ordinary Tourists—Dr Hayden worked for the American Fur Company in 1852 3 and 4. in 54 he was stationed for a time at Ft. Alexander [54] four miles from here—he showed me the old site and I cannot find anyone in the country who could do so though many like myself had heard of it—his accounts of that day surpass anything I have listened to— [55]

It is to be regretted that father and son did not have the same points of common interest in respect to the problems of securing pictures as they did in respect to darkroom techniques. Had such common points existed, perhaps Huffman would have written more about his experiences in the field. Of these, too little is known. The few bits which have been recorded indicate that much of what he accepted as part of his work and made little or no mention of was hardly commonplace. On one trip he crossed the Shoshone River on a horse that was weak in the front knees. The river was swift, approaching swimming depth in places, and the horse almost lost his footing several times. Once across, the only route out was a narrow game trail up a steep canyon wall several hundred feet high. As he could neither turn back nor lead the horse, Huffman had to ride him out. After several dangerous slips, any one of which could have been fatal, the horse finally made it to the top.

On another occasion, in the very early 1880's, Huffman was caught out on the "Big Open" in a blizzard and spent two days and nights talking to his pack horse in order to stay awake and keep from freezing to death. This experience he recorded in a fragmentary manuscript.

I, alone, twice crossed from the Yellowstone to the Missouri and back this butte studded, gulch sown, weird, lovely land which teemed with wild life. The first time [was] in the saddle during August. The second time [was] on foot in mid-winter, leading when leading was easy and driving when the leading grew hard, a "paint" pack pony dubbed Crackers because he had on each flank markings that suggested the possibility of his having been branded with a big Army hardtack [with] the pricks plainly noted. And Crackers too had a weakness for those same squares of soldier fare that it always gave me keen pleasure to humor him—when I could without stinting my own allowance too much—

Somewhere up in the Frozen Dog Hills,[56] two days out, we holed up, Crackers and I, to await a favorable turn in the weather which had taken of a sudden a threatening change with a pitiless wind that cut like a knife, and the seething, blinding drift that it bore pelted and swirled half snow and half alkali dust so we groped to the nearest washout we could find. We huddled there two days and two interminable nights that each seemed thirty hours long. Fuel, save a little sage and the buffalo chips, there was none. Except [for] a few tufts of salt grass that clung to the rim of the little washout we'd crept into, and an occasional mouthful of dirty snow . . . poor, patient Crackers had nothing. I dared not sleep, to sleep meant death in such a temperature as that so when not busy melting snow in an army cup or toasting hard bread and bits of bacon over my tiny fire I talked to Crackers of my scheme to make a great pasture of the "Flat Iron," [57] to fence it with a great woven wire to banish forever the skin hunters, maybe enlist them in the army of wardens. How and where the great park gates should be guarded, how tame wild things would get—bison, antelope and elk—and too how splendid t'would be when the yellow-green carpet of spring had come, to see it all teeming with life.

Then the seething of the snow and dust grew less and the wind fell to a fitful moan, the stars shone again and the cold grew, gripd to the heart as at daybreak we moved from our camp so benumbed that to lash on the load was no easy task. Everywhere as we plodded along the storm-driven herds of antelope and buffalo scarce moved from our path, the former stamping cactus,[58] the latter in dozens and hundreds slowly—it seemed mournfully—plodding and grazing.

The photographing of wild animals with cumbersome cameras and slow film was difficult; and, considering the habits of antelope, deer, and elk it is to be expected that he never secured close-up pictures of these animals. However, he was successful in photographing a group of mountain sheep; and, considering that these animals have extremely keen eyesight and are perhaps the most wary of all big-game animals, this was an achievement of which any wildlife photographer

20. "Mountain Sheep, a band grazing. The young ram looked me square in the eye and gave the hike signal."

could have been proud. One raw spring day Huffman dressed in a buckskin suit and hid in a dead cedar tree with his six-and-a-half-by-eight-and-a-half-inch camera. As a band of about 20 grazed on the mountainside in the vicinity of his blind, he succeeded in securing pictures.

Taking pictures of buffalo was a task that required courage as well as patience. Stories have been told that sometimes he employed a technique taught him by "Hi" Bickerdyke, the well-known hide-hunter who was one of his close friends. This was to camouflage himself with old burlap sacks and, hiding behind a piece of thick sagebrush, worm his way out on the plain pushing the brush before him. Huffman told, on one occasion, that some of the pictures were secured by hiding in a small washout with the wind right, and waiting for the buffalo to graze by close enough to photograph. Unfortunately it is not known how or where his splendid buffalo pictures were secured; but they must have been obtained at considerable risk of life and limb.

Huffman's pictures, while valuable in themselves, are most interesting when one knows the background and intimate details which the camera cannot record. This background of understanding begins with the man himself and requires a knowledge of something more than the photographic techniques used in securing the pictures. One needs to know something of the man's activities outside of his profession and, above all, something of those personal peculiarities which set one individual apart from another.

During the 52 years he lived in Montana, Huffman gave freely of his time and energy to other tasks. "By the way," he closed a letter to his father on April 5, 1885, "I was elected school twister [59] yesterday—wont I make a fine addition to that august body—never thought I would rise to such a political distinction did you." The following year, 1886, he was elected county commissioner. At this time

21. "Buffalo Grazing in the Big Open, North Montana, 1880."

Custer County embraced all of southeastern Montana, and one of the major problems was the collection of taxes from ranchers who regarded taxes on their highly mobile assets as an imposition to be dodged if possible.[60] This practice of the times did not escape his attention, and, as chairman of the board, the onus of the situation fell on his shoulders.

> I was "kid" commissioner, the youngest on a board of three, for a large un-organized territory, no high taxes, and no big expenses. The cattlemen in eastern Montana would throw everything over into North Dakota when the assessor was around, and when the assessing was completed would bring [the herd] back into Montana.

One of the outfits with which the commissioners had trouble was the VVV, then owned by Western Ranches, Limited, and managed by John Clay [61] and W. H. Forrest. This outfit ran cattle in what is now North and South Dakota, Montana, and Wyoming. Another trouble-maker was Joseph Scott, a prominent cattleman who managed the SH in the valley of the Tongue River. Huffman wrote later:

> I remember when John Clay came first into my view, standing before me . . . speaking of an injustice he felt I had contributed in putting up on him and his associates. . . . Joseph Scott, about that same day, in forceful manner publicly, and more than once privately, to my face charged me with bad faith about a similar manner. . . .

The problems of law enforcement were unpleasant—as they often are—but Huffman remembered gratefully that, in later years, Scott made what restitution he could for this unfair criticism.

In 1893 Huffman was elected a member of the Montana House of Representatives from Custer County. Here he introduced one of the first bills for irrigation in the state; and it is interesting to note that, while he was interested in the development of the country, he watched certain aspects of that development with feelings of regret. In 1907 he attended the opening of the irrigation project near Huntley, and his friend Sam Gordon, editor of *The Yellowstone Journal*, requested him to write his impressions of the occasion. Huffman closed this short article with a poignant note:

> Everywhere I go in the Yellowstone country, twice on long drives to the south and east, within the past few weeks, tells me this, that soon if I am to gallop the little gray mare it must be in a lane, and you do not care, but I do; that makes me sad. I would that there were yet a few waste places left untouched by the settler and his cursed wire fence, good in its way, but not for me. I can not help it.[62]

There were probably other activities which brought more personal satisfaction than those connected with public office. For example, he must have thoroughly enjoyed helping President Theodore Roosevelt in his program of establishing national forests. In 1905 Huffman took two horses, one of which served as a pack animal on alternate days, and located the boundaries and collected legal descriptions of the timbered areas which became the Otter Creek and the Medicine Rocks Forest Reserves. Another conservation activity which brought pleasure was the preservation of wildlife. The love of wild things which he had as a youngster remained with him to the end.

However, it was the little favors he did for people scattered far and wide which probably earned for him the distinction of being what the late Louis F. Grill, editor of the *Miles City Star*, termed an *"institution."* A casual survey of old correspondence and references in newspaper clippings gives some indication of the wide variety of these services which were based on his deep and understanding knowledge of the life and history of this part of the West. Huffman recorded the first of these services which is known today. When Granville Stuart came to Miles City hunting a cattle range in 1880, he engaged Tom Irvine[63] to accompany him and

. . . the second sheriff of that large unorganized territory that reached from Dakota to Bozeman, Montana came to my little log shack at Ft. Keogh and said, "Mr. Granville Stuart is coming down here in a little while. Lets go with the old man[64] and show him around." I was his guide because Tom did not know the country as well as I did.

Stuart was followed by many others. For Hamlin Garland, the writer, he provided an introduction to Wolf Voice and other old Cheyennes. George Bird Grinnell wrote to ask if Huffman would try to locate some skulls of the mountain sheep—"the so-called plains sheep"—which once lived in the badlands along the Missouri, Yellowstone, and other large rivers of the Northwest. Harlin Smith of the American Museum of Natural History asked for advice on how to make a profitable collecting trip—and would Huffman spend some time with him and show him his own collection. To Dr. W. T. Hornaday, then chief taxidermist of the U. S. National Museum, Huffman shipped the sagebrush and buffalo grass which went into the fine mounted buffalo group in this museum. These favors, and many others like them, did not make headlines—but they were more or less indispensable to the work of many other people.

As might be expected of anyone who had a wide circle of acquaintances and who was elected to public office in a frontier community where a man was judged for what he was and not for the connections which he had, Huffman had an enjoyable and interesting personality. In 1880 Granville Stuart wrote in his diary that "Huffman is one of the most companionable men I ever traveled with."[65] He was honest and sincere to the core. One old friend characterized him as "attentive, discreet, meticulous, keen penetrations, an analyst and appraiser of influences that eminated from experiences."[66] He was a student and lover of nature, and a champion of the underdog. In accord with the custom of the times, he would take a drink and play in a friendly game for low stakes, but he did not participate in either activity to excess. And, although not of a boisterous nature, he was fond of well-told stories and practical jokes.

Some idea of his sense of human values is contained in his article written in reply to John Clay's comment about a foul blow John Holt, one of the outstanding cattlemen of Montana, was alleged to have struck another prominent man at a cattlemen's meeting. Clay wrote:

John Holt fell foul of Dr. Azel Ames, taking him unawares as they left the first meeting—a mean sort of thing to do and always a black mark in my estimation against an otherwise successful cattleman. When you want a fight do it in the open; don't sneak up on your victim. [67]

Huffman took exception to the allegation and, in his peculiar style, described John Holt in a statement of considerable interest for its picture of the temper and moral codes of the frontier times.

. . . when things were new here and the outlet from the south had not been trodden by herds to any extent, I met John Holt. I did not know his name until long afterward, and we talked together and I sold to him that day the first horse he put a leg over in this country, I think. That happened near the Gray Mule [68] and not far from the old McQueen House [69] site, in view of the window where I now write. He paid me $30.00 down and rode away along the old Piper Dan [70] trail Tongue River way. . . .

John Clay, I think it of little importance relatively whether Con [Conrad Kohrs] or John had many or few successes in acquiring a multiplicity of cows, acres, or other material things, but it is important as you, above many men I know, understand that their cooperation and their acquiring a fine consideration for the feelings (and feelings are things like other things) of their fellowmen did and does measure fitness to manage men and large affairs, and who acquired not that has never gone very high, which is my way of saying also that a loose word or a despised fact may loom like Smoky Butte tomorrow. . . .

On another memorable day, also in view of this spot, LO [71] and SH cowboys reveled and drank and galloped the plank sidewalks fully armed and ready as always to slay, under certain provocations, and I saw John Holt seize in his strong hands and take off from an LO horse one of his boys and lead the abused horse away, and that armed and whiskey inflammed hand reviled him in language that would chill your blood, and John Holt reviled him not again, and who thus reviles not under such provocation must have had in him the elements of a great soul. Looking back over the years of my neighboring with John Holt I recall one special occasion, borrowing or returning his kraut cutter, I found him ill in bed. I sat beside him and he told me, among other things, calmly, unwhimperingly, that he thought it doubtful whether he should rise therefrom again. His manner and his words convinced me of something that nothing since has changed, or can change, when I try to estimate his real character.

Again, one never to be forgotten day while a guest of his ranch in the presence of his men I unwittingly broke a cardinal rule of the place, and he, in the presence of the amused throng, his face aflame, walked away without a word, and though we were alone much together after that, it was never mentioned.

. . .   .

There may be many men still members of the Old Miles City Club, who I believe know that he upon one occasion, resenting unbecoming language from a man of the cloth and believing that he, the man of holy orders, had cheated at a game of cards promptly threw him out of the Club, and I dare to say now because the one thrown out is still living, that I believe whatever he may now be, he was then and for a long time, sneaked and lied. So I am unable to believe that John Holt ever with malice aforethought struck below the belt or sneaked from behind, also I believe it possible that you, John Clay might have been imposed upon in getting the score of that encounter with Dr. Azel Ames, but if you saw it, and he did strike from the wrong side, he did it in the heat of passion, and after the lie had passed between the two men.[72]

Huffman's love of humor was one of his outstanding characteristics, and it permeates many of his fragmentary manuscripts. Some references, alas, are only short cryptic notes as "Fritz the sawed off cook and Monte. Tobasco for catsup," stories that have been lost to the past. Other incidents he outlined in more detail in sketches and letters. An example of the sort of practical jokes in which he sometimes took part is described in the account of the evening spent reminiscing with General Miles and a group of other old timers. Huffman recalled:

April Fool's day was a little different when we were three hundred miles from the railroad, and were just emerging from a long hard winter. We played a few pranks on each other and wound up by loading a lot of big fat cigars with anywhere from 45 to 70 grains of black powder [73] well tamped in. Now it is true that an Indian at that time would not smoke a cigar. He would light it, hold the muzzle towards him and when the donor of the cigar turned his back, break off the lighted end and stow the balance of the good tobacco to be ground up and mixed with his willow bark incense at some convenient period.

Now it must be confessed with all candor that a half dozen or more of us called upon the saddler of the post who was a mighty good fellow, and among the recent arrivals at the post was his wife. A sergeant, a dressy cavalryman who was present paying his respects to the saddler and chatting with the newly arrived young woman who was seated in an adjoining room, promptly espied the fine large cigar that we presented to the saddler. He watched his chance and slipped it from where the saddler had put it and, getting the large evening lamp between him and the young woman, proceeded to stick the aforesaid cigar into the light chimney to light it, whereupon what happened can be better imagined than described. The lamp was out and the lady was being rescued from near faint and the visitors, including myself retired swiftly toward the trader's store. There we made the mistake of presenting some of these loaded cigars to Spotted Bear, High Bear [74] and at least one other, who, when they lighted them, left the burning fragments, hiked their buffalo skinned garments or robes high above their ears and without casting any glances behind walked rapidly towards the Indian camp.[75] As I recall it now, we had our laugh before the general had us on the carpet; and I said to the general, "He laughs best who laughs last. You had your laugh thirty years after." [76]

Huffman continued to operate a studio in Miles City until 1890. He had invested in city real estate and had prospects of a comfortable income when the depression hit. In a heart-weary mood, he wrote his father on March 2, 1890, that he had closed up his affairs and was leaving for Portland and perhaps, eventually, California. Nor did he have any idea of where he would "fetch up" or what he would follow for a livelihood.

The next few years found Huffman working at various tasks at various places, one of them being at a photographic establishment in Chicago. In the end the wide-open spaces called him back, and in 1896 he established a studio at Billings. After operating this establishment for a couple of years, he sold out and returned to Miles City, where he opened another studio. This he operated until about 1905, when he closed it to casual business and devoted his time to the production and

22. "High Bear, Ogallalla Sioux."

sale of pictures from his old negatives. These he sold in a variety of forms ranging from postcards to enlargements up to seven feet long, and from packages of contact prints to painstakingly tinted enlargements. He was never able to find anyone who could do tinting which was accurate enough to suit him, and consequently all the colored photographs are his own work. As his skill with water colors and oils was unique, these tinted, signed photographs are collectors' items. Collections of his pictures were sold to many museums, libraries, schools, and private collectors; and he exhibited at various art shows in the state and elsewhere.

His pictures kept him busy until the end. Visitors to his studio were certain of a pleasant visit, for he never tired of providing the human-interest details and stories which went with the pictures. He particularly enjoyed the calls made by others who had lived during the days he loved so much. According to one old cattleman:

He was a man that was hard to understand. He thoroughly enjoyed having you visit his studio and took great pleasure in showing his pictures and would gladly make you a present of one but was insulted if you offered to buy one.[77]

Charles M. Russell, the guest of honor at the annual meeting of the Montana

Stockgrowers Association in 1918, summed up the opinions of cowboys and cattlemen when he wrote of this occasion:

> One of the attractions the visitors enjoyed at Miles was Huffman's collection of range pictures at the fine art studio he has built to keep 'em in. Huffman was post photographer at Fort Keogh in the old Indian fightin' days of the '70s, and is one of the real old-timers in this business in Montana, which his pictures show.[78]

In December, 1931, Huffman and his wife journeyed to Billings to spend the holiday season with their daughter Ruth. On the morning of the 28th he went downtown to read and visit with friends at the Billings Commercial Club. As he climbed the steps from the street, he was stricken with a heart attack and died a few minutes later. Thus passed a pioneer who had watched with pride the development of a frontier country, but who had loved best those wild, free days he recorded with his camera. Although he left behind a priceless collection of frontier pictures, it is to be regretted that he never completed his *Recollections of a Frontier Photographer*. The present volume can never be an adequate substitute for what he could have written.

Nove 26
1925

Ralf Budd

Dear Mr. Budd

    this is Thanksgiving day an Im thanking you for the good time you gave us last summer   turkey is the emblem of this day and it should be in the east but the west owes nothing to that bird but owes much to the humped backed beef . . . . the Rocky mountains would have been hard to reach without him   he fed the explorer   the great fur trade wagon tranes felt safe when they reached his range   he fed the men that layed the first ties across this great west   Thair is no day set aside where he is an emblem   the nickle wears his picture   dam small money for so much meat   he was one of natures biggest gift and this country owes him thanks. . . .

                your friend
                C. M. Russell [1]

HIDE-HUNTERS and SPORTSMEN

During the summer of 1855 a tall, lean, hawk-eyed trapper guided a strange party slowly down the valley of the Powder and, in the fall, to the wooded mouth of the Tongue. Here, eight miles above the site now occupied by Miles City, the party "forted" and spent the winter. This was the first big-game hunting expedition, organized solely for pleasure, to penetrate this region. The leader was 60-year-old Sir George Gore of Sligo, Ireland, and the guide was Jim Bridger, that canny frontiersman whose knowledge of the geography and the good hunting regions of the Northwest was unsurpassed by any of his associates.

Gore was a "bold, dashing, and successful sportsman" who followed the unique daily routine of sleeping until about 10:00 A.M. and then having a bath and breakfast. After this he would go hunting and often remain out until 10:00 P.M. He was well prepared for a leisurely trip with a minimum of personal discomfort. There were 43 men in the party of whom 40 were employees of various kinds; and his outfit consisted of "112 horses—some very fine ones—12 yoke of cattle, 14 dogs, 6 wagons and 21 carts." His supply of provisions contained many luxury items unknown on the prairie, and his equipment and rifles were the finest obtainable.

While Gore was not the first hunter to kill wantonly, he probably set a record for those days. Later, in St. Louis, he told a U. S. Army officer that "during his protracted hunt he had slaughtered the enormous aggregate of forty grizzly bears, twenty-five hundred buffaloes, besides numerous elk, deer, antelope, and other *small* game." This slaughter came to an end during the summer of 1856 when

Gore made his way down the Yellowstone Valley, with his baggage partly in flatboats and partly in wagons, to Fort Union, and then on down the Missouri.[2] However, the departure of Gore did not mark the end of wanton killing—it only marked the beginning.

The country through which Bridger guided Gore was one of the best big-game hunting regions in the West; and of all the animals that ranged this region none provided a greater thrill in the chase than the buffalo. Stories of its peculiarities and habits, the variety of ways in which it was hunted, and the many uses to which various parts of its body were put have surrounded this animal with a fascinating folklore of its own. Certainly no hunter can read stories of the swift dash of the early hunts without wishing to experience those thrills; and no epicure can read of the ways of cooking the various cuts without longing to sit beside a campfire and sample a hump baked in a pit, chopped tenderloin broiled in a section of the intestine turned inside out, roasted marrow bones, and the many other dishes which early travelers have never tired of describing.

Buffaloes were large game animals. Full-grown buffalo bulls stood five to six feet at the hump and weighed a ton or more; cows were smaller and seldom weighed over 1500 pounds. And although massive heads and shoulders gave the animals a clumsy aspect, their strength, speed, and agility were out of all proportion to their appearance. Generally speaking, the color of the hair was dark brown when the hide was prime in the early winter, fading to a seal-brown in the spring. However, there were several variations in color and texture of hair which were recognized by the hide trade. There were the extremely rare white robes, dirty cream-colored or "buckskin" robes, "black and tan" robes, "blue" or mouse-colored robes, and "beaver" robes. Among the tens of thousands of hides bought in Miles City in 1882 there was *one* "buckskin" robe;[3] and one hunter recalled that in the same year about one per cent of his hides were "blue" robes—which brought $16 each, as compared to $3.50 for an ordinary robe.[4]

Those who have written about the meat claim exceptional qualities for it and state that it had a better flavor than beef and that much larger quantities could be consumed without ill effects. Hornaday, who tried to make a critical analysis of this question and who admitted that certain buffalo dishes were food "fit for the gods," did "not believe any difference really exists [between beef and buffalo], unless it is that the flesh of the buffalo is a little sweeter and more juicy."[5]

In some habits, buffalo exhibited considerable intelligence and in others, little, if any. Their stupidity, coupled with inborn stubbornness, often caused herds to march steadily forward into places from which the animals could not extricate themselves. Their slowness to take alarm when an individual was wounded made possible the killing of large numbers in what the hide-hunters termed "stands." However, when wounded, an animal would separate from the herd and hunt a narrow gully in which to hide. If not pulled down by the wolves, they showed remarkable ability to recover from serious wounds. In grazing, they also showed a lack of good sense and frequently seemed to wander from good pasture to poor in an aimless fashion.

On the other hand, the animal had an uncanny faculty for locating the easiest grades across a divide, and frontier trails and railroads often followed old buffalo paths from one valley to the next. They rarely had disease or screw worms and, when bothered by heel flies, simply laid down and tucked their feet under them, whereas cattle would "roll their tails" and take off at a gallop. They never lay down with their feet uphill and so never had trouble getting up; furthermore, they rose like a horse—on their front feet first—and therefore were able to get up when weak.. As their eyesight was poor, they depended on their keen sense of smell, or on bands of antelope which often grazed nearby, to warn them in case of danger. Once alarmed, they ran upwind, relying on their noses to warn them of any new danger which might lie in their path. In winter storms they faced into the wind and sought protection in some sheltered valley or system of ravines instead of turning tail like cattle and drifting helplessly. And the bulls acted as guardians for the young calves, often taking more interest in warding off wolves than did the mothers.

Just as elk, deer, and mountain sheep came to lower altitudes in the mountains as winter approached, the buffalo made a similar compensation by moving southward. Thus the herds that ranged in Montana during the summer spent the winter in northern Colorado, Wyoming, and Nebraska; and those which wintered in the valleys of the Missouri, the Yellowstone, and their tributaries went north in March to ranges in Canada. This seasonal migration was a fascinating characteristic. Peter Koch recalled that

> In March 1870, I traveled from Muscleshell to Fort Browning on Milk River, and for a distance of forty miles I do not think we were out of easy rifle shot of buffalo. . . . we could see many miles on either side; but . . . the eye only met herd after herd of grazing and slowly moving buffalo. . . . Three days later I passed over the same trail on my return trip, and the vast herds had disappeared as if by magic. Only two or three old bulls were still wandering over the prairie. . . .[6]

Those who depended on the animal for food might live in a land of plenty one day and find starvation staring them in the face on the next.

This movement was sometimes slow, as Koch observed, but at other times rather rapid. James McNaney, who guided for the Smithsonian expedition under Dr. Hornaday[7] in 1886, reported that about the first of December, 1882, while his party was hunting on Beaver Creek approximately 100 miles south of Glendive

> . . . an immense herd arrived from the north. It reached their vicinity one night, about 10 o'clock, in a mass that seemed to spread everywhere. As the hunters sat in their tents, loading cartridges and cleaning their rifles, a low rumble was heard, which gradually increased to "a thundering noise," and some one exclaimed, "There! that's a big herd of buffalo coming in!" All ran out immediately, and hallooed and discharged rifles to keep the buffaloes from running over their tents. . . . The herd came at a jog trot and moved quite rapidly. In the morning the whole country was black with buffalo.[8]

About three weeks later a still more striking event occurred. For a few days previously the vicinity of McNaney's camp had been entirely deserted by buffaloes, not even one remaining. Then

> . . . one morning about daybreak a great herd which was traveling south be-

23.   Another view of Buffalo grazing in the Big Open.

gan to pass their camp. A long line of moving forms was seen advancing from the northwest, coming in the direction of the hunters' camp. It disappeared in the creek valley for a few moments, and presently the leaders came in sight again at the top of "a rise" a few hundred yards away, and came down the intervening slope at full speed, within 50 yards of the two tents. After them came a living stream of followers, all going at . . . "a long lope," from four to ten buffaloes abreast. Sometimes there would be a break in the column of a minute's duration, then more buffaloes would appear at the brow of the hill, and the column went rushing by as before. . . . For about four hours . . . did this column of buffaloes gallop past the camp over a course no wider than a village street.[9]

This privilege of being able to shoot from their "doorstep" was promptly exploited by the hunters who poured a continuous fire into the column as it galloped past, killing about 50.

After the buffalo moved in on a range and settled for a season, they usually broke up into small bands of about 20 to 100 and scattered over the countryside. This was the condition which existed when Huffman guided for Granville Stuart in April, 1880, when the latter made a long trip up the Rosebud and Tongue valleys to the Big Horn Mountains, down the Big Horn Valley to the Yellowstone, and then northward to Flat Willow Creek and the Judith Mountains in search of a good cattle range. Stuart's journal provides an intimate and detailed picture of the amounts and the tameness of the game observed, as well as the activities of the party.

April 26. . . . Just before camping time I discovered a band of buffalo bulls up a little draw to the south and Huffman and I went up and killed one. We took the tongue, the tenderloin, and the "fries." [10] Huffman considered them a great delicacy. I preferred the loin fried in a separate pan with strips of bacon. The others of the party [11] going to camp killed a white-tailed deer. There was a band of buffalo, about fifty in number, across the river from camp but we did not bother them. . . .

April 27. Had to mend a broken pack saddle which kept us in camp until nine o'clock. Buffalo all around us. Huffman and Eugene couldn't resist the temptation to have a run so they crossed the Rosebud and went for a bunch that was grazing along the edge of a ridge and after a lively chase across the bench land killed one. Only took the tongue as we had all the fresh meat that we could use. . . . This day's travel was through a good grazing country. . . . Hundreds of buffalo in sight all the time. We had lots of fun running them but had to forego much of the pleasure as the sport is too much for our horses. . . .

Wednesday, April 28. . . . The whole country is black with buffalo. Eugene killed one. Being a boy he couldn't resist killing just one, although we did not need the meat. He took the tongue. . . .
. . . . The country is now all broken up into low grassy hills and mounds. No timber but splendid grass everywhere and buffalo in every direction. . . .

April 29. . . . Saw four black-tailed deer, first on the trip. Small bands of buffalo in sight all the way down to Tongue river. . . .
After we rested and had dinner, Eugene Lamphere and L. A. Huffman packed up and started down the river on their return to Fort Keogh and Tom

24. "LAH and a Young Bull Killed with the Henry Saddle Gun."

and I are left alone. We miss our friends sadly. Eugene has all the enthusiasm of a boy of twenty-one, in a country where everything is new and wonderful to him, and Huffman is one of the most companionable men I ever traveled with. Tom Irvine is the best reconteur on earth, and we have had some great old times on this trip. This morning Irvine's little roan objected to being saddled and bucked into the campfire, scattering coffee-pot and frying pans, consequently we had plenty of ashes for relish.

Several days later, after making a reconnaissance to the Big Horn Mountains and back north to the Yellowstone River, Stuart crossed at Terry's Landing[12] and continued northward. Of the country north of the Yellowstone, he wrote:

May 10, 1880. . . . There has been a big herd of buffalo across here lately and they have eaten the grass off close. Saw a herd of buffalo running across the hills east of our camp. Indians after them of course. . . .

May 11, 1880. . . . Large bands of antelope and hundreds of buffalo in every direction. I killed one at camp. . . . Harry Wormsley and John Roberts stood guard tonight. Had to run out and shake our blankets to freighten the buffalo away and to prevent their stampeding our horses. . . .

May 12. . . . Buffalo by the thousands in every direction. Could have killed many as we traveled along but we did not need the meat. . . . camped at noon at a hole of rain water in a little dry creek. . . . While in this camp a band of antelope lay down on a point on one side of our horses and two old buffalo bulls on the other side are standing guard for us. Antelope and buffalo are very tame here. Will hardly run from us. . . .[13]

Such was the condition at the beginning of the hide-hunting days. Three years later all that remained were a few stragglers.

Stuart was not the only one who thoroughly enjoyed this trip. Thirty-six years later, in a letter to Tom Irvine, Huffman recalled:

. . . as Granville Stuart used to say—"We are burnin' daylight," when we dawdled along the trail telling stories when we went to the Big Horn [Tongue] with him in 1880 and maybe stopping to cinch up your old Roney and I'd get my gun out of the boot and cinch up old Paddie and we'd have a little wild west on the side, running buffalo, on the flats along the Rosebud not far from where old man Straw afterward built his home; and I can see you now on old Roney, who was gun wise, and I can hear you laugh when I get back, for Paddie he'd go hog wild at the first shot and break away for the Tongue river, you'd get the meat and you'd laugh and I'd get the ride. "We're burning daylight." [14]

No wonder Huffman loved those wild, free days!

"Arrived in Miles City about 5 P.M. April 17 [1880]," Granville Stuart wrote in the journal he kept on the range hunting trip.

From the Porcupine [15] clear to Miles City the bottoms are liberally sprinkled with the carcasses of dead buffalo. In many places they lie thick on the ground, fat and the meat not yet spoiled, all murdered for their hides which are piled like cord wood all along the way. 'Tis an awful sight. Such a waste of the finest meat in the world! Probably ten thousand buffalo have been killed in this vicinity this winter.[16]

Thus Stuart chronicled the early hide-hunting days in the Northwest—the change from hunting for meat and robes to hunting—if cold, businesslike slaughter can be called hunting—almost solely for hides.

The southern herd in Kansas, Colorado, Oklahoma, and Texas had been practically wiped out by the end of the hunting season in 1875 and the extermination of the northern herd had just started when Stuart bumped along the trail between Terry's Landing and Miles City in a "covered jirky." [17] Hunting had not been difficult along the Yellowstone the preceding winter. "Yellowstone" Kelly recalled that

The last killing that I remember was near the mouth of Powder river in the winter of 1879–80. The buffalo were massed along the Yellowstone in very cold weather, so cold the buffalo were stupid. We approached within 40 yards of them and they would scarcely run when we commenced firing.[18]

Huffman recorded the hide-hunting days in both photograph and story, but unfortunately some pictures mentioned in his writing are no longer known. In one rough manuscript, he put down a thumbnail sketch of these days as he saw them.

With all its hardships, privations and dangers, its wastefully cruel and bloody work, the life had its charm as I know. How well I remember that October morning on the Little Missouri—not far from the spot where Mr. Roosevelt a few years later made his ranch home and gathered the material for his most interesting books—when we sighted a few scattering buffaloes. Instantly every man of the seven we mustered was keyed to top notch excitement. Our wagons were parked. Some thought we were about to come in touch with the long talked of edge of the "main herd." But save the few stragglers first sighted none were seen though the country was scouted, horse and foot, far and wide, the last of our weary hunters not returning to the camp until late the following day. Elk and deer we encountered here in abundance and there was broiling and feasting galore by night with no end of sport and minor adventures.

Not until the Yellowstone lay many miles behind us and we had climbed the divide between the two rivers, where across the brown wastes Smoky Butte—butte of memories—came into view [19] bathed in the haze of October, did we at last see spread out before us, far and wide to the limit of vision, that mighty herd, here grazing in scattering hundreds on ridges and slopes, there massed—moving black and dense against the distant horizon. Then we halted and set about building rude camps of poles chinked with mud and roofed with the first green hides of our killings. There we wintered, adding our mite to the work of destruction.

Hard by that camp [was] a round rocky butte, its crest commanding as vast and noble expanse of yellow bunch grass, ravine sheltered, pasturage as can be found. . . . This was our watch tower. From here our hunters took their morning observations and planned their daily attacks on the herd that took refuge in increasing numbers as the short winter days drew on with intense cold and a blanket of snow. . . .

Few men ever became successful killers, ever acquired the knack, possessed the strength, iron nerve, patience and endurance required. The work was, for the most part, done on foot, [and] the favorite arm [was] the "Old Reliable" Sharps rifle, calibre .45–120 or .50–130, . . . weighing 18 to twenty pounds each. Any rifleman in those days could go out and stalk an animal or two and start a stampede but the man worth while, that could keep half a dozen skinners in work, must know how to get a "stand." [He must know] how to pick out and kill dead in their tracks at long range the leaders, the heads of families—bull or cow as the case might be, [and] time his shots—not too fast—with perfect precision, guessing his distances with a nicety beginning seldom nearer than 200 yards. [This] only comes of long practice, [and] form[s] the nucleus of a "stand" round which numbers would move as if dazed until not infrequently killings would total sixty or eighty lying dead in a group. One of Jim White's famous stands I recall near the old "Dry House" [20] north of Ft. Keogh tallied one hundred and twenty, killed in less than two hours when herds were storm driven, intense cold and a heavy blanket of snow furnished ideal conditions for successful slaughter.

What an awful waste it seemed to me then, and, as I look at these few old photographs which I made in and about our camps in those days, it seems more cruel and unjustifiable than ever. Almost none of the hunters, and they were legion—their camps, turned their attention to the curing of meat. They left it to rot where it fell once the robe—and sometimes the tongue—had been

25.   "The Deserted Camp."

taken. Smoked buffalo tongue was a delicacy famed of the steamboat days, and it did have an appetizing flavor and richness all its own found in no other tongue. At Dry House Springs only, as far as I remember, was any serious attempt ever made to cure buffalo meat in quantities for sale at the then far away "end of the track" and the steamboat landings. And there at Dry House springs to this day, beside the creek, you may trace dimly the rows of pits which were dug in the earth and lined with green hides [thus] forming the vats in which the meat was pickled before being dried and smoked.[21] This was pretty tough meat too, that "bull buff" that was freighted to market. Bulls yielded more pounds though and were far easier killing than the fat, barren cows and yearlings we soon learned to pick for our own eating. If there was ever a sweeter, finer morsel of flesh than those well marbled strips from the hump of a fat, barren cow, I have failed to find it.

Always there comes back visions of that wide fireplace of mud and stones, in the snug camp where we spent that first winter, 'round which at the end of those [short, winter] days of toil and adventure [we gathered for] that chief meal . . . of the day. [There] we rested and feasted on the very fat of the land, food fit for the gods, prepared by our faithful old "Hombra," the cook, at work in the glow of the fire before which he'd have swinging sputtering, spit-tasty, long slabs of choice "hump" skewered together, four inches thick, brown and "crumpy" without [and] red and juicy within, served with sour-dough dutch oven biscuits, big and generous and each garnished atop with its shortening—a "cracklin" of buffalo fat—and a dusting of "cinnamoned sweetnin." And now and again a dessert of "duff," good old "plum duff" [in] a plump sack, a lost art [that has not] come . . . down to the cooks of these times. And fellowship too, by the light and warmth to that fire piled high with fat pine [22] and crackling red cedar, we knew, of a sort which can only subsist twixt men who together have toiled, shared and dared in the wilds. . . . One among us, the bravest and truest with deep, vibrant, musical voice, stilled this many a year—its owner asleep in an unmarked grave, would sing to us, "Douglas, Douglas tender and true," and old Hombra's especial delight would wake when it came to the ones with the familiar refrain.

Hide-hunting was rough, dirty, and sometimes dangerous work; and the hunter was, in the opinion of one old ex-cowboy, "one tough hombre." Theodore Roosevelt, who saw them after the herds were gone, noted that they "formed a distinct class" and "were absolutely shiftless and improvident; . . . had no settled habits; . . . were inured to peril and hardship, but entirely unaccustomed to steady work"; and that many drifted into criminal occupations.[23] On the range they were rough-looking individuals—usually dirty, greasy, unshaven, and frequently lousy [24]—but usually hospitable and ready to help in time of need. John Goff, who had hunted in Texas before he came to Montana, was once described by a buffalo hunter, who was probably dirty and unkempt himself, as having "long hair and was the dirtiest, greasiest and smokiest looking mortal I had ever seen, as he sat there on a fleet-looking horse, holding in his hands a 44 Sharps' rather carelessly. . . . After we reached his camp he treated me like a nobleman." [25] However, when these individuals came to the little villages like Miles City and Coulson to refit and carouse, many of them raised hell and put a prop under it.

Not only did these men occupy one of the lowest rounds on the social ladder, but even the women of easy virtue patronized by them were considered below the girls of those honky-tonks frequented by the cowboys. Among them were men with prices on their heads. Huffman jotted down this note about Jim White, the hunter who got the stand of 120 at Dry House Springs: "Told Hanna [26] on getting over a spree in fall of '80 on Shell Creek that 5000 was offered as reward for him killing a wealthy Spaniard in mountains of old Mexico." White, who was later shot by a man named Miller on White's Creek, was also known in Texas as a tough character. On one occasion when a group of *ciboleros* [27] spoiled a stand he had started, he deliberately shot the horses from under four of the party. On another occasion, when a party was being organized to go fight Indians, he got drunk and tried to shoot another hunter.[28]

However, there were individuals who did not conform to this pattern. Huffman noted that

These hunters were not all uncouth, unlettered men, not all devoid of fine sensibilities or entirely neglectful of the little amenities of life. There were Clarks and Seviers, Boones and Poes among them—the best rifle-bearing woodsmen or plainsmen that ever faced the wilds. . . .[29]

Vic Smith, a marvelous shot with both revolver and rifle, was considered by many as the most famous hunter in Montana;[30] and, according to one who rode the ranges in his youth, this fearless man was idolized in Montana and Wyoming in later years.[31] Huffman numbered among his friends Jack Hawkins (the ex-Texas Ranger who believed that the buffalo would drift back from the north someday), "Hi" Bickerdyke (son of the famous Civil War nurse, "Mother" Bickerdyke), Oscar Brackett, Jim McNaney (who guided for Hornaday in 1886), John Cook, Joe Spence, and probably many others long since forgotten.

As soon as the Indian troubles in the Northwest had been settled, many of those who had hunted on the southern plains drifted up to Montana and Dakota. A few of these—John Goff, Jim White, Helmer, French Joe, "Hi" Bickerdyke, "Doc" Zahl, Conkling, Tripp, Buttermore, Joe Spence, and John Cook [32]—rise lifelike from Huffman's notes and manuscripts. As these hunters brought with them the techniques perfected on the plains of Kansas, Colorado, and Texas, the methods of hunting used on the northern plains were similar to the best used in the Southwest.

With the exception of a few U. S. Springfields—sometimes called "Long Toms"—and a few lever-action, model 1876 Winchesters, most of the rifles used by the hide-hunters were heavy-barreled, single-shot Sharps and rolling-block Remingtons. One old hunter who worked out of Miles City recalled that

The rifles were nearly all Sharps, .45–70, .45–90, and .45–120. Dan Levalley [33] had a .44–77 Sharps and there were a few Winchesters. My best luck was with a .45–90. Dan said his best gun was the .44–77 which there werent very many of this caliber.[34]

Such rifles, when fitted with a good telescope, cost well over $200 each. Huffman owned two Sharps, a .45–120 and a .40–105. The latter had a 28-inch barrel and weighed 16 pounds.

Although most of the rifles were Sharps, there was considerable divergence of opinion as to the proper cartridge. Hornaday states that the .40–90 and the .45–120 were favorites. These used straight cases which did not need resizing, and thus simplified the reloading problem. The favorite calibers for the Remington rifles were the .44–77 and the .44–90; the Springfield took a .45–70; and the Winchesters were chambered for the .45–70, 45–90, and .50–95. Sharps rifles were chambered for most of these cartridges, however, the big Sharps, or "Texas Fifty," was not so popular in the north as it was on the southern plains.

Killing buffalo at ranges of 200 to 600 yards required fine marksmanship but many other factors also contributed to the end result. With factory-loaded cartridges at 25¢ each and hides at a top of $3.50 each, the hunter had to reload his shells to keep expenses down, and, if he was to kill efficiently, he had to try for a kill at each shot. Many a hunter was as fussy as a hen with one chicken about the quality of his powder and the thickness of the paper used to patch the bullets. When using a rifle with set triggers, the touch of the trigger finger had to be sensitive—one hunter rubbed his finger with a rough piece of sandstone until it almost bled just to keep the proper touch!

Hunting parties varied in size. Some hunters skinned their own kills; others employed skinners, or strippers as they were sometimes called. Such a party might include one hunter, two skinners, and a cook; while in good hunting a skillful hunter might keep a half-dozen skinners busy. The kinds and amounts of

26.　"Five Minutes Work" *or* "A Killing of Cows and Spikes in the Smoky Butte region, North Montana."

equipment required are illustrated by Jim McNaney's purchases in 1882. To outfit a party consisting of himself, his older brother, and two helpers hired at $50 per month, he acquired the following:

　　2　wagons
　　2　four-horse teams
　　2　saddle horses
　　2　wall tents
　　1　cook stove with pipe
　　3　Sharps rifles (one each .40–90, .45–75, and .45–120)
　 50　lbs. gunpowder
　550　lbs. lead
4500　primers
　600　brass shells
　　4　sheets patch paper
　 60　Wilson skinning knives
　　3　butcher's steels
　　1　portable grindstone
　　　 Flour, bacon, baking-powder, sugar, molasses, dried
　　　 apples, canned vegetables, beans, etc., in quantity

This outfit cost them $1400 in Miles City.[35] Equipment bought at Fort Buford the following year, which involved eight wagons, cost "between $8000 and $10,000." [36]

27. "House of Green Buffalo Hides. Slabs of Hump at right, North Montana, January 1882."

In the field the hunters usually lived in rough log cabins—if near a timbered area—or dugouts built in the side of a steep hill or breaks along a drainageway. Judging from his notes, the old cabin pictured in one illustration was probably a hunting camp which Huffman once used; and the little washout roofed in with green hides represents the little, crude shelters sometimes used by a small party. McNaney set his tents end-to-end with the stove at the junction in the middle, cooking and eating in one and sleeping in the other.

The hunter usually sallied forth at daybreak with his heavy rifle, 75 to 100 cartridges, and—unless he employed skinners—knives and a steel. He usually went afoot and tried to work himself into a position 200 to 300 yards downwind of a small group of buffalo. There, behind a large rock, bit of brush, or the crest of a ridge, he laid out his tools and settled himself into a comfortable sitting or prone position. A sitting position with rest sticks was preferred by many, as it was believed this would lessen the amount of sound traveling along the ground which might alarm the animals, and it was easier to keep watch of the surrounding countryside for Indians or other trouble.

The hunter's problem was now to make his kill in as small an area as possible, and the ideal sought was to get a "stand." The time of day, what the animals were doing, manner of killing the first animal, and other similar factors affected the attainment of this ideal. One old hunter summed up his experiences as follows:

. . . I had better luck [for a stand] when not near water. As a rule, when going to or coming from water they seemed more restless. When getting up after a sleep was my best chances for a stand.

The best way to get a stand was to kill the leader, either bull or cow, and not shoot too fast. When the leader was killed they seemed to hesitate to see who . . . [would start to move] away. Then down him or her, then another

28. "After the Chase, North Montana range, M.T. Jan 82."

lull. The best stand we had got 17 out of 23. The main thing is to keep out of sight and scent. If they smelled or saw a man they were gone. Always kill . . . wound one and he would generally try to get away.[37]

The hunter usually shot the first buffalo through the lungs so that it would bleed and totter for a little while before it dropped. The others nearby would then become curious and smell or hook the wounded animal, thus concentrating their attention on the victim and not on the source of the danger. As wounded animals might bolt and spoil a stand, subsequent shots had to be heart or neck shots which would cause quick death. A stand which yielded 100 or more was exceptional, and Hornaday recorded the following: Vic Smith, who estimated that he killed about 5000 during the season of 1881–1882, got 107 in one spot in about an hour; Doc Augl [Zahl?] once had a stand of 85; John Edwards killed 75; McNaney knew of a stand that yielded 91; and Harry Andrews shot 115 shots from one position in less than an hour and killed 63.[38]

The number shot during a day was usually governed by the number that could be skinned; animals shot in the winter would freeze solid overnight, and those shot during warm weather would bloat overnight and stretch the hide so skinning was difficult. One hunter recalled that his quota for his skinners (probably two) was 25. Usually the animals were skinned in the manner shown in the pictures; but, if the kill was well grouped, a saddle horse or team might be used to roll the carcass as it was skinned, or, if a rough job was done, in pulling on the skin as it was being cut free.

In this type of skinning, the hide was slit along the belly from the throat to the tip of the tail, and down each leg to about eight inches above the hoof. Each side was then skinned out, rolling the animal as indicated in the pictures. On large animals, a "skinning wedge" was sometimes used to hold the body in position as it was rolled; however, it was easier to use a team and a wagon with a short, forked stick attached to the rear axle. By attaching a rope to one of the legs and to the rear axle, horsepower was used to roll the animal, the dragging "prop" preventing the wagon from rolling backward as the carcass was slowly turned. The head of an old bull was never skinned, the hide being cut around the neck. However, only the foretop around the horns was left on the carcass of a cow or younger animal—both of which are shown in the illustrations.". . . to skin such a quarry," wrote Huffman, "was not job for a boy or a novice."

Hides were cured in many ways. Sometimes they were salted, rolled, and piled where they would stay out of water from melting snow in the spring. Sometimes they were staked flat; but usually they were merely stretched out, flesh side down, on the prairie until picked up by the wagons and taken to market. They were folded lengthwise, hair inside to keep the hide bugs out, and piled in ricks like cordwood in the hide yards at the markets. The hides were shipped East by steamboat and by rail. Huffman recalled:

As the end of the steamboat days . . . drew near those old flat-bottomed stern wheeler steamers, as they went booming with the swift current on their return trips resembled great floating bales so heavily were they laden with bulky cargoes of robes and hides.

29. "Buffalo Skinners. Taking the Monster's Robe North Montana Jan 1882."

In May, 1881, the Sioux City (Iowa) *Journal* noted, "Most of our citizens saw the big load of buffalo hides that the *C. K. Peck* brought down last season, a load that hid everything about the deck below the roof of the hurricane deck. There were ten thousand hides in that load. . . ." [39]

Just how many thousands of buffalo were killed is not known. In 1886 Hornaday tried to arrive at an approximate figure and failed. One account of these days in *The Yellowstone Journal* states that Custer County, which then comprised the entire southeastern corner of Montana, shipped 180,000 hides in 1882, which was about 75 per cent of the kill in the northwest.[40] Huffman wrote:

Before me as I write is an old time pocket memorandum book used by a friend who bought hides in those days, wherein it is recorded that in a single month— June 81—at Miles City and the neighboring steamboat landings he received $25,500 [worth of?] buffalo hides—exclusive of robes [41]—at an average cost of $2.70 each. And there were scores of buyers. Hides were banked by the hundreds and thousands at every trading post and steamboat woodyard along the Yellowstone from Fort Buford at its mouth to the Big Horn and from the same place to Ft. Benton, the head of navigation on the Missouri.

When it was all over, except for the little herd started by Walking Coyote in 1874 on the Flathead Reservation with two bull and two heifer calves, only a few scattered survivors remained alive. Roosevelt, who began ranching on the Little Missouri in 1883, observed that

On those portions [of the plains] where the herds made their last stand, the carcasses, dried in the clear, high air, or the mouldering skeletons abound. Last year, in crossing the country around the heads of the Big Sandy, O'Fallon Creek, Little Beaver, and Box Alder, these skeletons or dried carcasses were in sight from every hillock, often lying over the ground so thickly that several scores could be seen at once.[42]

There remained one buffalo hunt of note. Dr. Hornaday, concerned because of the lack of choice specimens in the National Museum, began a frantic hunt for some stragglers. At Miles City in May, 1886, he verified the rumor that a few were left between the Yellowstone and the Missouri. Before coming back to hunt in the fall, he wired Huffman, "*I shall arrive Miles City 15th. Will you share with me the honors of the last buffalo hunt.*" But Huffman was too busy to go; and on December 22 he wrote his father regretfully,

Mr. Wm. T. Hornaday is with us—I shall have it to regret the rest of my life that I could not share in the glory with him as he kindly intended me to do —he has the finest collection in the world   25 in number (Bulls cows calves in nice graded sizes and ages)   The Smithsonian will take no back seat on the Buffalo question now. . . .

That was the end of the buffalo hunting. During the next few years bone-pickers scoured the plains and did their work so well that when Hornaday and Huffman went to Hell Creek on a hunting trip in 1901, even the bones had almost totally disappeared. The only evidences remaining of the vast herds were the narrow

30.   The hide-hunter's work.

paths their hoofs had worn in the prairie sod.

Unfortunately there is little specific information in Huffman's notes, and those letters to his father which have been saved, about his buffalo-hunting days. As his father liked to hunt, hunting—next to their "shop talk"—was the most common subject about which they wrote. On February 1, 1881, upon returning from a hunt, Huffman commented as follows:

> I made some good views of buff and sheep on my last trip—Just finished the titles ready for printing today   it was so intensely cold and stormy that I lost some [of the] best opportunities while among the Missouri Badlands near Poplar River. Glad you were pleased with the views.
>
> Yes I wish I could satisfy your curiosity and take a months ride through this land that to you there seems so very strange and wonderful. I wish you could change places with me and do some of the steady sitting of the saddle that I expect to do during the summer. Its not so interesting to me any more— yet I could not name a place that I had rather saddle up to go to than the Badlands and wild mountain parks of central and western Montana. no one can form a good idea of their vast extent who only reads and compares.

After his hunting trip the following year, Huffman sent his father the latest pictures which he had taken and, in answer to a letter from his father which apparently asked some specific questions, Huffman wrote on March 19, 1882:

> . . . You wonder who was with me on my Jan trip—and you also think it must have been jolly sport.
>
> I went in the same old California saddle that I always use and sent my outfit in the wagon carrying grub bedding and rations for two "skin hunting outfits"—The camp where you see the two grindstones is where we divided up one outfit stayed there and myself and one Joe Spence a professional skin hunter went north across the Mo with our pack a skinner and my little outfit— I wish you might have seen some of the sights but I cant wish that you should ever have to travel on a treeless plain in Jan for 8 days with only your overcoat and saddle blankets for bed. Camp Emmett is 160 miles in a N.E. direction from here and in some respects the most curiously formed country I ever visited—its in that region that in summer the Reds from over the line come to pound Pemmican and howl about the graves of numerous little bands cleaned up in scrimmages among themselves—Bull berrie thickets and cherry groves abound—the picture you refer to as having good grass and fertile appearance must be 188—5 minutes work—its on a lovely plain or valley 75 miles long and from 1 to 3 miles wide—right pretty to look at   well watered *winter and summer*   rich soil   good grass   and not a hoof track in it except Bison, soon to blossom like a rose—If I am any prophet   To strike Buff plenty would be at least 150 miles ride at this writing—dont know which way one would have to go next fall . . .

Huffman recalled these days in a manuscript which he titled "Pop Shots." The "Scotch Joe" noted in the story may be the Joe Spence in the letter just noted, though the date of the incident is earlier, probably 1879 or 1880.

> "Pop Shots," thats what "Scotch Joe" used to call the extra lucky ones that surprised by their accuracy and instant effectiveness out of keeping with average results when shooting at long range or at rapidly moving game. Joe

31. "Old Buffalo Camp."

was among the first of my hunting companions on the northern buffalo range in the seventies when I began to hunt for robes and butcher buffalo beef for sale to the army of N.P. [Northern Pacific] railway laborers then at work in the badlands between the big and little Missouri in Dakota, 150 miles southeast of our hunting camp in the breaks west of Prairie Creek and Red Water, north of the Yellowstone. One day Joe and I had made a killing of cows and spike bulls [43] in a bit of rough country near camp, had skinned and quartered it and were headed for the dugout, our pack pony well laden with strips of fat hump, tongues, and cartridge belts and skinning tools following close on our heels. The short winter day was almost at its close: it was bitter cold, the air full of flying, biting frost. Scattered bands of buffalo were in sight in all directions but one herd of maybe ten old bulls particularly attracted our attention by bunching on the edge of a little bench on the far side of a deep washout and exactly at the point where we must cross it on our way to camp. The leader—there was always a leader no matter at what season or the size of the bunch—stood out from the rest a few yards and would have been a fair target in a better light though 600 or more yards away.

"Have a crack at yon bull holdin the trail on us," says Joe.

Instantly I drew the hickory wiping stick from the barrel, threw the 18 pound Sharps to my face and fired—we almost never did offhand shooting with those 18 to 20 pound Sharps. We did our work sitting, using the wiping stick as a rest. Down went the big bull without a stagger or struggle.

"Pop shot," says Joe. "He'll be up and off in a minute. He fell too quick to stay down."

We drew nearer, crossed the washout, crept cautiously to the edge of the bank and looked over. There lay the bull, his head strained back, tongue out, eyes bulging but somehow looking strangely different from other dead bulls.

"Mark you his legs," says Joe.

Then I noticed that they did not lay relaxed but stuck straight out from his body like the legs of an overturned table.

"He's but numbed I tell ye," insisted Joe. "Mark my words, Kid. Never do you go up to put the knife to a bull that has his legs stickin' out straight the likes of yon."

But I lacked Joe's wisdom and experience. I was for saving that half ton of meat and pelt so convenient to camp. So while Joe waited for Crackers, "Crax" was the pack pony, I walked boldly up to his bullship. The next instant, before I could bring a gun to bear, those upturned legs gave a wild wiggle and the huge beast bounded to his feet and dashed by us like a runaway mongul [locomotive] down that narrow trail up which poor old "Crackers". . . at that moment was toiling with his load. That wise old nag managed to change ends before the headon collision occurred which precipitated horse and bull in a cloud of dust and stones to the bottom of the gulch. Crackers, handicapped by his pack, we found wedged wrong side up in the narrow dry creek bed . . . from whence we rescued him with difficulty. and the bull . . . went siftin up that badland hill like a bobcat up a shell-bark hickory.

Wolfing was the one other hide-hunting activity which depended on mass killing. The usual method of operation while buffalo were available—and the Indians were not too bad—was to make a circle trip of 40 or 50 miles from camp and kill buffalo along the route. The carcasses were half skinned, the abdominal cavity opened, and the meat slashed and sprinkled with about half an ounce of strychnine crystals which were well rubbed in. Although it was not uncommon in the early days for the hunter to be watched by a pack of wolves sitting on

32. "Wolfer's two-wheeled outfit used in rough country."

their haunches nearby—waiting until they could begin the "feast"—the wolfer preferred that the carcass freeze so that the wolves would have to gnaw frozen meat thus making the bait last longer and killing more wolves. A bait usually yielded ten to 50 wolves. The frozen bodies scattered around the bait were collected and piled, but the hunter had to wait for spring or for a chinook before doing his skinning.

The early wolfers traveled with a pack horse outfit, but in later years some of them used a little cart to carry their equipment as the one pictured here. The technique of wolfing changed with the passing years. As cattle were too valuable to be killed for bait, an old horse or the carcass of a cow or steer which had been pulled down was used for a decoy or bait; and in time the wolves became extremely wary. Huffman sometimes told of watching a wolfer who operated in the vicinity of Timber Creek:

I found him almost uncanny. He could locate the trail of a wolf in places where I could scarcely see the sign when it was pointed out to me. . . .

One weapon he used to kill wolves was balls of tallow and strychnine. In making these, he was very careful never to touch the tallow, lest he contaminate it with the human smell, but held the tallow in leaves when he rolled it, or in gloves liberally coated with tallow. Each ball, of about the size of a walnut, was split and a depression made in the center with a little wooden spoon. Into this depression he poured his strychnine, then pressed the two halves together again. Tallow was a tasty bit of food for a wolf; strychnine wasn't so healthy!

33. Market-hunters.

I myself, in one instance, saw where a wolf father had found one of the tallow balls and carried it to its puppy, bitten it in half, and shared the deadly morsel. We found the old wolf and the young one dead side by side.[44]

The group of later-day wolfers included some peculiar individuals. One ex-cowboy, who rode the range in the early days, recalled that wolfers usually had the uncanny habit of putting loose tobacco and cigarette papers in the same pocket with unwrapped strychnine crystals, of smoking all day, and being in good health at suppertime.[45]

In this game-rich country, deer, elk, antelope, buffalo, and wild fowl played an important part in providing provisions for soldiers and settlers. In a fragmentary note Huffman pointed out that the following quotation from General Miles' Memoirs was "a scrap of evidence" indicating the veritable hunter's paradise existing in the valley of the Rosebud when he and his partner established their ranch there:

In October, 1879, I left Fort Keogh, Montana, with a party of eight officers, twelve soldiers, and five Indians, for a hunt along the valley of the Rosebud. We were gone six days and had great success. During that time we killed sixty large deer, three antelopes, one mountain sheep, five elks, seventeen buffaloes, seventy prairie chickens and six ducks. . . . and on our return to the post we had ten six-mule wagons heavily loaded with the tropies of our rifles. There was a feast for the whole garrison of four hundred men.[46]

When Huffman arrived in Milestown, buff was a standard item of fare, and a few years later he wrote his father, "If you were here now you could take in your fill of game dinners as theres great rivalry among the new hotels in that direction. . . ." [47] In his spare moments Huffman hunted for recreation and, on one occasion at least, did a bit of market hunting. Some of these experiences he related to his father.

Yours of the 5th came while I was out on my fall hunt. We had a bang up time   6 of us in the party—one english pointer   one dandy spaniel   both dogs good trailers and crazy to run deer in the thickets. We gave them their fill in ten days   got a deer every day and one day two   had my canoe   one small row boat and one 18 foot clinker. Such a trip would make you young again   I cant get enough to eat since I came home—never had a trip brace me up like it—fact is I have not had a real old rough and tumble since 83

I acted as purchasing agent and paid all the bills for the boys and after everybody had what ducks geese chickens and venison they and their friends wanted I sold enough to place $7.25 to the credit of each one after paying everything. sold deer at 6 cts lb   ducks and chicks brought 2.75 per doz geese 75 cts each   We had a jag of it I tell you.

But best of it all is not as I used to think killing game. The Oct tints along the river's wooded islands—water clear as ice water—as your boat shoots along you can see the pebbly bottom from one to 8 ft below   clear frosty nights—long sunny hazy shimmering days brim full of running rapids—scrambles after wounded birds that fall on bars—now and then the sudden grounding and piling out into the water to save your cargo. then the reunion at night. supper over then comes the big camp fire and general exchange of experiences for the day. at a half hour before daylight everybody rolls out and by the time you can see to shoot each one has his stand for deer or is a mile or two out on a duck pass waiting for the early flight. I brought home one green head duck that weighed 5½ lbs   he was fat and we had him stuffed   made a good meal for three. . . .[48]

With such an abundance of game, it is not strange that sportsmen from the Eastern cities converged on the country west of Bismarck. As Miles City was the only town of any size in eastern Montana, many hunting parties outfitted and went out from here. One of these sportsmen whom Huffman knew well was the previously noted George O. Shields. In magazine articles and in an interesting book Shields described his trip up the valley of the Rosebud to the eastern edge of the Big Horn Mountains in 1881, and a trip the following fall up Clark Fork to the Absaroka Mountains.

On the first trip Shields came to Fort Keogh where he visited a friend, Captain Borden. The commandant, General Whistler, kindly put at his disposal Jack Conley, a packer, and three pack mules and the necessary camping equipment. The loan of a saddle pony from Borden completed the necessary items. Shields noted, "I also procured the services of Mr. L. A. Huffman, the popular and skillful photographer of Miles City, to accompany me." [49] Before the trip was over, Huffman had also doubled as guide and assistant cook.

Tuesday morning, August 30, 1881, found this party of three on the trail for the Big Horn Mountains. Hunting was excellent and the party had no difficulty in catching plenty of trout nor in killing deer, grizzly bear, mountain buffalo,[50] and antelope. They had no unusual experiences with game—other than the ease with which they kept their larder supplied with fresh meat. One of the most interesting experiences related details of the happenings of a night in camp near the head of the Little Big Horn River. After an all-night rain had soaked their bedding, Shields recorded:

It has rained nearly all day to-day and continues to rain to-night, so there

34. "Our Hunting Camp on the Little Horn."

is no possibility of drying our blankets. . . . we must sleep in wet blankets to-night. The cold chills run up and down our backs as we think of it. . . . The mercury has crawled down . . . to the freezing point, and a violent snow storm has set in. The wind sucks down through the canyon just back of our camp, and moans through the cottonwoods, driving the snow in blinding clouds through the brush, over the hills, and heaping it on our fire in such quantities that it soon drowned it out.

"Well what shall we do now?"

"Go to bed, I suppose," said Huffman drawing a deep sigh, and proceeding, with the aid of a forked limb, to extract his boots, which were as wet as the snow and water in which he had been wading, could make them. I struck a match and looked at my watch. It was nine o'clock.

"Well, Huffman," I said, "we shall only have nine hours to wait until daylight, and then we can get up and make a fire again."

. . . .

We had made our camp where a band of Crow Indians had camped a few days before. They had left some of their wiciup poles in position, and we had spread our canvas over them, thus making a very close, comfortable shelter, if not as roomy as we might wish for. Huffman and I crawled into our wiciup, and Jack into his. . . . We kept . . . [our soaked clothing] on, removing only our boots and hats. Our blankets were so wet and heavy that they stuck to us like a bathing-suit. Our bones ached and our teeth chattered. . . .

We finally got reconciled to our fate, however, and went to sleep, if being stupefied from the effects of hard work and cold water can be called sleep.

However, the conditions were too much for Huffman, who got up in the

35. Shields' hunting party with antelope killed on Bennett Creek, near where General Miles whipped a war party of Bannocks.

middle of the night and made a futile effort to start a fire. As the cold air outside was worse than the wet blankets, he had to give up and return to the wickiup. At the first crack of dawn, each pulled on his frozen boots and set about building a fire and getting breakfast.

   . . . As we became comfortable, and even jovial, we enjoyed the scene around us. The snow-storm was premature. The leaves had not yet fallen from the trees. . . . All these trees were heavily clad in their mantle of spotless white, and the contrasts between the green, gray, brown, golden and other colors, furnished by the autumn foliage, and the snow, made a grand picture.[51]

The day following that miserable night Huffman killed a bull elk and Shields got two deer. Shown in the picture Huffman made of this camp are Shields' two deer, and Shields' .40–75 Sharps-Borchardt (left), Huffman's .44 Kennedy (center), and Conley's .45–70 Springfield carbine. The blankets apparently rest on the antlers of Huffman's elk. Just beyond are the poles of one of the Crow wickiups with Shields seated nearby, two pack boxes with provisions, and Jack Conley holding Nig, the black pack mule which threatened to dunk Huffman's cameras and photographic supplies in the Little Big Horn on the return journey as related in the preceding chapter.

The following year found Shields and three friends headed up Clark Fork for the mountains on a three-week hunting trip. There, late in the forenoon of September 5 he met "away out there on that lonely trail, my old friend L. A. Huffman, the Miles City photographer . . . just returning from the National Park. . . ." As previously noted, he persuaded Huffman to turn back and photograph for him. Just above the mouth of Bennett Creek [52] the party camped and scouted this little valley for game. Here they spent a day hunting antelope with the results shown in the accompanying photograph.

The party then moved on up into the mountains following, generally, the old game trail to the Yellowstone National Park area which Chief Joseph had used on his retreat.[53] In the mountains they killed several elk and bear, one bull elk being a particularly fine specimen. One drizzly afternoon Shields and Sawyer each killed an elk within a short distance of each other and decided to forgo the butchering until the following day so the kill could be photographed. To keep the bears away, Shields camped beside them that night. The next morning a bull elk whistled about a half-mile away, and Shields made a successful stalk although it took eight hits to bring the animal down.

He was indeed a giant, much larger than Huffman's sorrel horse, which we knew weighed at the time over eight hundred pounds. He had by far the finest head of antlers I have ever seen. . . . Each beam measures four feet nine inches long, and the spread is four feet six inches. There are six points on one beam and seven on the other.[54]

Shields went back to his temporary camp to await Huffman; and when the two went to photograph the bull they found that a bear had torn it slightly but had not damaged either the head or the meat. After Huffman had photographed the animal, Shields and Wise started to skin out the head. When well started, they "heard strange noises on the hillside above us, and looking up we saw three grizzly bears charging down upon us." The situation was complicated. The horse on which Huffman was packing his things dragged him into the brush, the bears got between the hunters and their rifles, and the other horses were so crazed with fright that Shields and Wise could not attempt to mount. Not being able to flee or shoot, the hunters managed, by means of a brave front and much yelling, to bluff the grizzly and her two cubs. After a second charge and countercharge, the hunters killed the mother and one cub and the other took off through the brush. When it was all over they "dragged the corpses of the two down and laid them tenderly alongside of the elk, and Huffman leveled his camera on them" while

36. "Glory Enough for a Day."

Shields and Wise posed with their kill.[55] Thus ended the unusual experiences on this hunting trip.

The friendship formed between Hornaday, Huffman, and Jim McNaney in 1886 persisted through the years. On August 25, 1901, Hornaday, then director of the New York Zoological Park, wrote his former guide that he felt in need of a hunting trip. He complained that his muscles were soft, his head was no good, and that he needed to get on a horse again, sleep on the ground, eat off a tin pan, and hear coyotes instead of trolley cars. "We could have a bully time, Jim, as we always did. . . . If Huffman would go along, it would do him a world of good, & increase the fun. . . . And I will [hire the cook and] grub-stake the crowd."

Probably Hornaday's wheedling approach was unnecessary to interest his two friends in a trip to Hell Creek in the Missouri Badlands, but it was successful. Huffman wrote in a diary—which he failed to continue after the first week—that on "Wednesday Oct 2nd 1901 [at the] McNaney Ferry 3 PM W. T. Hornaday, Jim McNaney, Bert Smith, LAH [with a string of horses named] Bull Pup, Colorado Mustang, Jady, Sunfish, Lily, [and] Yellow Belly [left Miles City] Bound for Hell Creek." Unfortunately, like many fondly laid plans, the trip did not work out as it was supposed to. On the morning of the 5th Huffman noted:

This morning just after breakfast and while we were packing to leave, a solitary horseman appeared at a swinging gallop. . . . It was Calico Charley. We all wondered who was to have the bad news. It was Jim who at once galloped for Miles City 68 miles [distant].[56] The courier made it in the night.

37.   "Max Sieber, LAH, and Dr. Hornaday." (*Left to right*)

The diary indicates that "H & H" had a never-to-be-forgotten hunt. The first night out "Jim told us the story of Buck, Blucher, and Coaly," the hounds he had when he was wolfing. At the second camp "Young sage hens on the camp ground were soon in the salt pork and batter," and "Two Vests"—Huffman's nickname for the cook—told of an unsuccessful attempt to teach another how to dress a sage hen to avoid the sage taste. The camp at Sand Creek was bombarded with thunder and lightning from midnight until near morning; and at Sage Hen Springs, 12 miles from Jordan, the two deployed to a high round butte to take a new view of Smoky Butte, and Huffman recalled that "Round about its base and on the distant mesas I have seen, long years ago, sights which will never be again, miles on miles of buff as far as the eye could reach." And then they got lost in the edge of the breaks along the Missouri badlands, and, when about ready to turn back, "there came in view a neat little cabin with an overhanging roof like a Swiss chalet."

The cabin was the home of Max Sieber, a wolfer. The bachelor was away when the visitors drove down the trail, but he soon arrived:

38. "Interior of a Wolfer's cabin in the breaks of the Missouri."

hot and somewhat angry . . . as someone recently had invaded his home and borrowed tools and chains in his absence. When he had cooled a little and we had convinced him that we were not *scrippers* [57] or borrowers, he gave us a most cordial invitation to camp near by and make ourselves at home.

Sieber lost no time in extending his hospitality. After joining the party "at a good dinner," he announced, "now chentlemen, I failed for the first time to kill me a buck this morning and if you allow me I take you to the finest view about two miles and we can kill a buck, for sure, before sundown." Sieber guided them to a high rocky point, and, a few minutes after they sat down to enjoy the view and spin yarns, a buck broke cover nearby and Hornaday and "Two Vests" promptly downed him.

The hunting proved to be all Hornaday had hoped for, but it provided only a moderate part of the enjoyment. Sieber proved to be a kindred soul and he and Hornaday each had a

mine of good, heartsome stories . . . stored up—the one [having] spent 45 years a cowboy [and] buffalo hunter, the other a like period in search of animals in almost every foreign land. Behind some little butte we'd set down to blow, drink rain water from sandstone cups and spin our yarns.

39.   "Breaks of the Missouri. Hornaday in the foreground looking toward Snow Creek."

Perhaps the fellowship was the most enjoyable part.

But the results of this trip did not end when Huffman and Hornaday returned to Miles City. One day, while waiting under a protecting ledge of rock for a shower to pass, Hornaday picked up a bit of fossilized bone which he carried back to New York. The next spring he wrote to McNaney:

May 19, 1902

Dear Jim:—

A friend of mine who is connected with the American Museum of Natural History, here, wants to go out to Hell Creek to look for fossil bones, where I found some last October, and where M. A. Sieber found others, east of his ranch.

He would like to go up for a week or ten days, flying light, to see if it would pay to make a stay of a month or so.

Now, don't you want the job of taking Mr. Brown up. . . .

Barnum Brown's trip proved to be profitable, for it led to one of the largest finds of fossil bones in the West. Here the American Museum of Natural History in the course of several years uncovered the bones of hitherto-unknown prehistoric beasts.[58] The skull of one, when loaded at Miles City, barely went through the door of a boxcar.

. . . military life on the frontier is a compound of mud and romance.[1]

John F. Finerty

SOLDIERS—RED and WHITE

Ft Keogh M T Feb 6th 1880

Dear Father,

I have not heard from you for some time . . . The weather has been steadily moderating lately and things are unusually active about the post— On the 3rd the Gros Ventres and the Sioux had a big rumpus down the river a few miles—some ten dead and 12 wounded have been brought in   some reported to belong to S. [Sitting] Bulls band

Yesterday morning 3 men came in from Powder River one wounded in the shoulder and one in the fore arm—They were attacked while in camp at a hay corrall and barely got off with their hair—they put the number of Sioux at 40—Sargt Glover and 25 men started to look them up this morning—I heard Gen Miles tell Glover when he gave him orders at the Adjutants Office last night—"Glover make a success of this trip and I will make a *success of you*" so Glovers return will be looked for with much interest—Gen M arrived on Monday morning—was serenaded and bored generally as usual—I am doing well at business and enjoying life as well as might be expected—Am strongly urged to open a studio at Miles City the coming summer—Will think about it

I can think of nothing of importance to write—Hope to hear from you soon—With kindest regards to all the family

Late

The final results of the little expedition which Huffman mentioned in this letter were, contrary to his estimate, something "of importance." Sitting Bull and part of his followers had gone north into Canada in the spring of 1877. For the most part they maintained their camps north of the border, but small parties

40. "Spotted Eagle's Village Beside the Old Freight Road, 1880–1."

hunted and raided in the Montana and Dakota territories. In 1879 these raiding parties became so troublesome that Miles put a sizable force in the field during July and August and chased Sitting Bull back across the border. However, parties of lariat Indians still plagued the country and it was one of these parties which Sergeant Glover was sent out to "look up."

Miles recorded in his memoirs the outcome of Glover's trip:

He surprised them in one of their camps, drove them into a ravine, and held them there until Captain Snyder with his troops came up and forced them to surrender.[2] These Indians and those captured [later] by Captain Huggins,[3] were retained as prisoners, and information was sent to their people that they would be held until their relatives came in and surrendered.

In answer to this summons a delegation of eight stalwart warriors came in under a flag of truce from Sitting Bull's camp to ascertain upon what terms they could surrender. We treated them civilly, and tried in every possible way to impress them with the advisability of laying down their arms.[4]

"Every possible way" of impressing the delegation included demonstrating the telegraph with its sparks jumping between the contacts of the key, and the telephone over which the Indians talked to each other. Whether it was the "captured lightning" and the "whispering spirit" or the difficulty of finding enough to eat in Canada that was the deciding factor is not known, but part of Sitting Bull's followers did decide to come in and "in this way more than two thousand surrendered Indians were gathered at Fort Keogh." [5]

Huffman accompanied Miles' little party that negotiated the actual surrender with Spotted Eagle and Rain-in-the-Face after the Indians had moved down from Canada to Rainy Creek but, unfortunately, his impressions, if recorded, have been lost. Even after coming so far, these people were reluctant to give up their horses and guns so the negotiations could hardly be called a routine affair. Those who surrendered included the Sans Arcs under Spotted Eagle, part of the Hunkpapa, and various other bands under Broad Tail, Kicking Bear, and Rain-in-the-Face. These Miles located in prisoner-of-war camps along the Yellowstone just west of the post.

These were the first of Sitting Bull's force in Canada to come in. The others, some guided by Gaul and then finally, a year later, the remnants led by Sitting Bull, came in to the vicinity of Fort Buford and were taken down the river to the Standing Rock Reservation. Only with the surrender of these parties did the Indian wars in the Northwest come to a formal end. Huffman's pictures of life around Fort Keogh show the last large camps in the United States where Indians lived in buffalo skin tepees and subsisted chiefly on buffalo meat.

Among the surrendered Sioux were some interesting personalities. Of these Spotted Eagle was the most important. Miles described him briefly as "a wild, fierce chief . . . and one of the extreme type of wild savage." Finerty, who saw him at a council between Major Walsh of the Canadian Mounted Police and Sitting Bull's followers on July 30, 1879, set down a more detailed description of the man a year before he surrendered:

The Sans Arcs were represented by Spotted Eagle, who . . . was a fine specimen of the North American native—tall, rather slender and very graceful. He was about forty-five years old. While his features were very dark his eyes were rather light—a contrast very remarkable. He has no white blood in him, however. The Spotted Eagle was one of the foremost warriors of the wild Sioux, but never carried his martial hostility into camp with him. He knew how to fight and shake hands . . . Spotted Eagle was eloquent as well as valorous, but was not a mischief breeder.[6]

After the chief surrendered, he made an effort to learn the ways of the whites and to adjust himself to their customs. On one occasion he requested permission to attend the religious services of an itinerant preacher at Gould's Hall in Milestown, and Miles sent Tom Irvine as his escort.[7] The preacher used numerous emphatic gestures throughout his sermon; and Irvine was surprised to learn at the end of the service that Spotted Eagle had experienced no difficulty in understanding the "sign language" of the preacher. The Indian was also favorably impressed by finding in the benediction with the upraised hand of the preacher a kinship between his religion and that of the whites.[8]

Although not the most important man in the village, by far the best-known warrior was a handsome Hunkpapa who hobbled on crutches, lamed permanently by wounds received in the battle of the Little Big Horn. A noted warrior among his own people, Rain-in-the-Face's fortitude was attested by the feat of having hung six hours at a sun-dance ceremony. However, most of his fame—or notoriety —with the whites came from an alleged act which he probably never committed.

It was on August 4, 1873, that the first of a series of events took place which eventually made him almost as well known as Sitting Bull.

Having reached a point on the Yellowstone River, near the mouth of the Tongue River, and several miles in advance, and while awaiting the arrival of the forces of the expedition [wrote Lieutenant Colonel George A. Custer in his official report], six mounted Sioux dashed boldly into the skirt of timber within which my command had halted and unsaddled, and attempted to stampede our horses.

Thus began the first action of the Sioux against the escort of the Northern Pacific Railroad surveyors. In the ensuing fight the Indians were driven from the field at the cost of one man and two horses wounded.

But unfortunately two non-combatants, Veterinary Surgeon John Honsinger, Seventh Cavalry, and Mr. Baliran, of Memphis, Tenn., in endeavoring to come from the main column to join the squadron in advance, were discovered . . . and killed almost within view of the battleground.[9]

These two men had been reckless in carelessly wandering away from the column unarmed, and this time, near Lock Bluff—a few miles above the present site of Miles City—their luck ran out.

About a year and a half later, while drawing rations at the Standing Rock Agency, Rain-in-the-Face boasted that he had killed these two men. Custer had his brother Tom arrest the Indian and bring him to Fort Abraham Lincoln. When questioned, he frankly admitted the killing and gave the details. Custer

41.   "Sioux Chief Spotted Eagle—Wa ma laga lisca, 1880."

had him confined to the guardhouse and chained to a civilian prisoner, but friends of the latter cut a hole in the wall one night and the next morning the room was empty. Rain-in-the-Face went to the camp of the hostiles and sent back a message that he would revenge himself for his imprisonment.[10]

Immediately after the battle of the Little Big Horn, the story became current that Rain-in-the-Face had revenged himself by cutting out Tom Custer's heart and eating it. This story was soon amended to substitute the heart of George A. Custer for that of his brother. Unfortunately for this myth, the officer who helped identify both bodies on the battlefield wrote later that "General Custer . . . had been shot in the left temple and the left breast. *There were no powder marks or signs of mutilation.*" Of Tom Custer, he noted that "His belly had been cut open and his entrails protruded. No examination was made to determine if his vitals had been removed." [11]

Huffman had already made friends with and photographed many of the prominent Cheyennes and Minniconjou Sioux who surrendered three years before, and the photographic possibilities in the new Sioux camp provided an irresistible attraction. However, Miles limited not only the Indians' movements outside of their camp but also posted a guard to keep whites away. These regulations posed a problem to Huffman, but he soon made the acquaintance of a young Irishman who drove a delivery wagon. This individual was not only on good terms with the sergeant of the guard, but had struck up an acquaintance with Rain-in-the-Face, the Indian whose photograph was most desired.

Huffman and the Irishman had no trouble getting into the camp and Rain-in-the-Face, although surly and unfriendly toward the soldiers, soon made up with the two conspirators and fell in with the plan Huffman proposed. They hid the Indian in the back of the delivery wagon and drove back to the studio at the post. Here Huffman kept the warrior for three hours or more while he photographed him in different poses, and in full regalia. After he had taken pictures to his heart's content, Huffman and the Irishman smuggled the Indian back into camp in the same manner as they had taken him out.

Just before Rain-in-the-Face was returned, the adjutant happened to visit the camp and observed that the Sioux were greatly excited. Investigating, he discovered that they were worried about the long absence of their chief, and many feared that he had been removed by the soldiers to be killed or sent away. The details of the situation were easy to ferret out, and the officer headed straight for Miles' office. Huffman used to relate that he did not have long to wait before an orderly came and told him he was wanted at headquarters. When he went in the adjutant merely motioned over his shoulder with his thumb toward Miles' office. Miles did not look up as Huffman came in and it was obvious that he was "hot around the collar." "Young man," he said, "if you ever take another prisoner out of camp without permission from the adjutant or myself, *you will find yourself in very serious trouble.*" Huffman obeyed. Years later when Miles was an old man and had forgotten the matter, Huffman's story of this incident provided the general with a hearty laugh.

Unfortunately for the Sioux, the government did not see fit to leave them in the land where many of them had been born. During the summer of 1881 Miles received orders that they were to be moved to the Standing Rock Reservation.

42. "Eta-ma-gozua or Rain-in-the-Face taken when he was in the camp of Spotted Eagle's hostile Sioux near Fort Keogh, 1880."

The Indians were contented and anxious to stay, and the crops they had planted were nearly half grown and in good condition. The orders to move were like a bolt of lightning from a clear sky. Some of the warriors went to officers and others whom they knew, begging and pleading with tears in their eyes to be allowed to stay.[12] But there was no way to evade the orders.

Five steamboats, the *Eclipse*—flagship of the fleet with Captain Marsh in command—the *General Terry*, the *Josephine*, the *Black Hills*, and the *F. Y. Batchelor*, tied up at the landing midway between Milestown and Fort Keogh. To the captains this was no ordinary trip. It was a great opportunity for a race, and large sums were wagered as to which boat would arrive at Standing Rock first. Each steamboat was tied up stern to the bank so that no time would be wasted in getting off to a running start when the last unfortunate was herded aboard. Huffman recalled the loading day—"the silent, stubborn warriors, standing with folded arms, without weapons, awaiting with what appeared to be stoical indifference whatever fate might be their portion . . . women and children, many of whom were in tears, some displaying resentment. . . ." For once the Indians had the sympathy of the soldiers and civilians. Huffman photographed these scenes and, of all the negatives lost when a fire destroyed his studio, he

43. "Officers' Quarters, Fort Keogh."
(About 1880; looking west.)

regretted these the most.

Fort Keogh—the hub of military activity in eastern Montana—had begun its existence in the fall of 1876 as the Tongue River Cantonment. The Cantonment, built in what is now the western edge of Miles City, consisted of crude "shelters made of logs placed on end in a trench dug in the soil and 'capped' with a 'plate' or log, on which rested a roof of poles and earth; not uncomfortable, as far as warmth was concerned, but terribly damp and leaky in the heavy rains of the spring." [13] The following summer Fort Keogh was erected on the level prairie about two miles farther westward. This was a typical frontier post with a row of officers' quarters built in a semicircle around the western part of the parade ground, two-story barracks for the enlisted men—or swaddies as they were called in Milestown—a guardhouse, post trader's store, stables, officers' club, warehouses, and other miscellaneous buildings. Most of the buildings were of frame construction, but a few—including the studio Huffman occupied—were built of logs placed upright, stockade fashion.

Miles, an energetic officer, began winter operations shortly after the command had settled in their rough quarters. Crook's operations, which resulted in the destruction of Dull Knife's camp on November 25, had driven the Cheyennes and Oglalas together in the valley of the Tongue. These Indians readjusted themselves after this disaster, and had just split into separate camps when Miles took the field in the latter part of December. His scouts captured four women and three children on Hanging Woman Creek as they were going between camps; and Miles found himself in possession of Sweet Woman, Crooked Nose, and the widow of Lame White Man who were relatives of prominent Cheyennes.

The Indians discovered their loss almost immediately and made an effort to secure their release; and the next day Miles engaged the main body of the hostiles in the Battle of Wolf Mountain. The latter part of the engagement took place in a snowstorm "which added an inexpressible weirdness to the scene." [14] At the crucial stage of the battle Big Crow, a medicine man who had been dancing very gracefully and nonchalantly in front of the Indian lines, was mortally wounded and the Indians broke off the fight. Miles, being short of supplies, returned to the cantonment.

44.   "Sioux Chief 'Hump' and favorite wives."

Miles now employed the same technique that Huffman was to observe in 1880. He treated the captives kindly, and on the first of February sent Sweet Woman and Johnny Bruguier, the Sioux half-breed who was one of his scouts, to the hostile camp with two pack horses loaded with tobacco and presents. The efforts of this peace party were successful and Bruguier returned with 19 chiefs and important men. The leading chiefs were Old Wolf and Crazy Head, and also in the group were Two Moon, one of the nine little "chiefs" of the Fox warrior society, White Bull,[15] the medicine man, and Hump who represented a group of the Oglalas.

The account of this surrender which White Bull gave Grinnell would make it appear that Two Moon and White Bull were the most important people. Miles' memoirs indicate that Little Chief was the spokesman when negotiations finally reached the dickering stage. The general's picture of Little Chief in the council where he spoke for a delegation of about 100 Indians is of particular interest as Huffman's portrait of the man must have been taken 25 or 30 years later.

45. "Little Chief, Cheyenne."

46. "White Hawk, a Cheyenne brave, Ft. Keogh, 1879."

Miles wrote that after he had presented his conditions there was an absolute silence for several minutes.

At last a stalwart Indian by the name of Little Chief rose. Throwing back his buffalo robe from his shoulders, and letting all the covering he had on down to his waist fall gracefully about his loins to his feet, he looked an ideal chief, standing over six feet in height, and being slender, sinewy and muscular. His features were prominent, sharp and regular; his cheekbones were high, and his lips thin and severe; and he looked, as we afterward learned he was, the orator of the Northern Cheyennes. The scars of the sun dance were very prominent on his upper arms and breast, and dignity and grace marked his every movement and gesture.[16]

In the end the Indians split up. The followers of Little Chief, White Bull, Two Moon, and Hump surrendered to Miles. Dull Knife and Little Wolf, being favorably impressed with offers to surrender at Fort Robinson, took their people to the Sioux reservation in an attempt to remain with the Oglalas with whom their ties were strong. White Hawk, a little chief of the Elk warrior society, to-

47. " 'Red Armed Panther,' sometimes called Red Sleeve, a Cheyenne Scout, Ft. Keogh, 1879."

gether with a few others who did not wish to surrender, went off to join Lame Deer's band of Minneconjou, thus temporarily avoiding the inevitable.

Two incidents of note occurred during the surrender negotiations. When the delegation Bruguier had brought in returned to their camp, Crooked Nose, a handsome young woman of about 21, committed suicide with a small pistol she had secreted. It was thought that she believed that she had been abandoned by her people and, like a trapped animal which realizes that its freedom is gone, lost her desire to live. The other incident involved White Bull. Miles asked the first delegation to leave a hostage as evidence of their good faith, and finally White Bull reluctantly agreed to remain. White Bull's fears were groundless, however, for Miles treated him kindly and asked him to enlist as a scout. So the Indian "held up his hand to the sky" and promised to serve faithfully.

White Bull then put on a uniform and told the rest of the delegation what he had done. When this news was transmitted to the people at the camp, not all of them were favorably impressed. When he was an old man, Wooden Leg told his biographer, "As we looked at it, the surrendering to the soldiers was good if one felt like doing this. But an offer to help them kill friends showed a bad heart." [17] However, not long after the Indians came in, 30 of them had been enlisted as scouts. The second to volunteer was Brave Wolf, a highly respected minor chief and medicine man. In the end many of the warriors served as scouts during the next 15 years.

The Indians who had surrendered camped a short distance up the Tongue. Their ponies were sold and a herd of cattle bought for them. They were fed on soldiers' rations until spring, when an effort was made to get them to plant grain

48. "Taken too soon after dinner in honor of Col. Illges."

Lieut Sibley. 5th Inf. *Col Illges.* *Lieut Aris. 5th*
W D Knight (Yellowstone Journal) *5th* *Joe Culbertson Scout*
+ Tom Defrees 5th Inf) *Stitts*

and raise part of their food. A prize bit of humor of these days pertained to White Bull's reaction to the proposition of planting a garden. White Bull was definitely interested—but he wanted to plant raisins! When asked his reason, he explained that raisins were the best food the white man had, therefore, he wanted to plant them in his garden.

For all practical purposes, the soldiers on the frontier were helpless without scouts and guides. Among the first to serve at Fort Keogh was Thomas Leforge, the Crow squaw man who was one of the interpreters for the Crow scouts enlisted by General Gibbon. Had he not had a broken collar bone when Custer marched up the Rosebud, he might have ridden to his death. Another, Joe Culbertson, was a half-breed Blood, being the son of Alexander Culbertson, the noted fur trader, and Natawista Iksana, the daughter of a Blackfoot chief. Culbertson was Captain Baldwin's guide when this officer charged Sitting Bull's camp on Red Water Creek during a snowstorm and pushed the Sioux northward

Yellowstone Kelly 1878

©L.A.Huffman Post Photo
Ft Keogh MT.

49.   Luther S. Kelly.

toward the border in the early spring of 1877. "Yellowstone" Kelly, in writing of this action, commented that, "Joe Culbertson, a fine type of frontiersman, was guide on this occasion and did excellent work here and elsewhere." [18] In Kelly's opinion, John Bruguier was also a "very capable and trustworthy man." Big Leggins, as he was sometimes called, was a half-breed Sioux who fled to Sitting Bull's camp in October, 1876, to escape a murder charge. Here he remained for several weeks. Later, while acting as an interpreter at a parley between Miles and some Minniconjou, he attracted the attention of the colonel who engaged him. In 1879 his friends persuaded him to stand trial in the U. S. District Court at Fargo, North Dakota, where he was acquitted.

Among the lesser figures were "Liver-Eating" Johnson and George Boyd. Johnson acquired his sobriquet in an Indian fight at a little trading settlement at the mouth of the Musselshell in June, 1869. The often-told story is that he cut out a warrior's liver, put a part of it in his mouth and, Indian fashion, sliced off a bite at his lips with his knife. However, according to one who was in the fight, Johnson only held the liver up and looked at it, with the blood running down his arm.[19] Boyd was very much deformed, and was clubfooted in both feet.

His feet, on which he wore short, round moccasins, turned in toward each other, thus leaving a very unusual trail in the snow. Once when Miles made a remark about the peculiar appearance of his footprints, Boyd told him that

Several years ago when I was carrying dispatches my horse gave out, and I went the balance of the way to my destination on foot. The Indians struck my trail in the snow, and following it to the military post to which it led, came in and reported to the officer in command that they had found this singular trail and wanted to know what kind of an animal it was, and which way he was going.[20]

The best known of all the scouts was Luther S. Kelly, widely known as "Yellowstone" Kelly, and nicknamed by the soldiers at Fort Keogh, "Kelly the Silent," and "Kelly the Sphinx." Miles found him kind, generous, "exceedingly enterprising, reliable, and fearless," and with a knowledge of the topography and nature of the upper Missouri and Yellowstone valleys that was "exceedingly valuable." [21] He was a descendant of Hannah Dustin, the New England woman who made a remarkable escape from the Indians during the French and Indian Wars; and, while he loved the wild life and scenery of the Northwest, he was well educated and was fond of good books. Huffman remembered that of all the officers at the post, the only one whom Kelly regarded with some awe was Captain Eli Huggins of the Second Cavalry—Huggins could read several foreign languages and speak some of the Indian tongue.

The picture of Kelly reproduced here was taken soon after Huffman came to Fort Keogh. Huffman had just finished the photographs of several officers and these caught Kelly's eye as he came in the studio. The scout, dressed in buckskin with an old army cap on his head, looked enviously at the photographs and remarked that he wished he had a good-looking picture to send to his mother. So the photographer loaned him his coat and Stetson and made the picture reproduced here. Later Huffman loaned his only file copy to Miles when the latter was writing his memoirs. Miles lost it and many years later Huffman found a print in a curio store and made a copy negative.

Although he was not a scout, another interesting frontiersman who came to this area to live at a somewhat later date was the interpreter William Rowland. He had run away from home when a mere youngster to live with the Cheyennes in Indian Territory. In 1876 he was working at Fort Robinson from which the Spotted Tail and Red Cloud agencies were administered. Rowland had gone with Crook in the winter of 1876, taking charge of the Cheyenne scouts under Lieutenant W. P. Clark; and he was with Mackenzie's men when they charged Dull Knife's camp. He was married to a Cheyenne woman and later was employed on the Lame Deer Reservation as a military interpreter. Mrs. Nannie Alderson, who went to the Rosebud country as a rancher's wife in 1883, recalled years later that Rowland's wife kept a neat little cabin, and raised a "very nice family . . . all handsome as mixed-bloods often are." [22]

While the white scouts played an important role, the Indians provided valuable services in their own unique way. In many respects they were scouts without equal, having been trained in such work from childhood; and some of them, particularly the Cheyennes, were excellent irregular troops. The first Indian

50.   George Bird Grinnell and William Rowland interviewing White Bull, or Ice.

scouts at Fort Keogh were mostly Crows under Leforge; but the Crows got into difficulty when they killed most of a party of Sioux who were approaching the cantonment, presumably to sound out the possibilities for surrender, and left immediately for their home reservation. Thereafter, they preferred to serve at Fort Custer, which was closer to their reservation. As a result most of the scouts at Fort Keogh were Cheyennes, with a few Sioux.

It was not long after the first Indians surrendered that Miles tested the mettle of his red recruits. Lame Deer's Minneconjou comprised the only sizable band of hostiles left south of the Yellowstone; and Miles explained to his scouts that this band should be brought in. Early in May Miles marched against this camp with Brave Wolf, White Bull, and Hump acting as scouts; and a few days later the soldiers closed in on what is now Lame Deer Creek. Hump made a successful contact with Lame Deer, and Miles might have induced him to surrender had not a white scout made hostile movements and precipitated a fight. In the ensuing skirmish, White Bull was beside Miles when Lame Deer attempted to shoot the colonel, and Brave Wolf rode with Lieutenant Casey in the charge to secure the pony herd and block the escape of the hostiles.

The following fall when Miles had to throw in the forces at Fort Keogh to block Joseph's desperate drive for the Canadian border, he took 30 Indian scouts with him. As the troops advanced, some of these scouts fanned out over the country far in advance of the soldiers and picked up the trail of the Nez Perce.

According to the story Brave Wolf told later, he and another warrior established the first contact with the Nez Perce. They rode into the camp and were invited into the chief's lodge where they explained their mission. The Nez Perce immediately became very hostile and threatening, but Brave Wolf boldly signed that he would rather fight to the death than surrender his arms. While this discussion was going on, a band of buffalo passed nearby and the Nez Perce took to their ponies and gave chase, thus leaving the two scouts free to escape. Their leave-taking was embarrassed, however, by a pack mule which followed them. Whenever they got too far ahead, the mule would bray and they would have to slow down until it caught up in order to keep it quiet.[23]

The alerting of the main body of the scouts produced a scene of considerable interest to Miles. To him, they were "listless flankers" until the news wrought "an almost instantaneous transformation." They peeled off their hats, coats, and leggins and backed out of their shirts, throwing all their belongings into a pile except their breechclouts and moccasins. Then, bedecked with gorgeous headdresses of eagle feathers and war paint, their ponies stripped to a lariat with a double knot around the lower jaw, they "appeared to be perfectly wild with delight."

Miles observed that the soldiers, although they fully realized the dangerous nature of their task, were also lighthearted as they moved forward in battle formation. Laughs and an occasional witticism were heard, and "one officer complacently rode into action humming the air 'What Shall the Harvest Be?'—the melody of the song timed to the footfalls of his galloping steed." Out in front was part of the Seventh Cavalry with its commanding officer, Captain Hale, riding in advance. Hale—riding to a death he had predicted—was "an ideal picture of a cavalry officer" as he swept along "with a smile on his handsome face."[24]

51. "Brave Wolf and Squaw [being] interviewed about [the] Custer Fight. Squint Eye interpreter. June 20, 1901."

52. "Sioux Chief Hump and head warriors."

Miles wrote in his memoirs that this gallop forward of his 600 mounted troops was "one of the most brilliant and inspiring sights" he had ever witnessed on any field. The charge which followed rolled up to the edge of the Indian camp —but a little warning was all that Joseph needed. His battle-tried warriors, already the victors over the forces of two generals, quickly demonstrated to Miles that a general assault on his camp would be extremely costly even though he was outnumbered four to one. As it was, after the first flurry of fighting was over, Miles had 22 dead and 42 wounded. One of the first to fall was Captain Hale.

The horse herd was quickly captured; and the soldiers then besieged the camp, the action developing into a deadly sniping duel. It was in this part of the fight that "Yellowstone" Kelly watched Hump, "a bold, picturesque fellow," skillfully worm his way, flat on the ground, from one slight depression to another and kill two Nez Perce warriors. One of these had countered with "matchless skill and desperate courage" all attempts to dislodge him from his position, and had killed one soldier outright and disabled two others who came to grips with him. As Hump shot this warrior, he received a serious bullet wound which laid him flat on the ground for several minutes, and Kelly thought he had been killed until he began his painful return to a sheltered position.[25]

Miles was well pleased.

> As soon as the Nez Perce had surrendered, I called up the chiefs of our friendly Cheyennes and Sioux and complimented them on their loyalty and courage. . . . On their swift ponies they had dashed down the valley and aided the soldiers in stampeding the Nez Perce herd, chasing them and rounding them up at convenient points, and had then returned to the left of the line encircling the camp where the most desperate fighting was going on. Hump killed two Nez Perce . . . and was severely wounded himself. They maintained their position with remarkable fortitude and discharged all the duties required of them during the five days siege. At its close I directed the officer in charge of the Nez Perce to give each of them five ponies as a reward for their gallant service.

Then Miles was amazed to see the scouts take their ponies and their wounded —Hump being shot through the body, and White Wolf with a piece of his skull shot away—and head for Fort Keogh. They traveled 200 miles, swimming both the Missouri and the Yellowstone, and reached the post four days before the command.[26] While their triumphal return brought rejoicing at their camp, it brought consternation at the post. The Indians were able to indicate that Miles was safe but they could not identify the dead, and wives had to endure grim fear for a few more days.

In addition to the operations against Lame Deer and Joseph, the army had one gruesome task to perform in 1877. In the year since the battle of the Little Big Horn, the rains and the coyotes had uncovered the inadequately buried bodies of Custer's troopers, and in June it was necessary to send a detail to inter properly what remained of the bodies. Troop I of the Seventh Cavalry, the unit previously commanded by Captain Keogh, was chosen for this duty. The troop had been re-formed around a few survivors including Captain H. J. Nowlan who had missed death by being on detached service with General Terry's staff, and

53.   "Grave of Colonel Keogh."

54. "Graves of Unknown, Custer Battlefield."

Sergeant M. C. Caddle who had been detailed to help Captain Marsh on the *Far West*. Colonel Michael V. Sheridan, brother of Philip Sheridan, was in general charge of the party.

It was extremely difficult to identify the bodies of seven officers which were to be removed for burial elsewhere. Although Nowlan and Caddle had helped to mark some of the graves the year before,[27] when they came to remove the body of Custer, the first remains they picked up proved to be the body of a corporal. Caddle stated in later years that they found another body and placed it in a coffin—"I think we got the right body the second time." However, there was not much left to pick up. Tom Leforge, the Crow squaw man and scout, sat on the ground "not more than ten feet distant" and watched the soldiers go through the motions of disinterring and transferring to a box the body of Custer. All that was left of the body was one thighbone and the skull attached to a part of the skeleton trunk.

The photographs of this battlefield are from negatives acquired by Huffman during his first years in Montana.[28] In two of the photographs the foot parts of cavalry boots may be noted. As the Indians had no use for uncomfortable boots, they cut off the tops for leather. Some of these were sewn shut at one end, thus making fine sacks. The wooden stakes which mark the graves were later replaced by the white stones which dot the field today; and the first monument was a pile of horse bones enclosed in a wooden crib. As for the bones of the troopers, the burial detail probably did the best they could, but human bones could be picked up on the battlefield for 50 years.

55. "First Monument, Custer Battlefield."

In 1878, while Huffman was making the moves which finally brought him to Fort Keogh, the Northern Cheyennes were engaged in an epic struggle to escape from the reservation near Fort Reno, Indian Territory, and return to Montana. This struggle had its beginning late in March, 1877, when the peace emissaries from the Sioux reservations told Dull Knife and Little Wolf that if they would go to Fort Robinson to surrender, their people could live with the Oglalas with whom they had intermarried and had been closely associated. These promises did not materialize, and not long after their surrender the Cheyennes found themselves on the road to the Indian Territory.

The climate in what is now Oklahoma did not agree with these people. Many began to be stricken with fever and ague almost as soon as they arrived and, in the year most of them remained there, almost two thirds experienced illness. Many died. The rations, deficient in both quantity and quality, contributed to the difficult situation. Finally in the summer of 1878 they appealed to the White Father in Washington for permission to return to the Sioux reservations, but this was denied.

When it became plain that no official action would be taken, Little Wolf called a council of his people. Then he made one last appeal to the local officials. At the close of this meeting with the agent and army officers, he told them frankly that he was "going north to my own country," and requested that if they wanted to fight over his move that they let him get a little distance away so that they would not make the ground bloody at the agency.

In Little Wolf the Cheyennes had a great leader. He was honest, fearless, and forthright, and, unlike most of his race, he had foresight enough to plan for the future. In battle he not only set an example by his personal bravery but also exercised considerable control over his warriors—another unusual ability. And, although Dull Knife held a rank in camp of almost equal importance, it was Little Wolf's ability as a general which was to make this march of the Cheyennes a great achievement.

Although poorly equipped with arms and horses, Little Wolf and his 250 followers lost no time in starting for home. When the troops from the agency caught up with them at evening on the second day of the march, they learned that Little Wolf had been in dead earnest when he said they could have a fight if they wished it. Fighting or playing hide-and-seek as the occasion demanded, stealing horses to increase their mobility and arms to increase their strength, the Indians left behind them a wake of terrified settlers and frustrated soldiers from the Canadian to the Platte. No doubt the fearful settlers Huffman saw in western Kansas during the third week in September were typical of the ranchmen and settlers along the way. And although he tried to keep his warriors from committing excesses, Little Wolf admitted later that they did not tell him much of what they did because they knew "I would not like it."

When the Cheyennes crossed the Platte, Little Wolf ruled that depredations along the way had to stop; and so the Indians melted into the sandhill country and out of sight. Here the band split up. Little Wolf's people remained hidden, but Dull Knife's followers moved toward the Oglala reservation. The old chief surrendered to a detachment of troops, his people gave up their arms peaceably, and, finally, lulled by false promises, the Cheyennes agreed to go to Fort Robinson.

Here the unsuspecting Indians were quartered in barracks. For a time they were treated well as the authorities debated their fate, but when a warrior slipped away to hunt for his squaw, they were locked up and guards were posted around the buildings. Then the commanding officer began to try to persuade Dull Knife to return to the southern reservation. The answer was always the same—they would rather die than go back. When verbal persuasion failed the Cheyennes were denied food and fuel. All the water they had came from snow scraped from the windowsills. Near sundown of the ninth of January, after five days of this inhuman treatment in bitter cold weather, the Indians put on their best clothing, said good-by to each other, and took five rifles and 11 revolvers from a hiding place beneath the floor.[29] Then, when the post was quiet after taps, some of the guards were shot down; and the Indians poured from the windows of their prison into the bright moonlight and fled toward the shelter of the nearby badland hills. Moments after the first shots, the soldiers streamed from their quarters in their red underwear, and the final desperate fight was on.

When it was all over, of the 150 who were confined to the barracks, 64 had been killed and eight or ten were never heard of again. Of the survivors, about 58 were sent to the Pine Ridge Reservation and 20 to the southern reservation. Eventually some of these drifted up to Fort Keogh, and later most of them were transferred to the reservation in Montana. One of those who spent some time on the Sioux reservation and was involved in the Ghost Dance trouble later was Little Chief.

Dull Knife's youngest daughter was shot and killed in the initial break from the barracks, but the chief and five members of his family and his son's family became separated from the main body and hid in a hole in the badlands hills.

56.　Dull Knife (*right*) and Bobtail Horse at Huffman's old log studio at Fort Keogh (1879?). The split ears of the ponies indicate they were buffalo ponies, the "elite" of the horse herds.

57. "Comenha, my partner's [Eugene Lamphere] wife, 1880. Daughter of Dull Knife and now (1900) wife of Jules Seminole."

After starving in their hiding place for ten days, they reached the house of Bill Rowland, the interpreter at the Pine Ridge Reservation. A few years later when Lieutenant Clark was gathering material for his book on the Indian sign language, Dull Knife explained to him the meaning of the sign for *brave*, a word which not only meant fearless, but was a qualifying adjective for anything of outstanding quality. Clark wrote, "Dull Knife, the Cheyenne chief, used it when he told me of his escape from Fort Robinson, and the subsequent journey of eighteen days in an arctic climate with only one blanket and a few rosebuds and snow to eat—'brave' hardships surely." [30]

Little Wolf avoided all this travail. He kept his people hidden in the Sand Hills until the next March, when they continued their travel northward. Lieutenant Clark, whom Miles sent out to intercept the group, found them in the valley of the Little Missouri near Charcoal Butte. After counciling with his Indian scouts, Clark sent Hump, Wolf Voice, and three others to try to make a peaceable contact. The negotiations were successful, and Clark was able to persuade Little Wolf and his party of 77 people to go to Fort Keogh with him.

Miles immediately asked Little Wolf to enlist as a scout and, after a little delay to think it over, the chief and all his young men joined. Miles' handling of the situation stands in sharp contrast to the bungling that took place at Fort Robinson. Clark, whom Miles sent out to make the interception, had been stationed at Fort Robinson in 1877 and, together with Bill Rowland, had accepted the original surrender of these people. White Hat, as they called him, was well liked and he could "make good sign talk," a thing which increased the confidence the Indians placed in him, as it tended to eliminate the mistakes interpreters sometimes made. The enlisting of the men as scouts gave them something to do and, no doubt, provided grounds for not returning them to the reservation which they had left.

These few recruits fitted themselves into the military organization in admirable fashion. A few months later they were in the field with Miles' troops in pursuit of Sitting Bull, who was then south of the border on a hunting trip—an operation his warriors extended to other prey besides buffalo. John Finerty, who was the newspaper correspondent with this expedition and who climaxed his trip by crossing the border to visit Sitting Bull's camp, set down these observations of Miles' scouts:

> Little Wolf, the Cheyenne Chief, was regarded with respect by all the officers, on account of his honesty and fearlessness. He and Brave Wolf were accounted the two best Indians in the command. After these came "Old Smoke," a brave but ferocious Crow, who had killed twenty Sioux with his own hand. The Assiniboines and the Bannocks did not appear to have much fight left in them . . .
> . . . The Cheyennes are as proud as Lucifer, and rarely beg. They fight like lions, and are, taken altogether, Indians of the dime-novel type. Some of them are amazingly intelligent, and . . . are of gentlemanly deportment. Brave Wolf was as graceful as a courtier, and had a face of remarkable refinement.
> The Crows are the handsomest of all the Indians. Some of ours were better looking than the whites. Their eyes were very large and brilliant, with long lashes. They were mercurial fellows. One day they would fight like demons, and the next night take to their heels like dastards. They are not over honest. . . . They say they never killed a pale face, but this is questionable, as they are very savage in their dispositions, and are much more treacherous than either the Sioux or Cheyennes, although not accounted nearly as fearless as either. Their hatred of the Sioux amounts to a monomania.[31]

On pay day he made another interesting observation:

People who imagine that the aborigines possess none of the finer feelings of humanity, will, perhaps, be enlightened by the following list of remittances sent to their families by our allied Sioux and Cheyenne warriors:
Spotted Bear, $20; White Horse, $20; Spotted Wolf, $20; Brown Wolf, $15; Two Moons, $15; Hump, $10; Tall Bull, $10; Yellow Dog, $10; Little Bull, $10; Poor Elk, $10; Bobtail Horse, $10; Spotted Wolf, $10; Little Horse, $10; Old Two Moons,[32] $10.[33]

Bobtail Horse, who sent $10 to his family and whom Huffman photographed with Dull Knife outside his log studio, was another famous warrior. One day, as Sitting Bull was withdrawing to the sanctuary across the border, Johnny Bruguier and seven Cheyenne scouts came upon his camp. Bruguier, Bobtail Horse, and another rode into the camp to try to induce the Sioux to surrender. Most of the Sioux were angry and very menacing, but Sitting Bull, although he refused to talk to the half-breed he had adopted three years before, recognized and questioned Bobtail Horse. This wiry daredevil, although he realized that their lives were probably in danger, refused to be cowed by the menacing throng around them and explained their mission with a courage that aroused the admiration of the Sioux chief. Although they accomplished nothing, the three scouts rode out of camp unharmed.[34]

There was a good reason why Sitting Bull paid deference to Bobtail Horse. At the Battle of the Little Big Horn the Cheyennes were camped at the northern end of the great encampment; and when Custer started his swing down toward the river the unprotected Cheyenne lodges lay before him. Three Cheyenne and two Sioux warriors observed Custer's advance and rode out against him. Perhaps the boldness of this advance made Custer suspicious of a trap, at any rate—so the story goes—the soldiers stopped and began shooting instead of charging the camp. It is possible that the dashing cavalryman faltered at a crucial moment—and Bobtail Horse, who was one of the five, may have played a vital part in turning this battle into a great Indian victory.[35]

Although the major operations have received most of the attention, there were other tasks which kept soldiers and scouts busy. For ten years after the campaign in 1876, there was trouble with the Indians. Only scattered references to these troubles have been set down in books, but it was this host of little things that did much to embitter the white settlers—many of whom were intolerant to begin with—against the Indians. Small parties of warriors drifted through the country, stealing horses, killing cattle, attacking stage lines, and killing settlers and members of small parties. And not all of the trouble-makers were Indians —there were white outlaws who camouflaged their nefarious deeds by imitating Indians.

In chases after lariat Indians [36] the aid of Indian scouts was invaluable. The exact nature of their services is well illustrated by the incident Lieutenant Clark observed:

> There is, of course, great difference in the capacities of individual Indians as trailers, some being no better than many white men, whilst others are astonishingly capable, and became famous in their tribes for their ability. In 1878 troops were sent out from Fort Keogh, Montana, to intercept some Cheyennes, who had been reported by an officer as crossing the Yellowstone below the post. After the scouts had been two days out from the garrison, a Cheyenne scout, called "poor Elk," [37] was sent out with dispatches. He had ridden all night, and his pony was very tired, when he joined the column about ten o'clock in the morning, but he managed, with much whipping, to keep his pony alongside the troops. The country had been overrun by great herds of buffalo, the grass had been eaten and broken down, and there was a perfect labyrinth of buffalo paths. Some excellent white and Indian scouts were with the command, but nothing had been discovered until, suddenly, "Poor Elk"

58. "Man-on-the-Hill and wife, Sioux."

stopped (he was riding abreast of the middle of the column), and going a little distance to the right, to more thoroughly scan the country, came back at a shuffling tired gallop, and reported that he had found the trail of the Indians.

It crossed the direction of the troops at right angles, and one-half of the command had already passed over it. "Poor Elk" followed it for about a mile to where the pursued party had camped. He brushed away the ashes from the dead fires, and felt of the earth underneath; examined the droppings of the animals, counted the number of fires, and noted, by the marks made by the pins, the size of the lodges; carefully scrutinized some moccasins, bits of cloth, etc., that had been thrown away; noticed that the moccasins were sewed with thread instead of sinew, and were made as the Sioux make theirs; discovered that the calico was such as is used at agencies; found a bit of hair-braid, such as Sioux Indians fasten to the scalplock. A sweat-lodge had been built, indicating that they had remained in camp at least one day, and the droppings of the animals determined that the stay had been but one. The position of the camp, the tying of the animals near the tepees and wickey-ups, the number of lodges, the care taken by the Indians in leaving,—all these things furnished evidence as to the number of Indians and animals, and the number of days since they had camped there. Though moving stealthily, yet they were in no special hurry; were Sioux and not Cheyennes, as stated; had recently left an agency; had not crossed the Yellowstone at the time reported, but two days previously; were evidently a party of Sioux who were on their way to join the Indians north of the British line. In fact, the record left by these Indians was as complete as though it had been carefully written out.[38]

As the number of men, both red and white, wounded or killed in these forays was small, most of the stories were lost when the participants died. Although

59. Officers quarters, Fort Custer, M.T. This post was built in 1877 on the high bench at the junction of the Little Big Horn and the Big Horn rivers.

Indians were usually the objects of such searches, white men were sometimes involved. On one occasion Leforge, while scouting at Fort Custer, was sent after about 25 horses and mules stolen from the post. He and his Indian companion had no difficulty in tracking the thieves down, killing one and wounding another who escaped, and bringing back the stolen animals. The commanding officer congratulated Leforge on the success of the trip and inquired what became of the thieves. The scout replied that they had wounded one and—when pressed for details—stated that the weather was too hot to bring the other in. All of which scandalized the general, who did not condone the killing of *white* thieves—Indians would have been quite another matter! [39]

No doubt most of the service rendered by the army in such matters was helpful—but not all of it. Granville Stuart, whose ranch headquarters was close by Fort Maginnis, left an uncomplimentary picture of one commanding officer and military policy in general. General Terry, then commander of the Department of the Missouri, ruled that Indian horse thieves—no matter whether captured by ranchmen or soldiers—and the stolen property were to be escorted to the reservation where the owners must make any claims for the property. Such a policy guaranteed the thieves escort to their homes and practically insured possession of their loot. After a couple of incidents of this kind at Fort Maginnis, the leader of the next such escort met a stock detective and a couple of cowboys who demanded the stolen horses. After looking down the barrel of the stock detective's Winchester and evaluating the expression on the face of the man at the other end, the lieutenant transferred the custody of the property. "This," wrote Stuart, "was the last attempt of the military to hold horses, stolen from white men by Indians." [40]

For each scouting trip which produced positive contacts, there were many laborious and unproductive ones. Typical of the latter was a trip made in March, 1879, when Huffman accompanied "Yellowstone" Kelly and Jeff Phillips, a packer at Fort Keogh, in pursuit of lariat Indians. They made a 400-mile circle which took them into the valleys of the Rosebud and Little Big Horn and then north of the Yellowstone into the valley of the Musselshell and finally north and east past Smoky Butte into the Big Dry country. Although they picked up a few stray horses abandoned by Indians, they had no excitement. Huffman always remembered, however, that they kept well away from cedar thickets and other places that might provide cover for an ambush.

Huffman never forgot the return from one scout that did produce some excitement and one casualty. A small party of Sioux jumped Sandy Morris [41] and his partner when they were trapping on the Powder. The two men made haste to reach the fort; and Miles sent a small party under Sergeant Glover in pursuit. Kelly picked up the trail easily, and on the initial contact the Indians shot a cavalryman named Douglass. The next day White Bull persuaded the Indians, who had holed up in a shallow cave, to surrender. Kelly and Phillips rolled the corpse in a bed tarp, placed it face down across the back of a pack mule, and brought it back to the post. Here Huffman helped "off the loads from the mules" and heard the story of the encounter from Kelly and the other members of the party.

Although the surrender of the last of Sitting Bull's followers during the summer of 1881 removed one big source of trouble in eastern Montana, there remained sufficient outlaws and renegade Indians to keep life from becoming dull. Unprincipled whites bootlegged arms, ammunition, and whisky to the Indians or robbed them with impunity; Crook's aide observed that "rarely are any of these scoundrels punished." [42] Army paymasters in particular had to be continually on the lookout for trouble. On one occasion, at dusk in a gathering snowstorm, robbers attacked the ambulance of Major Whipple, one of the paymasters, when his escort straggled on coming in sight of Fort Keogh. With one arm supporting the dying driver, Whipple sent the four-mule team on the run to the post. [43]

By the mid-1880's, Indian troubles had simmered down to horse-stealing, cattle killing, scares over occasional murders, and incidents which it was feared might develop into uprisings. One of these uprisings which did not quite materialize involved a few of the traditionally friendly Crows. Like some other incidents, it was attended by unnecessary hysteria on the part of the settlers [44] and injudicious action on the part of the military. In 1877 Wraps-Up-His-Tail, a Crow medicine man, claimed to be invulnerable to bullets, and to be able to decapitate the whites by pointing his sword at them. Some of his demonstrations, such as painting his face by merely pointing his finger at the sun and cutting down pines by pointing his sword at them with a sweeping motion, [45] inflamed the Indians and gained for him a small following of about 20 braves.

Frank Grouard investigated the trouble and reported that it would be simple to arrest the potential trouble-makers; but the officer commanding the troops who were called out issued an ultimatum making it possible to attack the entire camp where the trouble-makers lived. When the troops drew up in line to charge the camp, Wraps-Up-His-Tail and a handful of his followers jumped on

60. Deaf Bull, a Crow Indian.

their ponies and charged. However, before the soldiers could become engaged, an Indian policeman fired, breaking the medicine man's arm. The Indians immediately broke and ran—all except Crazy Head [46] who raced after Wraps-Up-His-Tail, caught his horse, and insisted that he come back and face it out. The prophet had had enough. Two Indian policemen took charge of him and one of them tested his immunity to bullets by shooting him in the back of the head. "That," Grouard told his biographer, "ended the war . . . for which there was not the shadow of an excuse, anyway." [47] Grouard was probably right, for 20 years later the Crow men, when recounting their deeds of bravery, still pointed with scorn at the policeman who fired the fatal shot.[48]

For their participation in this "uprising," the Crow Indian police arrested seven of Wraps-Up-His-Tail's followers—Deaf Bull, Sees with Ears, Big Hail, Theodore Whitehip, Knows His Coups, and Crazy Head—and imprisoned them in the old Carlisle prison. Deaf Bull, whom Huffman photographed later, spent nearly four years in this prison. On one occasion he became restless and incited a riot in which he tried to cut the throats of his fellow prisoners. Crazy Head failed to subdue Deaf Bull, and eventually the guards entered the altercation and one of them struck him in the face with the butt of his rifle causing the prominent scar on his left cheek.[49]

When the first Cheyenne scouts enlisted, they were furnished with arms, ammunition, and horses, allowed to dress as they pleased, and subjected to no

61: "Cheyenne Scouts."

discipline other than that which was absolutely necessary. In this irregular capacity they rendered efficient, faithful service. In the winter of 1889–1890, Lieutenant Casey, believing that the Cheyennes could be subjected to military discipline, secured permission to enlist a troop of them. Big Red Nose, as the scouts called him, had no difficulty in enlisting men or in molding them into a fine troop. Frederic Remington, who saw the troop just before the Sioux outbreak of 1890 when he accompanied General Miles to Fort Keogh on an inspection trip, appraised it critically and observed that the men "fill the eye of a military man until nothing is lacking." [50] A few weeks later he was to be in the field with these scouts who were then playing their part in the final campaign which marked the close of what has been termed a "century of dishonor."

The causes for the Sioux Outbreak of 1890—the so-called Ghost Dance War —which took this troop of Cheyenne scouts into the field and Casey to his death are not difficult to understand. What caused the trouble was not the Ghost Dance religion but rather disillusionment over broken treaty promises, incompetent agents, crop failures for the two preceding seasons, and insufficient food issues. If the Sioux were as badly treated, as hungry, and as poorly managed as the Commissioner of Indian Affairs, the Secretary of War, and other prominent people later stated that they were, the wonder is not that they caused trouble but that they caused as little as they did.[51]

Matters reached a climax in December when John McLaughlin, agent at

62. Private David Sweetmedicine, Troop L, Eighth Cavalry, about 1890.

the Standing Rock Reservation, tried to stop the dancing in Sitting Bull's camp on Grand River. McLaughlin, in many ways an excellent agent, hated Sitting Bull, and when he issued orders for the old chief's arrest he added this postscript: "You must not allow him to escape under any circumstances." The Indian police took these orders literally, as they invariably did. In the flurry resulting from the killing of Sitting Bull, about 50 of his people fled southward to the camps of Hump and Big Foot on the Cheyenne River. Hump, considered the most dangerous man after Sitting Bull, evidenced a friendly, helpful attitude when General Miles, his old commanding officer of the days at Fort Keogh, asked his assistance in quieting the frightened people in Big Foot's camp. Unfortunately, before this could be accomplished, Big Foot's Minneconjou broke camp and headed southward toward the badlands of the Pine Ridge Agency but were taken into custody without any trouble by the Seventh Cavalry under Major Whitside.

Whitside moved the Sioux to Wounded Knee Creek where they camped—the Indians, who numbered only 106 warriors, surrounded by 470 soldiers and four Hotchkiss guns. Up to this time there had been a little skirmishing with Kicking Bear's band, but no serious fighting: but, when Whitside attempted to disarm the Indians in his custody, a melee started. When it was over the Seventh Cavalry had lost 60 men killed and wounded, and nearly 300 Indians were dead [52]

63. "Spotted Elk, Head Warrior, Minneconjoux Sioux, 1878."

—and the ugly story was born that the Seventh "picked a fight" to get even for the disaster on the Little Big Horn. Perhaps there was nothing irregular, but it was difficult to explain why soldiers should have killed fleeing women and children a mile or two from the scene of the "battle." Two weeks later the disturbance was over.

Casey's Cheyennes served as scouts during this "war" and, near its close, camped on White Clay Creek some 25 or 30 miles west-northwest of the "battle-field" on Wounded Knee Creek. Here they acted as a sort of watch guard for a hostile camp eight miles further up the creek. There was no serious fighting—not that the Cheyennes were not willing and able—but Casey controlled his troops with an iron hand and, on an occasion or two when it might have been touch and go, he rode out alone between the lines to talk with the hostiles. On the seventh of January at one such parley Plenty Horses, a young Brule, shot him through the head.

Frederic Remington left a vivid picture of Casey's Cheyennes in the field. When he joined at Rapid City, South Dakota, the troop was on a freight train "with the horses in tight box cars, the bacon and Chis-chis-chash [53] on flat gravel cars, and Lieutenants Casey and Getty in the caboose."

Expansive smiles lit up the brown features of the Indian scouts as they recognized me. Old Wolf Voice [54] came around in his large, patronizing way and said, "How?—what you do out here?" Wolf Voice was a magnificent type of the Indian, with a grand face, a tremendous physique, and enough self con-

64. "Wolf Voice. Cheyenne warrior in war costume."

tainment for a High-Church bishop. High-Walking nudged Stump-Horn and whispered in his ear, and they both smiled as they looked at me.[55] Lieutenant Casey walked out in the road and talked with General Miles, who sat on his beautiful sorrel horse, while two scouts and a young "horse-pusher" from St. Louis helped me to load one strawberry-roan horse, branded "52" on the nigh front foot, into a box-car with a scrawny lot of little ponies, who showed the hard scouting of the last month in their lank quarters.[56]

During the week spent scouting in the badlands, Remington and Wolf Voice spent much time together. Remington wrote that they discussed the tactics of the army versus those of the Sioux; that after his horse had slid on the ice and splashed icy water over him while crossing a half-frozen river, the Cheyenne "looked me over, and smilingly said, 'Me think you no like 'em' "; and that one night after the scouts had butchered a couple of beeves he watched "Old Wolf Voice and another swinging six ribs on a piece of rawhide over a fire, and later he brings me a rib and a little bit of coffee from a roll in his handkerchief. I thought him a 'brick' and mystified him by telling him so."

Remington noted also that the discipline of the army did not extend to facial decoration. When contact with hostiles was expected, "the vermillion of the warpath was on every countenance . . . [and] faces which had previously been fresh and clean now . . . [were] streaked and daubed into preternatural ferocity." On one occasion when the little party he was with had to fall back to camp at a gallop, he found "the scout camp in a blaze of excitement. The Cheyennes were in warpaint, and the ponies' tails were tied up and full of feathers." The current of the old days still ran deep and strong!

The close of the Ghost Dance trouble marked the end of the use of troops as other than a stabilizing force: the Indian police were capable of keeping order. A number of the Cheyenne troopers, among them Wolf Voice, Stump Horn, and Tall Bull, served in the civil police organization. However, it is doubtful if any ideas of military discipline were helpful in this work: camp discipline among the Plains Indians had long been administered vigorously and promptly by their own police.

While Huffman showed considerable interest in the scouts, both red and white, he left but a scanty record of the soldiers stationed at Fort Keogh. This is regrettable for he was well acquainted with many who had had all kinds of adventures. Scattered notes indicate that he knew intimately the history of these days as related by the soldiers who had helped make it. However, he never set these stories down.

Life at Fort Keogh was much the same as at any other frontier post of a similar size. There were pleasures and there were hardships—and for the wives there was always the difficulty of trying to do much with little. Of the early facilities for relaxation, Miles recalled that "the upper story of a large storehouse was turned into a hall for entertainments, pianos and comfortable furniture appeared, the valuable library of the Fifth Infantry was unpacked, and the fine band of the same regiment contributed to make the post an oasis of civilization." [57]

The arrival and departure of steamboats were occasions of unusual interest as they brought new faces, and goods and supplies ordered months before; and they took away children going to school, officers changing stations, and summer visitors. Horseback riding and hunting with hounds provided sport, and there were occasional trips to the Yellowstone National Park. Trips to the park were major undertakings, and in 1878 when Miles made a trip there with a party of "ten officers, four civilians, five ladies, three children . . . and one hundred soldiers" he ran head-on into the Bannock outbreak and had to take time out for a little fighting. [58] An amateur theatrical company helped to while away the long winter evenings, and a number of old programs among the Huffman papers indicate that this activity flourished for years. Unfortunately, it operated under the handicap of being liable to lose the male members of the cast when a detachment was sent out on a scout which might last up to several weeks.

Captain Baldwin's wife included in the memoirs of her husband some of her own intimate recollections of the post—how glad the wives were to move from the "vermin-infected, ramshackle huts" of the cantonment—how they had been busy for months before this move, preparing curtains of materials they salvaged in various places—and what life was like in their new homes at Fort Keogh. She related that in the new homes there were fireplaces for heating, in which cottonwood burned rapidly without giving off much heat, and pine, if not sufficiently

65.   "Guard Mount in Buffalo Coats, Ft. Keogh, Mont." (about 1880).

dry, charred to a dark mass that emitted little other than a shower of inefficient sparks; and she noted that the foundations were high and the winter winds sucked underneath, causing the carpets to billow up from the floor until a banking of horse manure and soil between the supports put an end to the discomfort.

One social event made a vivid impression on this army wife. When a band leader arrived to take the place of one who had died, it was decided that his debut should be an "elegant occasion." An empty barracks was decorated with flags, guidons, draperies, arms, and fur robes; an elaborate buffet dinner was prepared; and of course the ladies dressed in new gowns procured in the East at the cost of many weeks of impatient waiting and considerable expense. When the ball was at its height and the supper was being eaten, the door opened suddenly. A trumpeter, spattered with mud and drenched by the storm outside, burst in and strode up to General Miles. Saluting, he reported that there was a band of Indians nearby and that he had been instructed to request orders as to what to do. The terrified women hurried back to their quarters, and the soldiers quickly laid aside their gay uniforms for field attire and prepared to meet the task at hand. The alarm turned out to be of no great importance, but it effectively spoiled the grand ball and consigned to the closets the "lovely and long-waited-for gowns." [59]

Another experience left a lasting impression on Mrs. Baldwin. While the crude buildings of the cantonment were still being occupied, Miles took the field against the Nez Perce. To the women, particularly those who had never experienced it before, the leave-taking was a heart-chilling ordeal.

The evening before it was the Sabbath. We had all gathered in our little log drawing room to say goodby. I had in my keeping a piano, waiting for its owner to arrive later. We played and sang "Sweet By and By," "On the Other Side of Jordan," and other good old hymns of Long Ago. When Capt. Owen Hale, 7th Cavalry, bold, dashing, dauntless trooper that he was, sang "And just beyond the shining shore I can almost discover," and I expressed my surprise at his familiarity with the good old song, he replied, "Mrs. Baldwin, I had a dear Methodist mother and was brought up on such hymns, and I wonder if I will ever forget them."

He was ever of a gay and cheerful temperament; but on this particular evening he seemed quiet and depressed. His last words to me, as he took my hand and bade me and the others goodby, were, "Pray for me, for I am never coming back!" He never did! [60]

The close of the campaign brought an equally agonizing experience, as has been noted. As the Indian scouts returned a few days before Johnny Bruguier, the scout Miles sent with dispatches, this interval was tense with apprehension about the identity of the casualties.

Those three days were agonizing to me and to the waiting women of the garrison. . . . The "friendlies" who had come into the garrison explained by signs that two of our officers were dead—but who? Thus each waiting heart questioned! When it was finally known that they were Comrades Hale and Biddle what grief and tears followed! What a scene of excitement . . . ! Women seeking to encourage and comfort each other, while the few men at the cantonment . . . affected a composure which they did not really feel, as they sought to console and cheer those inclined toward hysterics.

The scout, Brughier, surveyed the weeping ones with compassion and remarked, "I suppose God Almighty made them that way, but I don't know what for." [61]

Today there is a vacant, haunting atmosphere about the old post. Part of Officers' Row still remains, but the barracks, stables, and the old guardhouse are gone. Only in the pictures of their memory can the few old-timers see anything that reminds them of the blue uniform of the troopers and the befeathered warriors who have gone on their last scout.

By the trails to the Past, on the Plains of No Care,
Stood Shorty's saloon, but now it's not there,
For Shorty moved camp and crossed the Divide
In the years long dim, and naught else beside
A deep brand on Memory brings back the old place,—
Its drinks and its games, and many a face
Peers out from the mists of days that are fled,
When Shorty stood back of his bar, there, and said,
　　"What's yours, Pard?" [1]

Johnny Ritch

BRIGHT LIGHTS on the PRAIRIE

When Huffman came to the plains, Milestown was the metropolis of eastern Montana; and what its lights lacked in numbers and brilliance, its citizens and visitors made up in their colorful conduct and unique business practices. In the frontier years which followed, Glendive acquired a reputation as a rough little cow town; Coulson—forerunner of Billings—by April, 1880, was a "tough little town" with 16 graves already in its boothill cemetery,[2] and when a disastrous fire swept Junction City[3] in April, 1883, the dominant feature of this wide-place-in-the-road was 14 saloons and three dance halls. But none of these could rival Milestown as a business and amusement center, and so this chapter must treat chiefly with one town, not just because some of Huffman's pictures deal with it, but because in the 1870's and 1880's it was *the* important town in the vast triangular-shaped area between Bismarck and Fort Benton and Helena.

Not only is this the story of one town but, for the most part, it is the story of one street in this town. Sam Gordon, veteran editor of *The Yellowstone Journal*, pointed out:

> Whoever attempts the story of the early days in Milestown, must spin his yarn around Main Street, where ninety percent of the incidents dear to the memory of old-timers occurred. Unquestionably Main Street should have been given a more appreciative title, but the founders of the town appear to have been without any conception of what they were building and so perfunctorily followed the usage and christened the main road to the outside world, plain Main Street.[4]

66. "Diamond R Bull train, Main Street, Miles City, 1880."

67. "Yellowstone Journal Office, 1879, Miles City."

Huffman's photographs show that for several years Main Street was only about three blocks long, and the entire town covered not more than five or six blocks. However, what happened in that small area was out of all proportion to the square feet of space occupied.

Milestown was born in the fall of 1876 when Colonel Miles, becoming tired of having the coffee-coolers [5] loafing at the Tongue River Cantonment, had a stake set about two miles east of the post, and ordered all the hangers-on to move to the other side of the marker. By evening on the day Miles had issued his ultimatum, these civilians had a few tents up and two saloons and a gambling house in operation. The members of this new community did not bear any hard feelings toward the commander who had summarily expelled them from the military reservation. As soon as a few log cabins had been erected, they gave a party to celebrate the founding of the new town and invited Miles and his staff to a banquet consisting of approximately 90 per cent wild game, eight per cent liquor, and two per cent "trimmings." Major Pease, who presided at one end of the table, toasted Miles as "our future president," and the colonel was told that the town would be named for him.[6] When the troops vacated the cantonment a year later, the ramshackle log huts were taken apart and the little settlement transplanted on the east bank of the Tongue where the business district of Miles City is now located.

This infant village was a vigorous, lusty, man's town which provided its customers with alcohol, the necessities to support life on the frontier, and women. When Granville Stuart arrived on April 17, 1880, to engage Tom Irvine, and eventually Huffman, to guide for him in his search for a cattle range, he

. . . put up with my old friend Thomas H. Irvine and we boarded at the jail with Sheriff W. H. Bullard. . . . The hotel accommodations in Miles City were not first class, in fact I do not think there were any hotel accommodations. The people that frequented Miles City in those days usually came to

68. "Bullard and the biggest whitetail buck ever. Weight dressed 212 lbs."

town to stay up nights and see the sights. They did not feel the necessity for a bed or much to eat. They were just thirsty.[7]

The majority of the visitors in 1880 were hide-hunters, trappers, enlisted men from Fort Keogh—known locally as swaddies—bull-whackers, and a few river men. As their thirsts were usually of two kinds, it takes little imagination to picture the kind of activity which kept visitors up all night.

The reputation for hell-raising which resulted from this night life moved both Huffman and his friend, Sam Gordon, to write in defense of these early days. Huffman noted:

We had an awful bad name abroad, but we really did not deserve it. Nobody was ever real mean and the overflows of animal spirits, such as used to occur whenever the "Diamond R" bull train rolled into town and was paid off, were

69.　"The Military Bridge, W. Main Street, Old Ferry, Diamond
R Corrall and Store. Miles City, 1880."

merely demonstrative of the combative instinct inherent in "bull-whacker"
and "swaddy" when the moon was about right.

Of these brawls in the saloons, honky-tonks, and elsewhere, Sam Gordon observed:

> We were a pretty well-behaved community too. True, there used to be some
> delightful shindies at the dance houses when the "Diamond R" gang, headed
> by Big Sandy Lane, Jim Kennedy and Charlie Northrup, ran afoul of a bunch
> of swaddies from Keogh feeling their oats, but it was all fists and boots and
> never a shot fired or a knife used. . . . To be sure these affairs were disturb-
> ances of the peace, but what could our one night-watchman do, had he been
> inclined to mix in, which he wasn't. . . . The students at the military insti-
> tute at Fort Keogh were inclined to be offensive when congregated in any
> considerable number and the bull-whackers and mule-skinners of the "Dia-
> mond R" could always be mobilized for an argument with the "sogers." [8]

Writing in *The Yellowstone Journal* of the early years before the coming of
the railroad, someone—probably Sam Gordon—set down concisely the reason
why the old-timer defended these lusty days.

> It was called a tough place, and doubtless harbored during these years as many
> hard characters as have ever gathered together on the frontier, but for some
> reason—possibly the near presence of the soldiers—there was less of the "man
> for breakfast" in the history of these days of license and freedom from re-
> straint than most frontier towns can boast of. Everybody had money in
> plenty. Society as then constituted demanded that all should meet on a level,

consequently the spectacle of the prominent citizen playing "a stack or two" against "the bank" or "settin' up the fizz" at one of the frequent soirees dansante of the demi-monde, excited absolutely no comment. It was a principle of trade, recognized by those in business, that money thus put out always came back with usurious interest; it was simply advertising, but the man who could not adapt himself to these methods either had to quit or get a partner who could—and would.

. . . Of these days only a pleasant memory lingers in the minds of the old timers. Not because of the freedom and license of the times so much, as of the spirit of good-fellowship and camaraderie that made it almost impossible for a man of standing to do a cheap or mean thing. Although the competitions of trade were present, there was present also broad-gauge courtesy that lifted men above the sordid conditions of life and made them closer observers of the golden rule.[9]

These were the days when "two-bits" was the lowest price asked for any article in a store, when charges on freight via bull train from Bismarck were three to seven cents a pound, when saloon-keeper John Chinnick—a recognized friend of the lawless element—provided the planks which served as seats at the first religious services held in Milestown, and when the cost of living was extremely high. In a solitary note about the prices of these days Huffman wrote, "Entertainment was stiffish in those days—fried buff [$] 1.00 to 'set in' the round with blue hen [10] [canned tomatoes], and coffee on the side." Just what the favors of the "bird in the gilded cage" cost has never been recorded.

The geographical location of the Tongue River Cantonment—which determined the location of Miles City—was sound from a broad military standpoint but, like many of the things the military did on the frontier, was not particularly wise from an immediate standpoint. The thick timber along the Tongue offered desirable protection from winter storms and a ready source of building material and fuel; but to canny frontiersmen like Granville Stuart there was unmistakable evidence that the location was undesirable. Stuart wrote in his journal:

Miles City stands on the east bank of the Tongue river and in a grove of big cottonwood trees of which a great many have had the bark torn from the upper side of them for several feet above the ground by an ice gorge here apparently twelve or fifteen years ago, perhaps longer: so some day the town will likely be destroyed by another gorge—bad location.[11]

Huffman's photographs show that Stuart's appraisal was reasonably accurate, for the following spring brought a flood which was long remembered by early settlers. A heavy snowfall during the winter, estimated at "two feet deep on the level all over the country hereabouts," had been partly melted by a chinook early in February. After breaking the ice, the river froze deeply a few days later. When the spring breakup actually came, the flood water formed an ice gorge at a bend just above the town and on March 3 the water poured over the banks and through the village. Sam Gordon pictured the activity which ensued:

Because of the dire anticipations based on the evidence of the old cottonwoods, about two hundred people, mostly women and children, vacated their homes

70. Borchardt's Corner and Post Office. Fourth and Main—
looking east. Ice left by flood of 1883.

in favor of tents pitched upon the inhospitable sides of Carbon Hill, where they
lived a cheerless life for about a week while the town fairly rioted in new sensations. It didn't take long to convince those who stayed on the job that the old
cottonwoods were liars if they ever said so and what with the novelty of going
about in boats and a general suspension of business, the first flood was a water-
carnival pure and simple, and few there were who did not join in the unusual
festivities. This custom was followed in all succeeding floods and the first
indication of an overflow was the signal for all good men and true to sally
forth to the rescue of the distressed. . . . There was nothing perfunctory
about our observance of these occasions. Action ruled supreme and whoever
had an idea, no matter how whimsical, found a following ready and willing to
carry it into execution. Unprepared as we were by experience for the first flood,
twenty-four hours had not elapsed before we had as numerous a navy as the
conditions demanded, including one big flat boat that would carry a hundred
passengers, which made frequent trips up and down Main street under the
pretense of rescuing some marooned castaway, but as these were always found
in the vicinity of a House of Cheer, the presumption was admissable that
rescue-work was not the main reason for leaving a safe harbor and braving the
terrors of the deep.[12]

Thus the inconvenience imposed by the flood was not without its attractive
features: and the citizens of the town came to regard the shortcomings of the

town's location just as they did the yellow dust and mud of the streets—something to be endured in the natural course of events.

The first buildings were of log construction and, as feelings of civic pride developed, these were sided with shingles, or boards laboriously "whipsawed" by hand. When lumber became more plentiful, framed buildings were erected; and all the commercial establishments had false fronts according to the prevailing custom in the frontier West. Some of the decorations on these false fronts were quite elaborate, and the artisans who did such work drew a minimum of $7 per day—and worked when they saw fit. Brick construction was desirable but expensive. The First National Bank was one of the first, if not the first, building to be built of brick, and "the brick used in the front came all the way from St. Louis, at a time when freight rates were out of sight and were said, at the time, to have cost about 75 cents apiece in the wall." [13]

One of the famous buildings on Main Street was the "steamboat building" erected from salvage lumber from the *Yellowstone* which was wrecked on Buffalo Rapids just below Miles City about 1880. In 1891 "Jimmy" Dance hauled the heavy oak timbers into town and worked them into the walls of a building. Later he brought in the cabin and reconstructed it as a second story, thus the "ghost" of the restless river came to life as a lodging house.

As the little town depended for its water supply on driven wells scattered along its streets, fire was a greater hazard to the closely built wooden buildings of Main Street than the flood waters. Several of Huffman's early letters to his father mention the building which resulted from fires.

> Oct 2nd 1883
>
> Building goes on rapidly   900,000 brick are being delivered to replace the burned district—so that our political war in which local predjudices—the Lariat and six-shooter figured during the past two years will work favorably for the town yet croakers and milksops notwithstanding—

> June 7 1885
>
> Miles City now needs only two more fires to entirely clean up every old landmark—the last two fires were hard blows even though they cost the Insurance Companys $100,000   there are now 13 two story brick buildings going up and chances are good that during the summer at least 6 more will be built

Firefighting was a community enterprise, and usually involved the use of a bucket line since there was no water system. Fortunately for the highly inflammable little settlement, there were "fire guards" on duty 24 hours each day the year around. Regarding the manner in which this fire-alarm system operated—and some of the false alarms which resulted—one early-day "fireman" recalled:

> In the old days we had no fire alarm. Saloons never closed.[14] . . . [and] when there was a fire the bar tenders on shift took their six shooters and went out into the street where they emptied them into the night air and the volunteer firemen would awaken, inquire the whereabouts of the fire, take a drink or two, pull out the old hook and ladder and put out the fire. Then they would return to the saloons, put on a real jag to offset the cold or wet and there relate their experiences. . . . A fire was a great affair and called for a good display of heroism.

Well, Frank Burkholder and I had a room over our store on Main street, facing on the street, and when there was a fusillade of fire arms we would throw up the window, without getting out of bed, inquire where the fire was and if of sufficient size, we might get up, if not we just pulled down the window and resumed our dreams. However, one early morning we heard the shooting and we threw up the window to locate the fire, and we heard and saw these bullets hitting and caroming off the wall of the very next building. I can hear those zinging bullets yet. We slammed down the window and found the shots were coming from the six shooter of "Dogy" Taylor, a bartender for Harry Bruce, and "Israel," a colored gent. They had a difference over the affections of one colored gal, Cloe by name. "Israel" was hit in the leg but he got the sympathy and affections of Cloe, so there was nothing done about it.[15]

These fires often got out of control and most of the early fires cleaned up whole blocks. As the inhabitants were a "careless, happy people," these excuses to fraternize and be sociable were utilized to the utmost. If the fire occurred during the day, the remaining hours were turned into a holiday; if the blaze took place during the night, the festivities were extended well into the next day. And they served a very useful social purpose in that those who worked the day shift had an opportunity to meet those who worked at night.

To properly understand Miles City, it is necessary to recognize the impact on the community of the customers who supported it. In the beginning the 1000 soldiers and civilian employees of nearby Fort Keogh provided the dominant feature. To this society were soon added bull-whackers, mule-skinners, and buffalo-hunters. Numerically, the latter were a small fraction of the society, but they made an impression of considerable size during the few years the herds lasted. As the importance of the hunters began to wane, the cowboys and the cattlemen came, and it was the cowboy who put a mark on the town that still clings to it.

Thus the development of Miles City was influenced by the people who traded at its stores and patronized its saloons, dance halls, and parlor houses. Eventually, when quieter and more orderly people came to dominate the scene, the irresponsible activities of some of the customers were slowly pinched off. First the cowboy was required to park his gun on entering town, then his time-honored custom of announcing his arrival by riding madly up the street, whooping and taking an occasional shot at street lights was discouraged,[16] and finally his coming and going became quiet and orderly. The coming of the railroad also had its impact, for with it came the end of the free-and-easy ways of the frontier. The toughs who followed the railroad into the area made it necessary to put locks on the doors, but perhaps the "cruelest" change—to the old-timer—was the dropping of the minimum prices of any article from "two bits" to five cents.

A city directory published in 1882 [17] indicates that a variety of establishments were operated at an early date. These ranged from general stores to banks, wagon-builders, and Chinese laundries. Some listed unique assortments of goods. Leighton, Jordan and Company, primarily wholesalers and retailers of groceries and provisions, also sold foreign and domestic wines, liquors, cigars, ready-made clothing, gent's furnishings, rubber goods, saddles, harness, wagon covers, agricultural implements, hunters' and ranchmen's outfits, and also were headquarters

71. "March 3, 1881." Looking east on Main Street from Fifth during the 1881 flood. Charlie Brown's place left foreground (just beyond Broadwater, Hubbell & Co.), Cottage Saloon opposite.

for "Falk's and Schlitz's celebrated Milwaukee lager beer." One baker and confectioner, in addition to bread and pastries, sold cigars, tobaccos, canned goods, fruits in season, teas, coffees, sugars, fresh eggs, and butter. A barber advertised that he was a "capillary manipulator, boss barber and hair dresser"; and William H. Bullard operated a brewery that supplied beer that was "absolutely free from drugs and adulterations" for $4 per quarter keg or $4.25 per case. George M. Miles, nephew of General Miles, and Charlie Strevell ran a hardware store which, in addition to carrying the "largest stock of General Hardware west of St. Paul," offered for sale tinware, sheet iron, copperware, and house-furnishing goods. And Huffman was also listed. He "publishes fine Indian portraits. Stereoscopic and Orthoscope views of the National Park, Bad Lands, Big Horn scenery and the grand scenic effects along the Yellowstone Valley."

Some of the business practices were as unique as the stocks of goods offered for sale. Store hours were from early to late—and, of course, the saloons never closed. As shipments of goods arrived but a few times during the year—steamboats came with the high water in the spring and freight charges via the bull trains were almost prohibitive except for certain classes of freight—shortages were not uncommon. Years later Charlie Strevell recalled that, in the spring of 1881 before the annual steamboat shipments arrived, an old-timer who was about to take out a contract to cut ties for the Northern Pacific came in to make some purchases. After asking successively and unsuccessfully for several items, he suggested, "If it is not too much trouble, will you please make out a list of what you have and I will look it over and see if I can use any of it." [18]

On payday at the post, the Cottage Saloon, the chief resort patronized by the soldiers, did a rushing business. As there was no time to draw beer, it was dumped into a couple of washtubs behind the bar from which it could be dipped conveniently and quickly—one shift replenishing these containers while another filled glasses for the thirsty swaddies. Some of the merchants had added attractions for their customers. J. J. Graham, proprietor of a hardware store, kept a keg of whisky and a tin cup where his customers could help themselves; and in the wintertime Charlie Brown, who ran a saloon on the corner opposite the Cottage Saloon, kept on his old-fashioned cannonball stove, day and night, "an immense tin boiler containing a savory 'Mulligan' which was free to all who hungered." [19]

Not only did the saloons provide a permanent fire guard but "Jimmy" Coleman's Cottage Saloon functioned in another unique protective capacity. Located adjacent to this popular emporium was the First National Bank, then the Merchants' and Drovers' Bank. Feeling in need of effective protection from bandits and burglars, the bank installed a foot plate which stuck up from the floor just under the cashier's window. This was attached, by a hair-trigger release, to a pull wire attached to a signal in the adjoining saloon. All that was necessary to summon an armed gang in case of a holdup or burglary was for this trigger to be touched. Although this assistance was never needed, one cashier who inadvertently tripped this alarm was amazed to see an armed mob pouring in the front and back doors and demanding to know where the bandits were. This bit of carelessness brought down on his head much harsh censure, and probably cost him several rounds of drinks.[20]

72. "Macqueen House. A memory now like many a one time guest we loved and neath the roof made merry with."

An establishment remembered by old-timers with a feeling of nostalgia was the Macqueen House. First named the Inter Ocean Hotel, this rambling frame building was erected in 1882 and ceased to exist, in a blaze of glory, in 1897. What the Cheyenne Club was to Cheyenne, this lodging place was to Miles City; and Major Macqueen its proprietor, a genial, affable, Southern gentleman from St. Louis, made attention to the customer a cardinal principle of the service rendered. Here some of the wealthy ranch owners wintered, owners of trail herds awaited the coming of the herds they had put on the trail in Texas in the spring, many of the town's bachelors boarded, and here each year occurred the social event which was the annual highlight of eastern Montana—the ball of the Montana Stockgrowers Association. When the cattlemen's convention was held, no man could reserve a room—or even an entire bed. Many a man had a bed mate whom he did not know, and on one such occasion Theodore Roosevelt slept with a stranger whom he never even saw.

In the winter each room was heated by a small stove which the occupant fired. The only bath was just off the barber shop so the ladies used a wash basin in their rooms; and one bride, newly arrived from the East in 1883, remembered that the walls were so thin she could hear every sound from one end to the other, with the result that she overheard several masculine conversations that both fascinated and embarrassed her.[21]

Stores and shops constituted about half of the business enterprises in the town. Saloons, dance halls, and parlor houses were equally numerous. The young bride previously noted, who came to Miles City from West Virginia, had been warned by her husband that the town was a "pretty hoorah place" so

I was not surprised by the horses hitched to rails along the store fronts, the wooden buildings and unpaved streets, nor was I surprised that every other building was a saloon. . . . [Mr. Alderson] didn't want me to go out alone, even in the daytime—not that I wouldn't be perfectly safe, but I might run into a drunken crowd or a fight.[22]

73. "Bill Reece's Dance Hall, the first 'Low-necked carriage, the Town Well, 1879."

It was the saloons, the honky-tonks, the variety shows, and the red-light district which accounted for much of the "business" and most, if not all, of the notoriety this Dodge City of the Montana prairies acquired. As one old cowboy observed, "Many a virtuous polar bear raises hell on the equator"—and as many individuals were far from the restraining influences of home, lack of restraint was not uncommon. It might be said that, in general, the frontier society recognized not ten but four commandments: (1) Thou shalt not concern thyself with thy neighbor's affairs, (2) Thou shalt not steal, (3) Thou shalt not commit murder, and (4) Thou shalt not speak disrespectfully of or harm a decent woman. The penalty for failing to obey the first was ostracism, and, if convicted of a serious infraction of either of the other three, the culprit could expect to pay the extreme penalty.

"Sporting life" in Miles City was composed of a mixture of gambling, alcohol, and sex. In that respect it was not unlike any other frontier settlement but, in contrast with modern vice, this license on the frontier was associated with some curious contradictions in human actions. John Chinnick, whose saloon and ranchhouse were acknowledged hangouts for any tough characters who might chance by, "was never misjudged by his fellow citizens. . . . but in his daily contact with the world he was in many respects a decent sort and always ready and willing to join in public movements." [23] Charlie Brown, the saloonkeeper who kept the pot of "Mulligan" on his stove, was regarded as being a "character." Yet, according to unwritten legend, he was the passer-by who, on hearing a tough named Rigney insult the wife and daughter of a fellow townsman, promptly took the ruffian to task—an argument which ended when he "bent" a pick handle over the culprit's head.

One old rancher recalled that a cowboy who had come up with a trail herd for the N Bar spent a week with Cowboy Annie and rode away leaving a debt of $70. When this became known to the foreman of the outfit, he fired the cowboy who then returned to Texas—where the story followed him and he was fired a second time for the same offense. "And the N Bar fellows took up a collection and paid her what he owed because they wouldn't have a thing like that standing against the name of the outfit." [24] The cowboy who could be expected to squander all his wages on his annual spree, drinking and treating his friends, bucking the various games, and staying with the girls at some parlor house, could also be expected to guard his employer's womenfolk, in the absence of the other men, as a mother would a new-born babe—and without even a thought of scandal on the part of the neighbors. Such people must be judged by the code of their times.

The saloon filled a needed place in the social life of the community. The traveler who wanted a place to loaf, to look at a paper, or to inquire about business possibilities went to a saloon. Here friends met, the unemployed sought work, and the employer hunted labor to fill his needs. The visitor could drink and play roulette, faro, blackjack, keno, and various kinds of poker if he wished. Some owners operated places which were above question, but there were others where shady practices were followed. One of these was to solicit the trade of sheep-herders who, after their checks had been cashed and they were drunk or drugged, were rolled and tossed out into the alley to sober up—broke.

Gambling was a licensed activity, but it also ran the gamut from games which were above suspicion to those operated by shifty characters who were not to be trusted. Although the game might be square, the odds were always carefully calculated in favor of the house, and those who hazarded their hard-earned wages usually lost their pile eventually. As the "gam's" [25] hours might be long and strenuous, he often carried, in the buffalo days, a piece of dried buffalo tongue to sustain him when the going was strenuous. Some of the gamblers were women. One old-timer recalled that

> Poker Nell was quite a character when I arrived here. . . . She was supposed to be the common law wife of Harry Bruce who ran a saloon at the southwest corner of 6th St. Poker Nell used to run one of the poker tables. One time I saw her playing and raking off in a game where the other players were a Negro, Chinaman, Italian, Indian, Jew, cowboy and another local gambler. She knew her cards and was quite a kind woman, and not at all bad to look at. . . . [26]

Some places of entertainment also had a dance floor, an orchestra of a sort, and girls who danced with the customers and saw to it that the latter spent their money liberally at the bar. In the early days there were a number of variety shows [27]—the prelude to the evening's entertainment being the appearance at the corner of Park and Main of two or three bands from these shows to attract customers for the evening. One unique feature of these early theaters was a "balcony" consisting of a row of curtained boxes around the outside of the main floor. These low boxes were "worked" by girls dressed in abbreviated costumes and who were known as "box rustlers." They peddled liquor, obliged with caresses behind drawn curtains, and solicited visits to their rooms. In speaking of these days, Huffman sometimes recalled that in a variety show at the corner of Park and Bridge streets one customer, while leaning over the railing of his box in a semi-intoxicated condition, had his throat cut by an unknown enemy who passed by on the floor just below. Perhaps the best known of these was the Cosmopolitan Threatre at the corner of Sixth and Main. In 1883 this establishment figured in a spectacular fire following a vigilante "execution."

At the lower end of the scale of entertainment were the attractions of the parlor houses or "social centers." These often provided, in addition to the girls, a piano and a parlor where patrons could also dance. One feature of these houses was "the professor," usually an elderly man, who, in addition to soliciting patrons, presided at the piano. However, just how or where the title "professor" originated is a bit of a mystery. For the most part, these establishments were concentrated in the four-block stretch along Sixth Street between Main Street and the Northern Pacific depot. One traveler, arriving in the town about the turn of the century, remembered that the first building across the street from the depot had a sign which proclaimed that it was the First Chance Saloon. When viewed from the other side, the sign read Last Chance Saloon; and painted on the front was a well-executed picture of a nude modestly displaying a rear view.

Two of the best-known establishments are still remembered. One was known by the name of the brand owned by an admirer of the madam—which the proprietress had painted on the front door. The other, Maggie "Mag" Burns' place —a palatial house which still stands on Main Street—had the reputation of being the "classiest" in town—and she sent engraved invitations to the merchants and businessmen when she had her formal opening. Certainly it was a paying business, for the cashier of a local bank remembered that the largest single certificate of deposit he ever made out was for $50,000. The depositor was "Mag" Burns. She and W. H. "Bill" Bullard lived together, so it is said, without benefit of clergy. Bullard was a very early sheriff, onetime owner and operator of a brewery, and later owner of a saloon and hotel on Main Street known as the Bullard Block: it has been said that Maggie's money kept him in business. In the end both retired and went South together.

Like other kinds of seasonal labor, the "girls" worked the locations where the most money could be had. In 1884 one cowboy, en route to Oregon to help bring back a trail herd, wrote a friend after a night in Virginia City that he had met Tiger Lily, "a red haired freckle faced girl you used to know in Miles City." She had requested that she be remembered to his friend, and had commented that she hoped to be back in "Miles" about "beef-shipping time."

A few of the girls married, some of them very well—for this was a woman-poor country. Generally they became very good wives and mothers, and no man dared to speak ill of them after they broke with their profession. Others, paying the inevitable penalty, slipped lower and lower. A prostitute's standing in her profession depended on her clientele and, as one old cowboy put it, when a woman "went to the dogs," she went to the soldiers, the lowest level in the customers' scale.

Some of the girls became famous. One of these was Cowboy Annie and another was Connie the Cowboy Queen. "Connie," recalled one old cowboy, "had a $250 dress embroidered with all the different brands—they said there wasn't an outfit from the Yellowstone down to the Platte, and over in the Dakotas too, that couldn't find its brand on that dress." [28] Mrs. Alderson, a young bride from the east in 1883, a year later came to Miles City for the birth of her first child and inadvertently met this courtesan. Both stayed at the Macqueen House where Connie, posing as a wife, was being kept by a wealthy cattleman.

Mrs. Alderson remembered Connie as a dark-haired, dark-eyed young woman who was striking in appearance and dressed smartly. And when she saw her, pinning on her hat in front of her bureau with hardly more than a stitch of clothing on, she also noted that she had a very pretty figure. To all outward appearances her conduct was very proper, with the exception that she would go down to breakfast wearing a very beautiful satin Mother Hubbard, hand-painted with floral designs, which was hardly appropriate for a public dining room. Not long after the two met, a madam noted Connie on the porch and tipped off the proprietor, who promptly expelled her and her supporter. Connie went back to the red-light district.

> But she did not stay there very long. There was a wealthy Englishman, among several such around Miles City at that time, whose brother later came into a title; and this man set her up in an establishment of her own with horses, carriage, everything, and was seen with her everywhere. She would even appear at the races—for the town boasted a race track in those days—dressed in his cream and scarlet colors. It was a most brazen performance, and scandalized even Miles City. [29]

Of all the girls who "worked" Miles City, the most famous was Calamity Jane. However, in the final analysis, Calamity cannot be classed as typical. To one who observed her when she was an old lady at Deadwood, she was a "shabby old lady with nothing romantic about her. She had no sexual morals, was a reckless and heavy drinker, and she undoubtedly was a cheerful liar when it came to her own life and exploits." [30]

Perhaps the thing which endeared her to her contemporaries was that her heart was as big as the country in which she lived. Estelline Bennett, who spent her pigtail days in Deadwood, remembered Calamity when the latter was working in a house in that boom town during the gold rush. One day when she and a playmate met Calamity on the street, she took them—shaking in their shoes—into a grocery store where she tossed a silver dollar nonchalantly on the counter and said, "Give these little girls some candy." After they had thanked her politely, she walked away. Years later on a late winter day she met Calamity on the main street in Deadwood wearing a pair of overshoes when there was no obvious need for their protection. Calamity explained that she had to wear her "ar'tics" because she had given her shoes to a woman she met that morning on a train coming into Rapid City. This woman wore shoes so worn that they "didn't cover her feet" and, as Calamity observed, the woman was riding 40 miles in an open wagon to a ranch while she was coming up to Deadwood in a comfortable stage. [31] Perhaps there is no mystery why old-timers, when commenting about her, had a

74. "Only and Original 'Calamity Jane.' Taken in 1880."

tendency to defend her and dwell on her good points in spite of her very obvious
bad ones.

While it is extremely doubtful if Calamity ever had any of the hair-raising
adventures which legend attributes to her, she did work at a number of masculine
occupations. In the early summer of 1876 when Crook's column was moving
against Sitting Bull, Bourke wrote in his journal:

> It was whispered that one of our teamsters was a woman, and no other
> than "Calamity Jane," a character famed in border story; she had donned the
> raiment of the alleged rougher sex, and was skinning mules with the best of
> them. She was eccentric and wayward rather than bad, and had adopted male
> attire more to aid her in getting a living than for any improper purpose. "Jane"
> was as rough and burly as any of her messmates, and it is doubtful if her sex
> would ever have been discovered had not the wagon-master noted that she
> didn't cuss her mules with the enthusiasm to be expected from a graduate of
> Patrick & Saulsbury's Black Hills Stage Line, as she represented herself to
> be.[32]

One old-timer in Miles City used to tell of another incident which occurred when she was a driver with a government wagon train. One hot day while stopped not far from a river, the drivers went swimming. Before long it became apparent that something unusual was happening, and the officers with the train investigated. By the time the officers reached the swimming hole, the drivers had dressed and left for the "tall timber"—all but Calamity who was standing with the water up to her breasts. These officers, being less tolerant than those with Crook's column, had her "drummed out of camp."

Her visits to Miles City apparently never resulted in anything out of the ordinary except, perhaps, on one occasion. In 1895 she moved into a little shack standing back of the Grey Mule Saloon on Park Street. While living there, she was taken before Judge Milburn and fined—as she put it later—for "being a celebrity." As she was often noisy and disorderly when in her cups, she was probably jailed for creating a disturbance while drunk. Not having the $100 she had been fined, she persuaded the judge to allow her to try to raise the price of the fine and, when freed, decided to leave town. She awoke Wirt Newcom, an ex-cowboy then working and sleeping in a nearby livery stable, to arrange for a rig to take her to Deadwood. Newcom had trouble finding a driver in the early hours of the morning but finally persuaded a man to leave a poker game. When Calamity came to leave, all she possessed was in a "war bag and . . . a cheap suitcase." As she shook hands with Newcom on taking leave, she asked him to tell the chief of police that "he ought to be ashamed of himself" adding, "Do you know it took him and two more men to put me in jail. Tell him for me some day I am coming back here to Miles City and I will whip the hell out of him." [33]

The night life of these lusty days was, in spite of its striking features, but a minor part of the over-all picture. The early practice of cowboys racing their ponies on Main Street, and the influence of the English remittance men,[34] brought the development of horse-racing and steeplechasing—complete with colors for the various owners of stables. Fort Keogh had a fine military band which gave concerts, and the military personnel had a group active in presenting amateur theatricals. The coming of the railroad made possible visits by artists and traveling shows, and the old-time variety house with its low humor lost its importance.

Some of the early shows were given under very trying conditions. On one occasion a performance of *Uncle Tom's Cabin* was given in Charlie Brown's saloon on a stage improvised from planks supported by beer kegs—all of which had an adverse effect on the realism of the scene showing Eliza's escape from the bloodhounds. Sometimes a troupe went broke and had to stay until they had bolstered their finances to the point where they could move on. When such misfortunes happened, the town would have a concentrated dose of the theater while the actors gave their entire assortment of plays. A skating rink covering some 50 by 150 feet was put up soon after the arrival of the railroad in 1881, and this not only provided a place for roller-skating, a fad here as "back in the states," but it also doubled as a theater, an arena for boxing matches, and a hall for conventions—or, perhaps one should say, *the* convention.

The Fourth of July was properly celebrated with parades, fireworks, and other accepted trimmings. In fact the celebrations on at least two occasions began at midnight with prank-master Huffman as ringleader. Of one of these occasions he wrote:

Dear Father,

Since my return from the "Magic City of the Plains" (Billings) the 4th and its business and bustle its headache dust and remorse caused by firing heavy charges of powder in an anvil with a cigar [35] on the night of the 3rd while still in a sommambulistic state has made writing seem too arduous a task to tackle— We had a —— —— roaring 4th—do you recollect how we boys built big bonfires rang bells and mined for blasts a few years ago in W[aukon] well one of those same boys went about on the 1st here and organized a gang of Nihilists to meet in the rear of his gallery at midnight of the 3rd. They came 16 all clothed in blue shirts and armed with 1 Barrell of Rosin—6 Kegs of Blasting Powder 10 gals of Kerosine—a dray to haul combustibles and a hand cart to haul the powder and strong iron cans of 6 lbs capacity to fire Blasts in —with an inverted oak whiskey Barrel a yard of fuse and one can of powder you can produce a noise equal to and more ear disturbing than a 10 lb Rodman —we went and conquered—making the night more hideous than one can describe—we ceased not until the Breakfast Bells and innumerable invitations to irrigate became too tempting—I had barely time to saddle my stud and don my gorgeous uniform for the 9 Oclock parade   I rode as aid to Gen Bochardt Marshal of the day. . . .

There were also other community-sponsored entertainments. On December 3, 1882, Huffman wrote his father, "Socially the winter opens up well—We have a hop at our new rooms [36] each Thursday night—a Dramatic Club and two other Social Clubs—which speaks well for Miles once noted as wickedest of the Wick. . . ." In a letter dated January 14, 1883, Huffman provided his father with further details of the social activities during the holiday season.

The Holidays passed with much music Dancing Sleighing and Feasting here and they are still at it—The sleighing is fine and the liveries make a harvest from their fine cutters the rental of which costs $2.50 per hour or $5.00 for a short drive of not more than two hours—It dont agree with my nervious system to sleighride   I doubt if a "mash" even would make me brave the danger at those figures. . . . I can say truly that this New Years day just past was the best one—all considered—I ever saw. I spent the afternoon with my roommates calling—homes were all curtained and lighted within in the good old style—ladies in white—Egg Nog—Raw Isters—Salads and some richly decked sideboards we found on our rounds—

The big event at Miles City—and in all of eastern Montana for that matter —was the three-day annual meeting of the Montana Stockgrowers Association. This convention, held annually in April, brought cattlemen and their wives, and cowboys from far and wide: and jam-packed the town to the limit. "It would be impossible to imagine a more typically American assemblage," wrote Theodore Roosevelt,". . . and on the whole it would be difficult to gather a finer body of men, in spite of their numerous shortcomings." [37] Here the rich stock-owner rubbed shoulders with the cowboy who worked for $40 a month; and while the latter raced horses in the streets, drank, gambled, and frolicked with the girls, the former met at Russell's skating rink and grappled with such problems as Texas fever, management of herds, rustling, and organization of the roundups.

In the early years these meetings got under way with a parade led by the

75. "Sidney Plagnet, 1889."

band from Fort Keogh, and closed with a ball held at the Macqueen House. Attending the meetings were such pioneers as Conrad Kohrs, John Holt, Granville Stuart, Pierre Wibaux, and Henry Boice all of whom left an indelible mark on the cattle industry. There were others of peculiar note as Theodore Roosevelt, Antoine-Marie-Vincent Manca de Vallombrosa—otherwise known as the Marquis de Mores—and the Eaton brothers who eventually found it more profitable to wrangle dudes than cows. One of the highlights of the meetings which became known far and wide was the daily banquet of roast pig put on by the Miles City Club, a social organization dating back to the fall of 1883.

The remittance men, who usually hung out while in town at Sam Pepper's saloon and the Macqueen House, added their bit of unusual color to the life in the town. Some broke with the past and accepted the rough ways and dress of the frontier; others clung to the aristocratic ways in which they had been reared. As class consciousness had little place in frontier society, any evidences of it were quickly noted. There are those who still remember the wife of one Englishman who, after being introduced to some of the townspeople at a dance, inquired of her husband who these people were. On being informed that they were the local merchants, she remarked, "Fawncy that—meeting the tradesmen!"

Typical of the "hail fellows well met" was Sydney Paget, a sportsman to the core and ardent lover of horse-racing. As the speeds of his little string of ponies were pretty well known, the town sharpies would promote a match whenever a faster horse came to town. As a result he was "taken" regularly, but this did not seem to dampen his ardor, and money was not too difficult to secure from home to meet his losses.

Although not a remittance man, another Englishman was long remembered by Sidney Sanner, a local lawyer. J. H. Price, a bachelor, lived in a little log cabin on his ranch near Knowlton where he raised fine polo ponies. In some ways he was a character—always wore a monocle, was dignified in bearing, and never used an obscene expression. On one occasion he appeared in court at Miles City as a witness. Seeking to belittle him in the eyes of the jury, Sanner found himself caught in his own trap when he began to question the Englishman.

"Mr. Price," said Sanner, "I have heard that you were a college professor. Is that true?"

"Yes, that is true," replied the man with the monocle.

"Well now, just *where* were *you* a college professor?"

"Oh, a little institution over in England called Oxford University," was the dry reply. Sanner told a friend later he wished he had been standing on a trap door and that it had opened suddenly. Price had taught at a college in Oxford, and Cecil Rhodes, founder of the Rhodes fellowships, had been one of his students.

Although Miles City was a tough little settlement, there were those who worked to bring religion to the community. The Presbyterians were the first to make a formal effort to establish a church. Reverend Sheldon Jackson of Helena journeyed by wagon and stage in cold that registered 35 degrees below zero to hold the first service on January 12, 1879. Major Borchard allowed the group to use the unfinished second floor of his store at Fourth and Main for the meeting; seats were improvised from planks supported by nail kegs—the kegs being supplied by a hardware store and the planks by John Chinnick who was building a saloon and dance hall nearby. Subsequent meetings were held in private homes, the schoolhouse, the old log courthouse with its sawdust floor, other stores, and an undertaking establishment; and in 1883 the congregation finally moved into its own church. Other denominations had similar pioneering experiences.

One of the first Methodist ministers to hold services was Reverend William Wesley Van Orsdel who had arrived at Fort Benton in July, 1872. Brother Van, as he was affectionately known, earned his passage up the Missouri on the *Far West* by preaching and singing, plus a promise to raise $50, half the customary fare.[38] The character of this outstanding minister of the gospel and the nature of some of the men among whom he labored in Montana are mirrored in a letter Charlie Russell wrote to him on the occasion of a formal birthday party in 1918.

> . . . I think it was about this time of year thirty seven years ago that we first met at Babcocks ranch in Pigeye bason on the upper Judith   I was living at that time with a hunter and trapper Jake Hoover who you will remember He and I had come down from the south fork with three pack horses loaded with deer and elk meet which he sold to the ranchers and we stopped for the night with old Bab, a man as rough as the mountains he loved but who was all hart from his belt up and friends ore strangers were welcom to shove there feet under his table   this all welcom way of his made the camp a hangout for many homeless mountain and prairie men and his log walls and dirt roof semed like a palice to those who lived mostly under the sky
>
> the eavning you came there was a mixture of bull whackers hunters and

prospectors who welcomed you with hand shaks and rough but friendly greet-
ings

I was the only stranger to you so after Bab interduced Kid Russell he
took me to one side and whispered

boy says he I don't savy many samsingers [39] but Brother Van deels square

and when we all sat down to our elk meet beens coffee and dryed apples
under the rays of a bacon grease light, these men who knew little of law and
one among them I knew wore knotches on his gun   men who had not prayed
since they nelt at there mothers knee bowed their heads while you, Brother
Van, gave thanks and when you finished some one said Amen   I am not sure
but I think it was a man who I heard later was ore had been a rode agent   I
was 16 years old then, Brother Van but have never forgotten your stay at old
Babs with men whose talk was generally emphasized with fancy profanity but
while you were with us although they had to talk slow and careful there was
never a slip. . . .[40]

A minister of the gospel had to "deel square" and be a man from the ground up
to earn more than polite respect from the rough men of the frontier; and Brother
Van, like Father De Smet, had those qualities in abundance.

Although Montana was a Northern state, frontier politics usually involved a
striking clash between Republicans and Democrats because of the presence of
many Southerners. In fact, so many Confederate soldiers came to the state after
the Civil War that it has been said that the Rebels captured Montana without
firing a shot. Therefore, not only did all of the colorful characteristics of early-
day elections blossom here in full strength but there was also the unique feature
of a nip-and-tuck struggle between the two major parties conducted in a manner
only possible in a frontier town. On November 9, 1882, Huffman wrote his father:

Election day was a Daisy here—Many thousands changed hands on sherriff
Joe Leighton [41] had 4 $1000 bets and lost all—excitement ran high—Brass
Bands and Banners—Gunpowder and gin were used extensively on both
sides   Democrats and Republicans for the first time took decided stand
against each other—3 Republicans managed to get Nominations for Council-
men and sherriff on Dem ticket and result was the Dem ticket was elected
throught

I think if you people in the states keep on fooling with the Dutchmans
Beer and the Irishman whiskey you will have a Dem Pres next Rattle

Not only were elections colorful affairs where close friends sometimes fought
—literally and figuratively—until the votes were all counted, but they were
characterized by unique manipulations. Sam Gordon recorded additional details
of the election about which Huffman wrote.

Recalling the location of the "Diamond R" store at the northwest corner
of Main and Fifth. . . . the northeast corner . . . was known as the "Charley Brown" corner, where—in a single-story log building extending nearly, if
not quite, back to the alley, Charley Brown, a character inseparable from the
history of early Miles City, held forth. . . . It was in the rear end of this place
that the polls were held in the general election of '82, when many soldiers from
Keogh were temporarily equipped with citizens' togs and voted. If memory
serves, there were about 1,700 votes cast by a population of a possible 1,200

men, women and children. It took the election officials five days to canvas the vote, which procedure was in progress, off and on, for all of that period, at a faro table in the rear of the saloon, frequent adjournments being taken to indulge in the other attractions close at hand. It was currently reported, at the time, that the delay in announcing the result, was in deference to instructions from Helena to hold off until it could be ascertained how much of a Democratic majority would be required from spacious Custer, to cinch the deal. This was the election which had for one of its features the "Wooley's Ranch" vote, a precinct that returned a hundred odd votes, all of a kind, that has never yet been located on the map of Custer County.[42]

Nor was this "Wooley's Ranch" affair the only one of its kind. One old ranchman, recalling the activities of a slightly later date, wrote:

In the good old days you did not have to register to vote and you were not questioned about your age or how long you had been in the state. Just drop into a precinct and if you could write your name you could vote. Then you could drop into another where you were not known and vote again. One election a bunch of cowboys voted in Birney [and] then started for Miles City a distance of 100 miles [away]. They had fresh horses stationed along the route. They voted at every precinct and rode into Miles City in time to cast another vote before the polls closed.

At times the elections were very close [and] a candidate would win by as few as two or three votes. And in the outlying districts where they only had try weekly mail service—that is the mail went out one week and *tried* to get back the next—the votes would not get into headquarters for a week or so. The votes would not be sent in by registered mail but any rancher who was coming into town would bring them. In one election the vote for Sheriff was nip and tuck. Every precinct heard from would change the vote. The republican would have a lead of two votes, next the democrat would lead by one vote. Finally the last precinct was in and the republican had won by three votes. The Judge said, "This ends it boys"; but a democrat sitting there listening to the votes being counted jumped up and said, "The votes from Butches ranch are not in yet." They asked, "Where is Butches ranch, and how many votes are there?" He replied, "It is about 160 M. from here over in the Missouri river brakes and they have seven or eight votes. He lives forty miles from the P.O. and the country is very rough. I tell you what I will do. I will send a man out there and he can ask every one he meets on the road if they have the votes then he is to go on and get them." So he voted eight tickets, sealed them up, gave them to his man, told him to get out in the country and hide for ten days and then bring the votes in. When the votes were counted the Democrat had won by two votes. And to this day if a vote is close some one will say, "Have we heard from Butches ranch yet?" [43]

Like the election, law enforcement conformed in general with the accepted pattern—except for variations growing out of individual or local interpretations: Miles City, as county seat of Custer County, was concerned with lawbreaking in the surrounding countryside as well as local problems. And, by and large, the lawlessness had a peculiar "wide-open" quality which was typical of a frontier community—a quality which was particularly true of the days before the railroad.

In the beginning the tough element ran the town about as it pleased; and it was to be expected that the swaddies, buffalo-hunters, tin horns, bull-whackers,

76. "Montana Man-Hunters of the Seventies before the railroad came."

and mule-skinners would get into a brawl near the "shank" of the evening. Homeless men, loose women, and alcohol have always produced an explosive mixture when mixed in proper proportions. The easiest way to handle such trouble was to let it settle itself—and this the law-abiding fraction of the population did. However, as the town grew it was necessary to curb what Sam Gordon termed "elephantine antics"; and so the early town marshals began to put an end to the more offensive horseplay and brawling.

Although Miles City was never noted for gunplay like the Kansas cow towns, a town marshal had to be a man of decision and courage. One story Huffman told illustrates well the qualities required to maintain order. This incident involved Henry—better known as "Hank"—Wormwood, one of the first, if not the first, town marshal. Hank had one personal peculiarity which set him apart—he wore his sandy-colored hair long, like a dandy who wished to attract attention. One evening the report reached Hank that a swaddy in Strader's saloon and gambling hall was getting "tough drunk" and swearing to his friends that "no red-headed, long-haired son of a so and so could do anything to *him*." Hank, realizing that his hand was being called, stepped into the saloon and, being careful to keep his hand away from his gun, walked straight up to the soldier in a friendly fashion. All activity stopped immediately and an ominous quiet settled on the room in which there were at least 25 other soldiers. Looking the soldier straight in the eye, Hank said, "What's this I hear? You wouldn't do anything to hurt me, would you?" The soldier, a powerful man but not as tall as Hank, hesitated, and while he hesitated Hank's hands suddenly shot out and his long fingers encircled the man's neck. The marshal quickly lifted him off the floor and held him against the wall with a grip like a hangman's noose. The soldier choked, his tongue popped out of his mouth, and his face went purple. Supporting his victim with one hand, the marshal took the soldier's gun and then set him down. Holding his prisoner at the point of a gun, Hank glanced coolly around the saloon and then addressed those present: "I'm goin' to take this boy back to the fort. I advise you fellows not to interfere." Not a man moved as the officer walked his man out the door.[44]

From the mid-1880's on, the cowboys caused much of the trouble with which the local officers had to cope. Some of this originated with characters like George Geddes.

Peter Geddes, a multi-millionare of New York City, bought a big cattle ranch on Tongue River for his son George. . . . He never stayed at the ranch, spent his time in Miles City soaked to the gills. One day he loaded up on the remedy for snake bites, got on his horse, rode down to the depot, and roped the smokestack of a freight engine. When the train was ready to pull out the engineer told him to take his rope off. George said he would not do it [as] he intended to hold the train until he got ready for them to go. The engineer threw in the throttle. George set back on the horse. Faster and faster they went until the horse was jerked off his feet and dragged. It should have been curtains but the rope broke. When George got up he had left part of his hide mingled with the cinders and for once in his life he was duly sober. He finally drank up the ranch, and was accused of hiring a negro to kill an inoffensive boy. When he came to trial he got a change of venue to Billings. The trial lasted several months, broke Custer Co. Geddes got one year in the penitentiary, the negro drew 20.[45]

However, most of this trouble was made up of oversized doses of horseplay. Recalling this activity, one rancher wrote:

> Back before the country became civilized . . . the cowboys only got to town once in six months. They came in for fun and one of their pleasures was to harass the town marshall. The job was too strenuous for one man so they hired a deputy, but they made a mistake and hired a guy from the East. When he got a six-gun strapped on and a big Stetson hat he was a sight for sore eyes and duck soup for the boys. In those days the streets were not well lighted. One night when the mud was about knee deep he was standing on a corner. A cowboy ran his horse past him and splashed mud all over him. The next night the cowboy rode up to a saloon [and] left his horse at the sidewalk. In those days the old wooden walks were about three feet above the street. This horse would stand without dropping the reins. While the cowboy was in the saloon, the Copper came in the side door. The Cowboy broke and ran, the Copper after him. Just as he straddled the horse the Cop reached for him, he spurred the horse, the Cop's hand landed on the horses hips and the horse jumped from under him and he landed face forward in the mud. The cowboy just remembered that he was urgently needed at the ranch and left town on the double quick. When he got back to town some months later that Cop had moved on to quieter pastures. I knew this cowboy well. He was not vicious, was called a good fellow, he thoroughly enjoyed innocent fun and for some unknown reason was never arrested.[46]

E. C. Abbott—better known as Teddy Blue—related another bit of horseplay to his biographer. Abbott was singing "The Texas Ranger" and two of his friends were attempting to accompany him, one on a violin and the other on a piano, in the parlor of "Number 44," the well-known sporting house. The madam did not appreciate the "music" and finally objected to the treatment to which her piano was being subjected. The cowboys took offense and, after an interchange of remarks which need not be repeated here, Abbott went across the street to the livery stable, got his horse "Billy," and rode him into the parlor. The madam thereupon locked the door and called the police. The only way out was a large window which was low to the ground, and Abbott and Billy took it and left for the ferry on the run—with the law one jump behind. Abbott recalled that he escaped safely to the north bank of the Yellowstone and that the next day it all blew over and he came back to town.[47]

It should not be assumed, however, that Miles City was without incidents of serious trouble. There were shootings—some apparently accidental and unsolved, some drunken gun-waving that had serious consequences, and some deliberate shootings. One of the latter which Huffman recalled in later years involved James Pym.

> Jim Pym seemed to us in Miles City very rough and ordinary. To show you the kind he was, I once saw another man pull a gun on him in front of my shop. He took the gun out of the fellow's hand, tossed it away, knocked his assailant down, kicked him, and told him to leave town and not show his face in it again. The fellow left.
> Jim lived with a woman who was not his wife in a little log shack near Bill Reece's dance hall. That didn't matter to us as weddings weren't any too

common in the early days. Jim was good to her, and that counted. But she got to having an affair with a younger man. One day this chap was with her at Jim's house, and Jim came home unexpectedly and found them.

What was the younger man to expect, caught like that, from a man like Jim Pym? Certainly he looked for no mercy; doubtless he felt that he would be killed like a rat. So he pulled his own gun without a word and shot Jim dead.[48]

When they came to lay Jim out, the neighbors found that the dead man, formerly a trooper in Company B, Seventh Cavalry, had been awarded a Congressional Medal of Honor for a hazardous trip down the bluff to the river to bring water for the wounded on Reno's Hill in the Battle of the Little Big Horn.[49] Few of those killed in shooting scrapes were heroes of such high standing.

While shootings like the one just noted have largely been forgotten, two incidents involving law enforcement stand out boldly from the haze of the past. One of those involved a bold outlaw who sometimes used Miles City as a hangout. This man was George Parrott, better known as "Big Nose George," whose gang was well known on the Northwest Frontier from the stage and freighting routes which connected Cheyenne and Deadwood on the southeast to the Fort Keogh–Bismarck trail on the northeast, west as far as the Sun River country, and south and west to the line of the Union Pacific Railroad near Medicine Bow, Wyoming. Like other outlaws, he appeared briefly here and there and then vanished into the wilderness of prairie and badlands—often, so it is said, to that favorite outlaw retreat, the outer fringe of the Big Horn Mountains.

In January, 1879, shortly after Huffman came to Fort Keogh, Morris Cahn made plans to go East to purchase a new stock of goods for his store on Park Street. Cahn made no secret of his prospective trip although he took the precaution of traveling with an army paymaster going from Fort Keogh to Fort Abraham Lincoln. Beyond the Powder River Crossing, where the trail dropped down into a little coulee and paralleled the stream bed for a short distance,[50] the paymaster's ambulance and its escort—the latter riding in a wagon several hundred yards to the rear where they could render no effective protection—were stopped by Big Nose George and his gang. Cahn was relieved of $14,000—an expensive christening for such a minor piece of topography as Cahn's Coulee.

After the holdup the outlaws crossed to the north bank of the Yellowstone and stayed overnight at a ranch near the present village of Kinsey. The following night Big Nose George was back in Miles City spending freely large amounts of money, the source of which no one was prepared to effectively question. A couple of months later Hank Wormwood arrested the gang near Buffalo Rapids, just below Miles City, but they were released on perjured evidence to the effect that they were in Canada when the robbery occurred.

On July 15 of the following year Parrott was back in Miles City. This time U. S. Marshal John X. Biedler had received word from the authorities in Wyoming that they wanted Big Nose George. In fact, they were willing to pay $1000 for him. In 1878 Parrott's gang had been foiled in an attempt to derail a Union Pacific train with a pay car. Two men sent to trail the gang had been murdered and later, when a member of the gang squealed, Parrott's part became known and the authorities had put a price on his head. Jolly—but coldly efficient—"X" had a tough job on his hands.

This is Huffman's account of what happened:

One day I was standing in front of the old Bella Union Theatre in Miles City talking to Tom Irvine, the sheriff. X Biedler, United States marshall and a famous man hunter of the vigilante days, came along.

"Don't turn around and look," he cautioned us, "but when you get a chance, notice the two fellows sitting in front of Chinnick's shack. That's Big Nose George and Bill Carey.[51] I've got to get those men and I don't know how I'm going to do it."

. . . They sat in full view, but their position was highly strategic. John Chinnick's shack, from where we stood, was not more than two and a half or three city blocks, but the ground all around it was open and unobstructed. Any man who undertook to cross that open patch was under their eyes and if they didn't like his looks it was certain as daylight he would soon be full of lead. X Biedler had a game leg and was known by sight from one end of Montana to the other, and then some; and he had absolutely no chance of getting near the two desperadoes where they were then and taking them alive.

Chinnick, in front of whose shack they were resting, was himself a product of the country and the times. Known as a business man and trader, he had various irons in the fire, and would make money any way he could, did some freighting, owned a saloon and dance hall, had an interest in a ranch, and also knew various outlaws, staked them, and shared in the proceeds. Nothing was ever fastened on him; furthermore, his word was as good as his bond. . . . Horses belonging to the outlaws were now running in Chinnick's corral.

"I can't go get those men for you, X," Tom said to Biedler. "They know me as well as they know you, and would shoot me just as quick. Don't take any notice, but there's a man across the street who can get them for you, if anybody can."

"Who is he?"

"Lem Wilson." [52] [Wilson was acquainted with the task by a mutual acquaintance and accepted it.]

Lem Wilson that day was wearing high-water overalls, an old shirt and hat, and a pair of rough shoes. He looked like a farmer's half-baked son. But Lem was a lot smarter than he looked just then.

. . . . Lem fastened two six-shooters inside the top of his ragged old [bib] overalls in such a way that to all appearances he was unarmed. Then he walked straight up to Chinnick's shack, and what followed was very simple: It usually was, when the man going after something or somebody knew exactly what he meant to do.

"What do *you* want?" the outlaws asked.

"I'm goin' to see Chinnick," Lem replied.

He walked right past them. A minute later, being at their backs, he gave a command and their hands shot into the air fast.[53]

The men were put under heavy guard and, in due time, delivered to the authorities in Wyoming. Parrott was tried in Rawlins and sentenced to hang. While awaiting execution, he attempted a jail break, which the jailer's wife foiled, and a mob took him from the jail and hanged him, clumsily but effectively, from a telegraph pole.[54]

The second well-remembered incident pertaining to law enforcement happened after the coming of the railroad. The problem of handling tramps and toughs who drifted into town, attracted by its wide-open reputation, was considerably different from that created by men of Parrott's type. As Sam Gordon put it:

> The voting majority were of one mind on the point that a too technical enforcement of the law was not desired and so they elected officials who they knew would not be too officious. Not but that there was due protection for life and property but there seemed to be a tacit understanding to let smaller matters adjust themselves, and into a community permeated by this teaching and in this frame of mind, the injection of the lawless element the railroad brought to us, was distinctly disturbing.[55]

One individual of this lawless type succeeded in perpetrating a major affront on the one subject about which the frontier was extremely sensitive—abuse of decent women—and that sudden, violent wrath of which the frontier was capable promptly evidenced itself.

Early Saturday morning, July 21, 1883, William Rigney and one of his boon companions—drunk and ugly after an all-night carouse—turned up in the residential section of town. The two forcibly entered the home of Mr. Campbell while he and his family were at breakfast and, when ordered out, refused to go. Then they proceeded to give vent to "foul language and fouler allusions" to the mother and her daughter, Grace. A passer-by, said to have been saloon-keeper Charlie Brown, took a hand, and when Rigney became abusive "promptly dealt the worthy a blow that laid him out senseless." The second tough took to his heels, and Rigney was promptly deposited in the courthouse jail.

According to the published stories, the jailer, Jim Conley, was "stuck up" the following evening by a "posse of men" who removed the prisoner and suspended him by his neck from a railroad trestle a half-mile east of town. However, the old-timers—when they reminisced among themselves—told a different version of what happened. According to this account, Brown did not hit Rigney with his fist—he walloped him over the head with a pick handle (or a neck yoke). Rigney was laid out senseless—so senseless, in fact, that when he was taken from the jail he was either dead or in imminent danger of dying. As the men of the community approved of Brown's handling of the situation, they quickly formed a vigilante committee and took the thug out and hanged him, thus effectively camouflaging the situation and eliminating any danger of Brown being tried for manslaughter.[56]

The following Sunday morning, before many knew that the town had a man for breakfast, another major event took place. Just as dawn was breaking, fire was discovered in the Cosmopolitan Theatre at the corner of Sixth and Main. The major part of the block westward to the bank near Park Street was a row of solidly packed frame buildings—all without adequate fire protection.

> Care had been taken that the fire started in the theatre that Sunday should do its work. Almost as soon as discovered, it had enveloped the entire building and shortly afterward a series of explosions spread the fire in every direction, terrorized the few who had begun to fight the fire and doomed the entire frame

77. "Cosmopolitan Theatre, 6th & Main, 1883."

78.   "Old Trader's Store, Main Street, Miles City, 1879."

row to destruction. In less than an hour the stretch from the corner to the bank was a bed of smoking embers. . . .[57]

"It was never settled whether the fire had any connection with the Rigney hanging or was an independent piece of deviltry." As Rigney had been a hanger-on and part-time employee at the establishment where the fire started, it appeared logical to a good many that Rigney's pals had lit the fire as an act of retaliation. "On Sunday afternoon a secret meeting of the committee was held and a patrol force organized whose ticklish duty it was to wait upon the leaders [of the tough element] and direct their immediate departure." As the toughs, captained by steady, tough-fibered John Chinnick, could be expected to stand their ground and as the law-abiding people had reached a point where they were determined to clean up the town, "the town and the people were on the verge of an event." [58] Perhaps, had not kind Providence intervened, that "event" would have taken place the following day with John Chinnick's cabin as the center of a pitched battle that would have equaled any gunfight the West ever had.

Chinnick

was one of the first to be told by "the committee" to leave. He was due to depart Monday evening, and just to show that he was a good fellow he spent Monday forenoon around town, going from one resort to another and discussing the situation with a complete absence of rancor, but at the same time with a bravado that indicated that he did not intend to comply with the ultimatum.[59]

Sam Gordon, who lived at the corner of Third and Pleasant, was home during the noon hour watching the "camp of the enemy . . . through a field glass. As I looked I observed a sudden commotion among the many who had been lounging about and shortly a messenger was seen to leave the ranch for town. On his return, which was speedy, he brought a doctor." Chinnick, who had gone to town in his shirt sleeves and obviously unarmed in the morning, had decided to carry a gun in the afternoon. His wife endeavored to dissuade him and, in the ensuing scuffle over the revolver, Chinnick was accidentally—and fatally—shot in the abdomen. Although the leader of the toughs lingered on for four days, his following, lacking the reckless nerve and assurance of their leader, "scattered in all directions under the friendly cover of that Monday night." The next day life in the community resumed its "accustomed peaceful flow." [60] Here, as in the mining camps of Alder Gulch, hemp and gunpowder in the hands of determined citizens were effective agents in creating respect for law and order.

It should not be assumed that the people of Miles City were not familiar with proper steps in law enforcement. When Fort Keogh was the dominant establishment, George M. Miles was U. S. Commissioner for eastern Montana. The nephew of the general held office from July, 1877, to March, 1879, and during this time heard 20 cases ranging from assault with deadly weapons to theft of government property.[61] The first term of court in Custer County was held during May and June, 1879. Thompson P. McElrath, a visiting member of the bar, put down his impressions of this special session of the territorial district court in a letter to the *New York Times* dated June 8, 1879.

> The courthouse of Custer County, presided over by the Hon. Henry N. Blake of Virginia City, is a primitive structure . . . a cabin built of hewn logs and containing a single apartment. . . . Cotton sheeting, the single ornament in the room being the brand of the mills in which the cloth was manufactured, emblazoned in blue letters on the center of one wall.
>
> On a small platform in the rear Judge Blake sat at a pine table, the unpainted state of which was partially concealed by red cloth. Near the entrance several pine benches afforded accomodation to the spectators, while the center, in front of the judge, was occupied by the lawyers, who were seated at a large table, ornamented by the district attorney's feet, as that functionary tilted leisurely back on two legs of his chair. Shirt sleeves were the prevailing fashion for both council and lookers on.
>
> The courthouse is a fair type of a majority of the buildings in the place, though frame structures, built of pine boards at $52 a thousand feet, and covered with shingles at $12 a thousand, are the prevailing fashion for builders this season. . . .[62]

Mention was also made in the letter that one Gros Ventre and three Cheyenne warriors were sentenced to hang during this term of court for the killing of white men. McElrath, noting the speed with which the Indians were convicted, remarked, "The theory that the only good Indian is a dead one is in full force among the civilians throughout our frontier, though the army, appreciating their bravery and recognizing their powerlessness, take a more merciful view of their red-skinned opponents." Regarding the Cheyennes, he added:

Two of the condemned Cheyennes . . . were found dead in their cell on the

79. "Inside old stockade, Main St., Miles City 1878." (1879?)

following morning. They had sought death in a cool deliberate manner, so un-paralleled as to provoke the admiration of even their white foes. Although hand-cuffed and chained by the ankles to a bull-ring in the floor, they had succeeded in hanging themselves by a belt-strap to an iron bar in the aperture of the cell door. The same strap was used by both, one waiting until the other was dead, and then lifting down the corpse, deliberately removing the strap and adjusting it for his own hanging.

As Huffman's picture indicates, these were not the only Cheyennes to be be-wildered by the workings of the white man's law.

Like the smell of tobacco in the bowl of a discarded pipe, the flavor of the frontier clung to the town for years. Sometimes these bits of the past were en-countered in unexpected places. One stormy, winter day, well after the turn of the century, a loafer in the gunshop of A. D. McAusland found that close-mouthed, veteran gunsmith in the mood to reminisce. Reaching into a box under his lathe, he brought out a stick about 15 inches long. Tied to it were three small, round pieces of rawhide—each with a long braid of coarse black hair. "Friend of mine gave me these," he remarked. "I promised him I'd never tell about them while he was alive; but he's dead now so I'll tell you the story."

McAusland's friend was a trapper. In the winter of 1876–1877, he built a little camp well hidden in a clump of cedars on the Little Missouri six or eight miles above where the OX outfit later built their headquarters. Knowing that the

80. "Billings [Montana], June 1882."

country had too many roving hostiles to be safe, he cached a repeating rifle, one of two he had, in a dense cedar about 50 yards from his camp. After a fairly successful "trap," the day came to make the last round and take up the traps. When he rode into camp on his return, he found it torn down and his furs and camp outfit packed on three ponies.

Before the trapper realized what had happened, three warriors stepped out of the thicket and he found himself looking down the muzzles of their rifles. Relieving him of everything except his clothing, the Indians "signed" that he could walk home. There was nothing he could do but accept that ultimatum. Feeling secure with their victim disarmed and stripped of his property, the Indians turned back to the task of packing—and the trapper walked to the cedar with its hidden rifle. It was all over in a matter of seconds. Taking his horse and packing his things on a couple of the Indian ponies, the trapper headed for the cantonment at the mouth of the Tongue. Hiding by day and traveling the high country away from possible camp sites, the trapper reached the post two days later.[63] His story ended and his loquacious impulse satisfied, the old gunsmith tossed the little stick and its grim mementoes back into the box and abruptly turned back to his work.

That, very briefly, is the story of this cow town. Born amid hostile Indians and great herds of buffalo with a handful of "coffee coolers" for midwives, it spent its infant days under the rough tutelage of swaddies, hide-hunters, and bull-whackers. With the coming of cattle and sheep, the village grew almost overnight from Milestown to Miles City and, although it assumed the importance associated with mature stature, it never lost the irresponsible ways of adolescent youth. At its peak, it basked in the importance of its central location and boasted of such noted and colorful visitors as "Teddy" Roosevelt, Calamity Jane, Granville Stuart, "X" Biedler, C. A. Broadwater, Conrad Kohrs, the visionary Marquis de Mores, and Oliver Wallop, later the Earl of Portsmouth, with his untidy clothes. Then, as the honyocker crowded the cattlemen, the town slipped slowly into more prosaic ways. "Mag" Burns is gone, and gambling isn't legal any more—although there are still games where one can buy a stack of tokens and spend them on tables with green felt covers. The old town of the cattleman and the roistering cowboy refuses to die completely.

In 1876, Cheyenne, Wyoming, was an important outfitting and supply center for several small military posts and the Black Hills area. A freighter on the trail to Deadwood met a second freighter returning to Cheyenne for another load. The following conversation took place:

Inbound freighter: "What yuh loaded with?"

Outbound freighter: "Twenty barrels of whiskey an' a sack of flour."

Inbound freighter: "Whatin hell are you goin' to do with so much flour?"

A frontier joke

HAY BURNERS
and WOOD BURNERS

The line of horses with packs on their backs, the steamboat with churning paddle wheel slowly nosing its way upstream, the bull-train with creaking wagon boxes and wheels slowly grinding ruts in the prairie sod, and the stagecoach with its body rocking easily on leather thorough braces and the bouncing buckboard—these were as necessary to the Western frontier as trains and ships are to modern cities. The steamboat and the bull-train were extremely important to Fort Keogh and Milestown in the very early days. In a way one supplemented the other, as the steamboat provided the necessary cheap transportation for heavy, bulky freight, while the bull-train provided year-round service as well as a means of supplying points distant from the river.

Steamboats had their heyday on the Missouri in the 1860's and 1870's when they were the backbone of the transportation for the gold fields and the fur trade; however, transportation on the Yellowstone was never so extensive. Traffic began on the Yellowstone in 1873 when General Stanley established a supply depot at the mouth of Glendive Creek to support the troops detailed to protect the surveyors locating a line for the Northern Pacific Railroad. The *Far West*, *Key West*, *Peninah*, and *Josephine* brought supplies to Stanley's stockade, and Marsh even took the *Key West* upstream to the mouth of the Powder.[1] Two years later Marsh nursed the *Josephine* 483 miles above the mouth of the Yellowstone to Hell Roaring Rapids; and the following year he pushed the *Far West* to the mouth of the Little Big Horn to bring out the wounded from Custer's battlefield. This year also saw the beginning of "commercial" transportation on the Yellowstone when supplies were set ashore at the mouth of the Tongue for Miles' troops.

In Huffman's day most of the steamboats shuttled back and forth between Bismarck and the upper Missouri ports, and Miles City on the Yellowstone: those carrying buffalo hides generally dropped down to Yankton, Sioux City, or Omaha with their cargoes. Only small, shallow-draft, stern-wheel steamers were used to negotiate the swift, shallow water of the Yellowstone. Although there usually was enough water for navigation between May 15 and September 1, the heavily loaded steamers could operate best during the "June rise" which took place between the middle of May and the middle of July.[2]

In the 1860's, during the peak of steamboating, freight rates from St. Louis to Fort Benton were eight to ten cents per pound. Later, when the railroads began to compete with steamboat traffic on the lower part of the river, they dropped to about three cents per pound. However, the costs, f.o.b., Fort Benton, Cow Island, or Miles City were only a part of the freight-cost picture. Although the steamboat provided the lowest cost transportation and was able to handle bulky freight that was difficult to move, its usefulness ended at the wharf—which was usually a long way from the ultimate consumer. This gap was bridged by the wagons of the freighters who added additional carrying charges to the merchandise. In 1876 it was estimated that the charges on freight shipped from Eastern cities to the mining towns of Montana were about $100 per ton.[3]

When the gold fields were booming, the freighting charges from Fort Benton to Helena and Virginia City added another six cents per pound to the costs. Like steamboat rates, these decreased as competition became stronger, and finally dropped to about one cent per pound.[4] Charges of two to three cents per pound were not uncommon to outlying points (depending on the difficulty of travel) even to the close of the freighting days.[5] The small amount of freighting into Miles City was done mostly during the late summer, fall, and winter. "This was expensive and only used for the transportation of luxuries that could stand the tariff of anywhere from three to seven cents a pound, according to the season and the necessities of the patron."[6] These charges, it might be noted in passing, provided a convenient explanation for high prices. It was not unusual for a merchant to charge an exorbitant price for a paper of needles and lay the blame on the high cost of transportation.

The cost of local freighting in the very early days of Fort Keogh and Fort Custer is indicated in a contract between Paul McCormick and M. Carroll and Co.[7] covering the moving of supplies from a dump on the Yellowstone to the location where Fort Custer was then being built some 30-odd miles up the Big Horn River.

Tongue River Montana
July 30th 1877

Messrs M. Carroll and Co
Tongue River
Montana

Gentlemen:
I will furnish you my ox train of six (6) teams of six (6) yoke of cattle and two (2) wagons to each team: capacity of train forty eight thousand (48000)

pounds eight thousand (8000) pounds to the team to work under your contract with the government of the United States for transportation of army supplies from depot on Big Horn and Yellowstone Rivers to post #2 on the Big Horn on the following conditions:

The train to report at the depot now established near the mouth of the Big Horn for service on or before August the twentieth (20) 1877 and continue in service so long as you may have work for them.

One ration for each man necessarily employed while in the service to be furnished by the Government.

Payment to be made on the following terms. For each team of six (6) yoke of cattle and two (2) wagons of eight thousand (8000) pounds capacity you pay to me seven (7^{00}) Dollars per day for each and every day the teams are in readiness for service and in condition for service as herein provided until discharged.—When fifty (50) days of service shall have been performed payment to be made me by draft on Helena Montana or St Paul Minnesota for said service:—payment for remainder of service if any to be made on completion service as above.

Your acceptance of this letter to constitute a contract binding and obligating on both parties.

Yours truly
Signed/Paul McCormick [8]

Accepted
M Carroll & Co

In a notebook titled *Rules and Regulations for Freighting*,[9] kept by S. C. Ashby, agent for Garrison and Wyatt in Helena, are recorded several interesting notes regarding freight rates charged by this firm during the 1870's:

On large lots of Frgts, say of 150 tons or more we are willing to go as low as 1½ from B to H [Benton to Helena?] but talk and hold out for 1¾ or 1.80 Contract to move 50 tons upon arrival & the balance in 50 ton lots in 20 days —the above is for three trips

If any large shippers have 200 or 250 Tons come to Benton—we are willing to drop as low as 1.37½ to 1.25 if nothing else will catch above that—This is with a distinct understanding that the Shipper is will to ship in 50 ton lots & ship every 20 days or thereabouts by the same Train.

When you talk to Freighters as to the prospect of the price of FRGHT never come under 1.80 & up to 2¢ from Benton—

Small lots of 25 Tons or a little less—ask 1¾ to 2¢ to be governed by the time the shipper wants his goods forwarded—if the Shipper in these little lots claims that his goods must come upon arrival—be stiff at 2¢

If any of these small shippers had a reasonable amount of Frght & were willing to have it come about the third trip you can then go as low as 1.60 or 1.50 but do as much better as you can   All fo [also?] the Benton Frghts mentioned—Storage & Handling is included—

Corinne Frgts.[10] To leave Corinne about 25th of April talk this but when I close contract put it in about May 1st if I can

RATE.   From Corinne to Helena on the first trip on any lots of ten or fifteen tons ought not to go lower than 4.25 and try to get as near 5¢ #   as possible on First Trip

Anything of a Jew Lot of Frght get from ¼¢ to ½¢ better than above rates.

Ashby's note regarding the hiking of prices when dealing with some people is interesting, and indicates there were difficulties in addition to those of competi-

81.   Bull-train in Miles City, 1880.

tion. Alexander Toponce, a freighter active in the 1860's and 1870's, regarded some of these early-day merchants as being "as crooked as a dog's hind leg." Finally, in self-defense, he adopted the practice of not allowing freight to be moved after he had unloaded it until it had been checked over, accepted, and the freight paid. He recalled that the three Kleinschmidt brothers in Helena were about the most difficult to do business with, and that they had a "whole bag of good tricks." After being clipped a couple of times, Toponce laid for them and neatly turned the tables.

As this freighter told the story, he went to the mouth of the Marias River just below Fort Benton to pick up a shipment which contained, among other things, 50,000 pounds of sugar. This was packed in 500 sacks of—supposedly—100 pounds each. As they loaded the sugar, the wagon boss remarked to Toponce that he thought the bags were heavy, and, when they pulled through Fort Benton, Toponce made a check and found that each sack weighed 120 pounds. Buying some empty sacks and borrowing a set of platform scales, Toponce removed 19 pounds of overweight from each sack, bagged it, and put the excess in the trail wagons. In Helena he unloaded 500 sacks of 100 pounds net weight and collected for the freight. One of the brothers, in checking the wagons, noted the sugar in the trail wagons and asked if it came off the boat. Toponce replied that it had, whereupon the merchant promptly claimed it saying, "Well, it belongs to me. My brother loaded that sugar on the boat at St. Louis himself." "Prove it," said Toponce handing him the bill of lading specifying that the shipment contained 50,000 pounds. The merchant cried, wrung his hands, and pleaded, "Oh, Alex, you know it was my sugar." But he was over the proverbial barrel, and, in the end, the merchant got the sugar—at 50¢ a pound. As the going price was about a dollar a pound, it was not unreasonable at that price, but $4750 for this 9500 pounds of hidden overweight made the scheme a bit expensive.[11]

Horses, mules, and oxen were used in freighting, the choice being governed by some very practical considerations. Mules, while less intelligent in some ways, stood more hardship than horses on the same amount of feed. Both horses and mules were capable of rapid travel, a factor of some importance when competition was keen. Matthew Carroll, part owner of the famous Diamond R, went to the field with the mule train which supplied Gibbon's troops during the Sioux campaign of 1876. His diary shows that when the troops tried the pincers movement against Sitting Bull's camp on the Little Big Horn, this Diamond R train was capable of as rapid movement as Custer's cavalry.[12]

But horses and mules had their disadvantages. In addition to requiring grain, which was bulky and expensive, costly harness, and considerable care, they were often the object of undue attention from thieving Indians. On the other hand, the slow, plodding oxen, which lived off the country as they went and required only a rough yoke for a harness, had some sterling qualities. The only use Indians had for oxen was for meat and rawhide—both of which buffalo supplied in a more desirable form—consequently bull-trains went through where horse and mule trains ran considerable risk of finding themselves "afoot."

The practice of hooking two or more wagons together as a unit was started in 1866 by the Sutherlin Brothers who freighted supplies into the gold fields from the head of navigation on the Missouri.[13] A few years later it was a common oc-

82. "Covered Wagons on west Main Street, 1882."

currence to see as many as four wagons coupled together with nine to 12 yoke of bulls strung out in front. Such a unit could carry 16,000 to 20,000 pounds of freight. Huffman's pictures indicate that the Diamond R trains freighting into Milestown were made up of units of two or three wagons with a *team* [14] of five to seven yoke on each. Eight or ten teams usually made up a train, and if the number was larger than this, they were usually split into two trains, each with its wagon boss.

Methods of handling wagon trains varied according to whether bulls or horses and mules were used; and there were, no doubt, additional variations depending on the ideas of individual wagon bosses. The method of hitching bulls and mules to the wagon or wagons was essentially the same, however. A long, heavy chain extended from the first two animals to the lead wagon. The other pairs of animals, with the exception of those nearest the wagon, were attached to this master chain which passed down the center of the *team*. The last pair of animals, attached directly to the tongue of the wagon, both pulled and guided the vehicle. These animals, chosen for their size and strength, were called the *wheelers*. The *leaders*, on the opposite end of the string, were usually the smallest in size and carefully selected for their intelligence, for they were the brains of the entire *team*. Those in the center were called the *swing* animals; and when six animals made up the *team*, they were usually graded in size according to the position in which they were hitched.

The bull-whacker plodded along on the near—or left—side of his wheelers, directing his team, for the most part, with four commands: "get up" to start, "gee" for a turn to the right, "haw" for a turn to the left, and "whoa" to stop— much colorful profanity, and a long whip which required two hands to control. This whip, with an 18- to 20-foot lash braided of many strands of buckskin, was the whacker's only tool, and he took pride in being able to control down to the last inch the placement of the popper on its end.

A string of mules or horses was handled by a mule-skinner, or teamster, who rode the *nigh*, or left, wheeler. Running to the left side of the bit in the mouth of the nigh leader was a single line. The *off*, or right, leader was connected to his teammate by a jockey stick, a short stick connecting the bit on his bridle and the adjacent hame of his partner. This jockey stick rigidly controlled the direction of his movements. By jerking or pulling on this single rein in certain ways, these signals sometimes being supplemented by gees and haws, the teamster guided his nigh leader and, consequently, the entire team. A team handled in this manner was known as a *jerk-line* team, and the keystone of the string was, obviously, the nigh leader.

When two or more teams traveled together, an extra man or a wagon boss supplied additional help in difficult places. On hard pulls he rode alongside on horseback and, with a heavy whip, supplied the necessary "touch" at the proper time and at the proper place to keep the team pulling effectively as a unit. "It was quite a sight," recalled one old bull-whacker, "to see 20 yoke of bulls, with 40 wriggling tails, putting their necks into the yoke, and three men with cracking whips urging them on." If there was danger of getting stuck, the extra man helped hitch two teams together for the pull or uncouple the wagons so that each could be moved individually, as the situation required. Recoupling wagons which had been taken apart was a difficult task, for they were attached, one to the other, by a short length of chain from the fifth wheel of the preceding wagon and a coupling for the short tongue of the trailing wagon.

When the wagons stopped, horses were unharnessed where they stood, the tugs being left hooked to save time when hitching up and to avoid danger of getting kicked by a mean animal. The animals were then fed on the spot, either on the ground or in a nose bag. With a horse or mule train, 20 miles was a good day's travel when loaded; in fact it was not possible to drive much faster when traveling empty. And the day's drive involved much more than making a drive—camp had to be made and broken, harness repaired, animals shod and taken care of, wagons greased, and often the roads had to be repaired.

With a bull-train, the bull-whackers rolled out at daybreak. The herder brought in the cattle and each man yoked up his team, the animals being trained to come to their proper places and put their heads under the yoke. Then, with the wagon boss directing the best driver to lead and set the pace, the train rolled without further delay. In a normal day's drive, the train kept moving until about nine o'clock when it would *corral* and turn the oxen out to graze under the care of the herder. The men would then prepare breakfast, do various odd jobs, and rest. If there were new oxen to be broken, these would be worked with at this time. This proceeding was not without its excitement when some steer objected strenuously and bucked around with the end of the yoke flying until the pin broke out of the bow. Then the whackers would crawl out from under the wagons, where they had taken refuge, and repeat the procedure.

About noon the train would again yoke up and drive until about four o'clock in the afternoon when another stop would be made to graze the cattle and to prepare the second meal of the day. After the cattle had grazed, if the next watering place was not too distant, the train would yoke up again and push on until it was too dark to drive, when it would camp for the night. For this, without time off for holidays and Sundays—there were no Sundays west of Omaha—the bull-whacker received about $50 a month.

There was some division of labor in a bull-train. With each train there was a wagon boss who supervised the movement and the work, a herder to drive the extra cattle and watch them while they grazed, and sometimes in the early days, a hunter, a guide, and even an interpreter when Indian goods were being freighted. For cooking and eating, the men divided into messes. Each mess had its cook, who was one of the teamsters, but who thus earned exemption from standing guard, and rustling fuel and water. This last task rotated between the remaining members of the mess. At night a guard was put out consisting of two or more men, and this was divided into two or three watches. Each driver slept in or by his wagon where he was available in case of emergency. In the days when there was danger from Indians, each whacker was armed with a rifle and revolver, the rifle often being a 16-shot Henry. Thus, in addition to his regular work, he acted as an armed guard or soldier—a task not foreign to the majority of the men.

Of the cooks who served the trains, not much has been recorded. Late in 1873 "Yellowstone" Kelly guided and hunted for one train, and he recalled later that the cook for this train was a big, bearded fellow whose gruff call of "grub pile" brought everyone immediately to the iron kettle of coffee and the Dutch

83. "'Jerkline Twelve' on the old Freight Road, 1883."

oven filled with meat and biscuits. Kelly also remembered that the cook had choice names for some of his "concoctions" and that these were not listed in any menu save the "unwritten one of a bull train." [15]

Ashby's *Rules and Regulations for Freighting* contains the following detailed information as to what at least one freighting company provided for their men in the 1870's.

Beef	¾ lb pr meal pr man 9 men				
Rations for 9 men for 10 days.					
Flour	1½#	per day to the man (15#)			150#
Bacon	¾#	" " " " " (7#)			70#
Coffee	2½ oz.	" " " " "			14#
Beans where there are no potatoes			4 oz.		22#
Syrup	1 quart per day 10 qts.				2½ gals.
Potatoes where there are no beans			2#		180#
Fruit	2 oz. pr day to the man				11¼#
Salt	1 oz. " " " " "				5⅔#
Matches					1 box
Soap	2 bars				2#
Soda	1 paper to the sack				
Axle Grease 4 half gallon cans					

The Wagon Masters of each Train must preserve the sacks
& furnish them from time to time to put the Grub in

Two bars of soap, even though they weighed a pound each, would not provide for much washing other than that required by the cooking utensils and the tin plates; and the axle grease was obviously not intended for human consumption!

Regarding the lives of these men whose only *home* was a bull-train, Sam Gordon, the veteran journalist of Miles City, observed that

It was a dog's life as far as the comforts and amenities went. The menu rarely went beyond black coffee, sour-dough bread and "sow-belly" fried in a skillet in its own grease thickened with flour and of camp shelter there was none for the men were too tired at night to arrange any but the most primitive protection and they "pulled" too early in the morning to do any "breaking camp." Summer was bad enough but the slow and uncertain creep of a bull-train on the road in winter was an experience to be endured only once by anyone but a real bull-whacker.[16]

Many of the bull-whackers who plied their trade in eastern Montana were deserters from the army or "galvanized Yankees," [17] as the ex-Confederate prisoners were termed who had been released on their word not to bear arms again against the Union in the Civil War. Often they were known only by a nickname. Gordon noted that

There were old fellows in those trains who had never done anything else but "whack bulls" all their lives. They had started in when the Union Pacific was building across the continent just after the war, freighting to points beyond, and when the railroad took their job away they found it again freighting from rail points into the north, but finally the railroads had beaten them back into this strip of "No Man's Land" in the Yellowstone valley; that the Indian had held supreme control of until a year or two before. Here the faded glory of the "bull-train" was for a time restored and here it vanished for good and all. The mule-train, a companion picture, was never as interesting as the bull-train. The "mule-skinner" rode a "wheeler" and guided his team with a jerk line. Any loafer could do that, but it took an artist to pilot a string of bulls along a side-hill road with a top-heavy load and the trail wagon pulling dead against you.[18]

Although the bull-whacker led a life of toil, privation, and hardship, there were a few moments they enjoyed to the fullest. In Miles City

. . . it was surely a sight when a "Diamond R bull-train" pulled into Main street en route to Keogh from Glendive or Buford, loaded with government freight. With eight to twelve yoke of "bulls" to a team, hauling two and often three wagons loaded to the top and with a real "bull-whacker" walking along back by the wheelers, a pageant was paraded to the life, of a phase of civilization that was just then passing off the stage. Ranking with experts in any vocation, the professional bull-whacker in action was a most satisfying sight, and the pull up Main street was their dress parade. With a whip, the stock of which, about six feet long, had been carefully fashioned out of properly tough timber and with a lash that would reach four or six yokes ahead, and a popper on the end that would bite out a bunch of hair wherever it landed, the dirty, tousled pilots of the creaking, swaying craft would wake the town with their sonorous and melodious warnings to their teams, punctuated continually with the sharp "spit" of the popper as it landed on some poor, patient brute's hide and jumped away, responsive to the backward swirl of the lash, deftly imparted by the expert twenty or thirty feet away. . . . It was a fleeting glory though, for an hour after the train had been parked all hands were too drunk to tell their own names and were swallowed up in the swirl that eddied around the "Diamond R" corner and by pure centrifugal force were one by one thrown off into "the park," there to lie and sleep off the overpowering effects of the dope they had taken aboard.[19]

Although freighting was a rough-and-ready sort of business, some standard regulations and procedures were desirable for the guidance of wagon bosses in handling their trains and the drivers under them. Ashby set down in his notebook the "rules and regulations" imposed by the company which employed him. The rules which applied to both the wagon bosses and teamsters were combined in one section entitled "Rules and Regulations for Wagon Masters."

Wagon Masters are positively forbidden to camp together when out upon the roads when traveling in the same direction or in an opposite direction—Unless they are compelled to use water from the same place and even then their corrals must be, no less than 300 yds apart.

Wagon Masters are instructed to inform each Teamster when they load up & start out that they will be held personally responsible and any man coming in and upon the delivery of the frgt find that there is anything short upon his wagon—he will be charged with the same—& wagon masters must tell their men plainly these facts in the start   Each driver will be made to pay for any sheets damaged by his carelessness also with any sheet ropes lost and bows broken in his wagon by his neglect or any Frgt damaged by his neglect or carelessness on his team or any wagon or wagons that are upset & damaged by carelessness or neglect will be made to pay for same

Night herders will be charged with the loss of detention by loosing cattle from his carelessness or neglect   In case of Hard Storms at night the Night Hearder shall report to the Wagon Master that he is unable to keep the cattle

In approaching or leaving town where grass is always scarce [wagon masters] will particularly caution herders against loosing any cattle near Town.

The above Rules and Regulations as to the running of our Trains—Wagon Masters will do well to see fully informed and any failure upon their part to carry out these orders—They will be held personally responsible.

In addition to these general instructions, several other restrictions, and notes on operation are both illuminating and amusing:

When a train comes in and the Drivers want money they must be putt off until they are done unloading as if they are paid as soon as they come in they are very apt to go off and get drunk
In case of any teamstors get drunk [when unloading?] the Wagon Master is to send drunken man or men to camp & hire other men in their place & whatever is paid these laborers—the same is to be charged to said drunken men.

The Wagon Master in making Beef Bills & Repair Bills & Stable Bills if any necessary is to certify to same being correct before Ashby pays any such bills

When the Wagon Master comes in ask him how much Grub he has and hand a list of what he has to Col Vawter [20] to be put up so that it will be ready when the Train is unloaded & not keep the Train waiting for their grub.

In shoeing Kyus [cayuses?] only shoe when absolutely necessary & then only in front. In shoeing Mules if they need it badly they can be shod all around if not needed only in front

In making notice for Bull Whackers never specify how many are wanted simply *"BULL WHACKERS WANTED."*

Avoid Irishmen—unless for Burnett—let him have what he wants

No discussion of the bull-train days would be complete without mention of the Overland Freight Line—better known as the Diamond R—owned by E. G. Maclay & Co. This was by far the largest single enterprise in the state during the 1870's, and its brand and trademark was to be seen everywhere on the trails of the Northwest. At its height it had an Eastern General Manager with an office on Broadway, New York City, and contracting offices in New York, Boston, Philadelphia, Chicago, St. Louis, and St. Paul.[21] Estimates of its size vary. According to one, it had 350 horses and mules, 500 yoke of oxen, scores of wagons, besides saddles, horses, and buildings valued at a quarter of a million dollars; [22] and, according to another, it employed "no less than twelve hundred oxen and four hundred mules, besides a large number of horses." [23] It was, indeed, one of the largest freighting organizations the Western frontier knew.

The Diamond R was founded by Nicholas Wall and John J. Roe.[24] The oxen it used in the beginning were acquired by some sharp dealings with Joseph La Barge, a famous captain during the early days of steamboating on the Upper Missouri. La Barge, when an old man, was still very bitter about the affair when he related the details to his biographer. In 1861 he had gone to considerable trouble to get Wall, whom he then considered a friend, out of some difficulties growing out of the latter's sympathies with the South. Then he transported him and his goods to Montana free of charge, and loaned him $700 to get to the gold mines. There Wall prospered and went into partnership with Roe. A year later the new firm contracted with La Barge to take a shipment of goods to Fort Benton which, because of low water, the captain had to discharge at Cow Island, a considerable distance below. There were some damages and the following spring Wall and Roe presented the firm of La Barge, Harkness and Co. "a claim for forty thousand dollars' damages, on goods that were not worth at the outside ten thousand dollars in St. Louis." La Barge's offer to pay the full value of the goods in St. Louis and to forget the freight was refused. Returning to friendly territory to bring suit, Roe and his ungrateful partner, Nick Wall, succeeded in "nicking" the captain for $24,000. As the litigation tied up a stock of furs which spoiled before they could be freed for market, the affair cost La Barge an estimated $100,000.[25]

"Among the ill-gotten gains of John J. Roe . . . were a large number of oxen which La Barge, Harkness & Co. had brought up the river to transport freight between Fort Benton and the mines. Roe organized a transportation company, using these oxen as a nucleus for the business." [26] Just exactly when the company started is not known. La Barge stated that the case was settled in 1865. Toponce, himself an old freighter, listed among the stores he remembers doing business in Helena in 1865, "The 'Diamond R' Company, general merchandise, from St. Louis. . . ." [27] Had the freight line been in operation at this time, it seems unlikely that reference to it would have been omitted. It appears probable that the Diamond R began operations in late 1865 or early 1866. According to one story, Edward G. Maclay, then employed by Wall and Roe as a secretary and bookkeeper, noted on the books of the firm considerable numbers of livestock and vehicles and suggested that they be put to some profitable use. The freighting business started with this suggestion.[28]

From this beginning the business mushroomed. In 1868 E. G. Maclay, George Steell, and Matthew "Matt" Carroll bought the Diamond R equipment and brand—116 wagons, 700 oxen, and employing 70 men—for $75,000.[29] Organized under the name of E. G. Maclay & Co., it carried the title of Overland Freight Line.[30] Later Colonel C. A. Broadwater, once a wagon boss himself,[31] bought a share in the enterprise. The firm operated with these four partners until 1873 when Steell withdrew, Carroll followed in 1878, and Maclay, in 1881. Broadwater closed the firm out in 1883 after the railroads had taken most of the business, except for local freighting handled by small operators. Thus the locomotive and its long train of "wagons" robbed the bull-whackers of their occupation. In 1895 old-timer Sam Gordon, musing over this change, wrote: "The advent of the iron horse sounded the knell of the freighter and he went, no one knows whither."

Unlike the bull-whacker and the mule-skinner of the big freighting companies who ate simple food and slept in the open, the small teamster who followed them traveled in some little comfort. The mess wagon of the large trains was modified into what was sometimes called a *coaster*, a light two- or four-wheeled vehicle loaded with camping equipment tied on behind the trail wagon. Camping equipment sometimes included a small, four-hole sheet-iron stove which could be set up

84.   Jerk line on the Old North Montana Freight Road.

in a tent or used in the coaster. Drinking water was carried in two kegs, one set on either side of the bed of the lead wagon; and, if the haul required a dry camp, a tank wagon was sometimes hooked on behind the trail wagon to provide water for the stock, a feature which can be clearly noted in another of Huffman's photographs.

While the life of the solitary teamster was more comfortable than that of the bull-whacker, it was not without its excitement. One April day as Huffman was walking down Main Street, he noted a "husky, hairy individual" unloading a fresh bearskin at one of the stores. A few days later he met the man, a freighter named Martin Wehinger, and inquired how he came by the pelt. At first the German was reluctant to tell his story, but when Huffman asked, "Where'd you shoot him?" the reticence disappeared and he replied, "I didn't had any gun. I choost schopped hein V de ax."

I been loaded v grub for Dan McKay's ranch last week over by Ekalaka undt when I come by Fallon grick its about noon so I stop to rest unt feed my horses. Some of dem horses been pretty vild bronchs und it takes me quide a vile to unhitch and take dem one or two by each time down thru dew brushes to de vater und pack. Und ven I comes pack v de last ones to put him py dese nose bags he is begin to blow and schnort and pull me all around trough boud two hunert [200] of de sage brushes und I have to lick him pefore I can make him der nose pag on. Den one old prown horse, one of dose wheelers, he is stand up kind of bow-necked und steef legged und commence to look vild and plow [blow] und schnort vorse as der bronch und I been pretty hongary unt mad I schwore to dese old prown rone dat if he dont come up close py de vagon und pohave I make example of hemself unt so I choost get hims py de head unt make one schlap when I look up on my front vagon unt dere is de bear—sure yes! Up on de vagonunt he been handle dem pundles unt little poxes of dried fruits choost like a man. Every horse choos make one pig schnort unt preak avay v' der hills unt while de bear vatch der horses schkin oud I zay to mesalv, "Martin you been afoot unt you can't run fast enough to keep warm." Choos about den I tink der ax been under de side of de vagon unt I choost get it in time for meet him when he is start to come over de front of de load. Luckl for me dot I get one good chop in de side py his head vitch is kinder stunted hem til I give him two more vitch preak his pack close to der heat by his neck.

Zay! py got tammit, if ever I got some hell of a times dese is ven I round up dose horses unt try to hitch oop again. I cant move deer vagons unt so I roll de bear into der sage pushes unt so quvick I pring one horse up he is blow unt trag me aboud two honder feet sideways v' wild plums trees unt I dont yet left enough by one leg of my overhalls to make vad v' single barrells shotgun. Aboud it been pretty near night pefore I can pull oud dese place been tramped all de same v' circus camped.

Although considerable freighting activity took place through, or from, Miles City, it was not involved in much stage traffic—nor was any part of eastern Montana for that matter. The chief enterprises in this part of the state involved the army, hide-hunters, and cattlemen, none of whom were heavy users of this sort of transportation. So there was but little of the big stagecoach traffic which plied between Deadwood and Cheyenne to the southeast, and in the borderland of prairie and mountains to the westward. Most of the staging along the Yellow-

85.　Martin Wehinger.

stone—if it can be called that—was closely associated with the movement of the mails. Of the prerailroad days, *The Yellowstone Journal* noted:

> The mail, a semi-weekly service, came over this route on a schedule of four days from Bismarck, the distance being about 300 miles. Day and night travel was contemplated by this schedule, but at this time it was more "night" than "day" on account of the danger from small war parties of Indians, who on several occasions made their presence known and once ambushed a lonely stage driver and left his bones to whiten on the plain.[32]

This service, as noted in connection with Huffman's coming to Fort Keogh, involved the use of buckboards and what were called "jerkies." The latter, a smaller vehicle than a stagecoach, had sides and top of canvas and a boot fore and aft, and was less comfortable for the traveler.

Shields, who came to the Little Missouri country to hunt buffalo in 1880, left this picture of the accommodations on the eastern part of the Fort Keogh-Bismarck trail:

> Just before reaching [Cabin] creek we struck the Keough stage trail, a tolerably fair road leading from Bismarck to Fort Keough. There is a line of stages, so called, buckboards in fact, running between these two points, which carry the mail, express matter, and any passengers who have courage enough to risk their scalps in making the trip. They run every day so that Fort Keough, Miles City, and other towns situated from three to five hundred

86.   "Medora, [North Dakota]." (De Mores' packing plant at left.)

miles west of Bismarck, get daily mails when the weather or Indians don't interfere. During the winter, however, the line is frequently impassable for weeks at a time, and at other seasons of the year much trouble is experienced from the Indians. Since the opening of the line several drivers and station keepers and a few passengers have been killed and a good deal of stock stolen.

There are feeding stations every seventeen miles, and relay stations every thirty-four miles along the line where fresh ponies are supplied. These stations consist merely of a log cabin, or "shack," a stable and a stack of hay. The garrison consists of one, and in some cases two men, and the armament consists of a rifle for each man. The passenger tariff on this line is fifteen cents a mile and the passenger runs his own risk of being scalped.[33]

In October, 1884, the Marquis de Mores invested some of his father-in-law's money in a stage line connecting Medora, North Dakota—which this visionary Frenchman was trying to promote into a meat-packing center—and Deadwood, South Dakota. Although this venture relapsed into nothingness—as did all of the Marquis' promotion schemes—it provides a picture of the equipment necessary to operate a stage line.

The road connecting the two towns was 215 miles long, and along it were 15 stations, five of which had eating accommodations for the passengers. The line was organized to provide triweekly service, and a trip over the route took about 36 hours. One hundred and fifty or 160 horses were required, each of which cost from $90 to $150. Four Concord coaches, each costing $1500 when new, were purchased second hand for a total of $1200. Each six-horse unit covered about

25 miles a day, and each driver was required to put in a daily stint of 100 miles. Ten minutes was the time allotted for changing teams at the stops. The fare was ten cents per mile and express was charged for at the rate of ten cents per pound. In May, 1885, the venture folded for lack of a mail contract and an adequate number of passengers.[34]

Travel by stage was never comfortable by present-day standards of comfort. It was bad enough during the heat of the summer when the fine, powdery dust raised by the horses sifted through the coach, covering the passengers and, unless they wore tightly woven dusters, thoroughly permeating their clothing. Winter was worse. In the fall of 1883, John Clay and a companion named Dorr Clark came up by stage from Sidney, Nebraska, to the VVV spread on the headwaters of the Little Missouri. In the jerky with them were a tall, lean gambler, his wife, a young, soft-spoken, fresh-looking girl, and their baby, a "little tot, wrapped up like a bundle of old clothes."

It took 72 hours for the trip, the thermometer marking zero every night. It was a small coach holding only four passengers. . . . Clark and the gambler were old enemies, and as both had six shooters, it was a rather uncomfortable situation. The wind swept with wicked glee across the divides, carrying sifting snow through the canvas covers of the coach. Inside we sat face to face, the gambler, his wife and the baby on the back seat, Clark and I opposite clad in big overcoats and covered with buffalo robes. The coach creaked, jolted, swayed, crawled uphill, made reckless dashes downwards, crossed ice bound streams, performed all kinds of stunts except turning over, halted thrice a day for meals, changed horses frequently and drivers occasionally.[35]

Nor was early spring a desirable season for travel either. On April 13, 1880 Granville Stuart, en route to Milestown on his range-hunting reconnaissance,

Left Bozeman at 4 A.M. in a snow storm with a high cold wind, when partly up the range it turned to a regular old-fashioned state's sleet, the first I ever saw in Montana. Coated twigs and grass with ice one-eighth inch thick and our clothing also. The stage was a little open spring wagon and played-out team. We had to walk most of the way to keep from freezing. The team mired in the snow in the sage and had to be dug out, wagon unloaded and pulled out by hitching a long rope to the tongue and then all hands pull. There were fortunately no women in the party so we all helped the stage driver to swear. Each time we mired down we all got wet to our hips and our trousers froze stiff so that we could hardly walk. . . . The sleet turned to snow when we reached the Yellowstone with a bitter N.E. wind that nearly "peeled the bark" all the rest of the day and all night. At Sweet Grass creek we changed horses and had a better team but the driver missed the road and we wandered around on an old wood road half the night tired and wet and half frozen.[36]

Huffman left no photographs of stages, and only one fragment of a manuscript. Although this story is apparently fact, it cannot be related to any known tragedy.

. . . back yonder when I used to be driver and passenger by turns or maybe crawl into the boot with "Gigsy"—Gigsy was the messenger—and sleep a sort of cold, nightmareish kind of sleep all mixed up with jolts, curses, the jouncing of the express pkgs, guns, Gigsy, kegs of whiskey and mail pouches, and dim yet distinct impressions of toiling up short and long winding badland hills, then the quicker chuckle of the wheels as we neared the high broad bench land. Mart was on the "swing drive" one of those nights and when we were fairly on the bench he sounded a new note to the four and shifted his whip to the rein hand while he reached down into the front boot among us, Gig and I and the guns and the kegs, to get some rocks to encourage his nags.

It grew colder, I reckoned the miles, would my feet be quite frozen and would they have to come off like old Flinch's who drove us the winter before across the same bench without overshoes. "Run down" he was by a spree in the town. He was weak and up there he sat and mumbled and swore while the tender . . . unhitched and forbore to complain because Flinch didnt get down to help, or go in to get warm as before but fell in a heap on the double-trees from his perch when he'd tried to come down. He's got cork pins now, five fingers in all, and a "nick" of a nose.

Listen to Mart, "Easy. Easy. H-e-i-t ya-a-a. Baldy—you mink!" And the sing of his lash, *k a b u h.* Then to us, "Damfh thaint snow on the bench an shes coldern hell." Then he walloped his hands right, then left. Then the galloping slackened, the trace chains all a-rattle, and the rattle of gravel, smell of steaming horsehide, and the squeal of the brake told that we were nearing "The Point" where in the chill of the morning we'd "change" and get a mouthful to eat. Then we plunged down a hill and roared over a bar and up to the shacks facing each side of a corral.

Mart shouted, "Hi there, Wickem. Get a move." No answer. Mart walloped his numb hands some more and jabbed his feet savagely at the iron heel rod on the dash and said, "Hold these leathers and I'll go wake up the ———— ——ch." I remember how Mart's coarse "soldier" boots clumped on the hard frozen ground as he hustled down with an oath and plunged for the door in the half dark. I was wide awake now. The horses tugged. One lifted his head and stilled his heaving sides as if in alarm. Grigsy was alert now and scrambled out. Mart said, "Jesus, Grig!" And Grigsy said, "Christz, thats so." Not a horse in the corral and the east shack burned out so the roof's ready to fall.

That was all Huffman wrote! For a frontiersman skilled in "reading sign," perhaps there was no need to write more. He would know there was a scalped body somewhere.

The coming of the railroad pulled down the curtain on the picturesque days of the bull-train and the stagecoach. However, the arrival of the track-laying crew of the Northern Pacific Railroad in Miles City in the fall of 1881, and of the Chicago, Milwaukee, and St. Paul Railroad in 1907 provided Huffman with some new and interesting subject material for photographs. The crew of the Northern Pacific used a horse to pull a dump car carrying 18 ties and two rails from the supply car to the end of the track—in fact "Old Nig" pulled this car all the way from Bismarck to the junction with the western division of the railroad at Gold Creek, Montana.[37] This load was sufficient to lay one length of track—no effort being made to "break joints" on the rails. When the ties were in place and the rails laid, three ties would be spiked and the supply train would move ahead, leaving the other ties to be spiked later. All of the ties used were chopped and hewn flat; and several tie-chopping crews came to grief when they depended on the streams of the area to float ties from the place where they were cut to the line of the railroad where they could be picked up.

87.　"Miles City, Sept 1881. Steel gang laying NP steel. 'Old Nig'
at right. The horse that hauled the car to the front from Glendive
[Montana] to Idaho."

The photograph of the Chicago, Milwaukee, and St. Paul crew shows a
different method of laying track. Here an endless conveyor belt brought up the
ties, and pairs of men working at its end had only to pick them off the belt and
drop them in place. The boom at the end of the supply train picked up the rails
and, with the aid of men to balance them, put them in place. As soon as the rail
was in place the "fish-plate" man immediately joined it to the preceding rail and a
few spikes were driven to hold it in place while the train moved ahead. In this
manner four hours were sufficient to lay a mile of track. Even though the construction crews were unglamorous, they had their colorful expressions—for example, the flatcar on which were loaded the spikes, bolts, and fish-plates was
dubbed the "jewelry car."

The Engineering Department of the Northern Pacific had a fine mess which
accompanied their construction work. Shields, who stayed at one camp while
hunting in the Little Missouri country, recorded that "they provide themselves
with nearly every luxury that the Eastern markets afford," and he also noted that
"good cooks were employed . . . and in many instances the cuisine equals that of
the Palmer House. . . ."[38] Among Huffman's papers is the invitation he re-

88.   Chicago, Milwaukee, and St. Paul Railroad track-laying outfit at work (about 1907).

ceived to a Thanksgiving dinner when the Northern Pacific first reached Miles City. The assortment of foods served was staggering—to say the least! This invitation read:

NPR

Your presence is desired at Headquarters of Engineering Department, Yellowstone Division, N.P.R.R. at Miles City, November 24th 1881 to join with the Engineers of the Division at a Thanksgiving Dinner.

Yours cordially
J. B. Clough
Eng. Yellowstone Div

R.S.V.P.

THANKSGIVING DINNER
at
ENGINEERS HEADQUARTERS
N.P.R.R.   MILES CITY
November 24, 1881

SOUPS

Oyster, Vermicella, Vegetable

OYSTERS

Fried, Scalloped, Raw

FISH

Trout   Salmon

MEATS

Roast Turkey,   Roast Chicken
Roast Beef
Roast Mutton,   Venison
Mountain Sheep
Buffalo Loin,   ELK
Chicken—Pie

VEGETABLES

Mashed Potatoes, Sweet Potatoes
Squash, Cabbage, Tomatoes,
Celery.

SIDE DISHES

Peaches, Cherries, Jelly, Plums
Cranberries   Apples

PASTRY

Apple Pie, Lemon Pie, Peach Pie,
Cranberry Pie, Strawberry Pie.

CREAM

Lemon   Vanilla

CAKES

Fruit Cake, Pound Cake, Jelly Cake,
Sponge Cake,   Dough-nuts.

FRUITS

Peaches, Apples, Strawberries.

Coffee,   Tea,   Chocolate.

Although the railroad wiped out most of the picturesque features of frontier transportation, road ranches remained for many years scattered over the country-side. These were rough log shacks of one, two, and sometimes three rooms where travelers might find food and lodging for the night; and they were patronized by patrons of the stage and by settlers going to and from town. Food, though usually satisfying, was invariably plain, and sometimes cooked and served under conditions far from appetizing.

The most interesting feature of these places was the sleeping accommodations. The "bed room" was usually a room with a few bunks. If there were more customers than bunk space, the late-comers rolled out their bedrolls and slept on the floor. If the bed was a double one and the place filled to capacity, the single

89. Small freighter of later days.

traveler would be expected to share it with another. When ladies were present, the problem was complicated for the facilities were designed to serve but a single sex. While en route to their ranch in April of 1883, the Aldersons stayed at a road ranch the first night out of Miles City. Mrs. Alderson remembered that they had a comfortable room to themselves with a good bed which the hostess must have given up since the ordinary accommodations consisted of a kind of bunk room which was occupied on this occasion by fully 15 men.[39] As women travelers became more and more common, this sort of courtesy gave way to making simple provisions for such guests. This usually consisted of hanging a curtain around a bed to provide a bit of privacy. The men added the necessary bit of courtesy by retiring to another room or outside while the lady or ladies went to bed—this also being the usual procedure for a stranger at a settler's home.

Some of these road ranches were of the sort to be remembered. One of these was a rough cabin by the Musselshell River on the road between Jordan and Lewiston. When one visitor stopped overnight, the things which impressed him most were the thick layer of sand and dirt on the floor, the muslin covering of the wall—from which dust cascaded at the slightest touch—and a very dirty bed in which he felt it wise to sleep without undressing. The operator of this establishment, a bewhiskered recluse named Mosby, had a government license for wholesale liquor sales. Allegedly, he was the son of J. S. Mosby, the famous raider of the Civil War who was exceedingly annoying to the troops of Major General Sheridan.

Another of these stopping places remembered by many who traveled to Miles City was "Piper Dan's." This road ranch, about 35 miles to the south on the road up the Tongue Valley, was a stop where the mail stage changed horses. Piper Dan, a tall, lean, bearded Scotsman who played bagpipes, was given this descriptive name to distinguish him from other Dans who had also seen fit to cloak themselves in anonymity. Mrs. Alderson, the first bride to stop at his place, remembered that

His place was clean enough, but rough and untidy, and the walls of his two-room log house was papered from end to end with the pink pages of Police

90.   "Old Piper Dan Road Ranch, Tongue River."

Gazettes. I'd been warned I'd better not look at them, so of course, as soon as the men went out to put up the horses, look at them was the first thing I did. . . .

For dinner we had a buffalo steak, cut from one of the last buffalo in that part of Montana. The rest of the . . . [meal?] was the usual bachelor fare of boiled potatoes, dried fruit and sour-dough bread. Dan was supposed to be a woman hater, but he was most kind, even to cooking the one egg for "the missus" which his hen had laid that day. . . .[40]

Piper Dan, like other close-mouthed individuals on the frontier, never told anyone his name, nor whence he came. The story is told that for a long time he received a newspaper from Canada. Then the paper stopped coming and not long afterward Piper Dan disappeared—his coming and his going constituting another of those mysteries of the frontier. His log shack finally burned, and with it went the host of bedbugs which the walls harbored.

Of the old-time transportation, just as with the vast herds of buffalo, hardly a trace can be found today. Of the steamboat days, nothing remains but the bell of the *Yellowstone* in a museum in Miles City. A few of the old stages—a very few— may be seen in collections of frontier relics, but the vehicles of the freighting train belong to the past. The trails they traveled are, except for a few scars here and there on the virgin prairie, buried under the modern roads which follow the routes the buffalo "surveyed" across the divides. So quickly and so completely have these days passed that few there are who would recognize an ox shoe, should they find one along one of these old highways.

91.   "Advance of Civilization. N.P. Express."

Nature taught her child
    To read, to write and spell,
And with her books before him
    He read his lesson well.

Each day is but a page
    His God, the sun, has turned.
Each year, a chapter nature taught
    Her child has read and learned.

A broken twig, a stone is turned
    Disturbed by passing feet
His savage eye has caught it all
    For tracks spell war or meat.

Nature holds his Bible
    With pages open wide,
He questions not her miracles
    'Tis done; he's satisfied.

He loves his mother country
    Where all her creatures trod,
Yet he is called a heathen
    Who has always lived with God.[1]

Charles M. Russell

NATIVE AMERICANS

O ne of the great tragedies of history," wrote a Western rancher, "is that the Indian and the white man had to meet. No two races could have understood each other less." [2] Not only did the Indian and the white man not understand each other, but the white men, who have been—and still are—cursed by an "inveterate tendency to judge others by the extent to which they contrive to be like" themselves,[3] have written most of the histories. Those who would study the Indian are indeed doubly handicapped.

With broad fundamental differences between the two peoples, and with these differences further exaggerated and inflamed by the guerrilla warfare which was waged by the irresponsible factions of each, it is not strange that the mass of the people on the frontier recognized no middle ground. Typical of many white settlers was an old-timer, a resident of Montana since the early 1860's, who showed a cowboy the contents of one of his war bags.[4] In the bottom, underneath some buckskin clothing, was an old, faded calico sunbonnet; and tears came to the old man's eyes as he told how his wife had been killed at the door of their cabin by Indians, and how he had shot two and clubbed a third to death to keep from being killed himself. Ranchers who had horses stolen and cattle wantonly killed by red raiders also believed that there was little good in the Indians. On the other hand, the Indians, who had been dispossessed of their homeland, who had had their camps attacked by parties of trappers and soldiers, and who had watched their friends and relatives starve to death on the reservations because the government failed to supply adequate food, entertained equally positive opinions of the white man.

92. "A Cheyenne Warrior, with war drum."

This feeling was so strong that Huffman, in making a complimentary remark in an article he wrote about the Cheyennes in 1900, felt it necessary to preface that comment with this statement, "Say what you will of the cruelty and savagery and bloody deeds of butchery and of his present sloven look and sad estate, and even at the risk of having hurled at me the old-timer's most withering taunt, 'Indian Lover,' I say that it is my belief. . . ."[5] Such attitudes could be modified or changed only with the coming of a new generation.

Perhaps the most candid observers of the Indian were the army officers and the scouts. As fighting men, they had a ground for common understanding, and respect for, the warriors; and they could view the horrors of warfare more objectively than the pioneer who sometimes suffered its brutalities.[6] Those who knew the Indians when they walked "uprightly and proudly" have indicated that they were different:

> The tribes of western Montana were hospitable, truthful, and scrupulously honest, until the whites taught them otherwise.[7]
>
> *Granville Stuart*

> While visiting an Indian village in one of the Dakotas, many years ago, I rode up to the head chief's lodge, where I expected to remain for the night. The chief came out and received me, while, at the same time, his squaw unsaddled my horse and placed the equipment alongside their tepee. I asked the chief if they would be safe there, whereupon he observed, "Yes, there isn't a white man within two days' ride of here." [8]
>
> *Bishop Whipple*

The change from the wild, free life on the plains to that of the reservation with its dole brought inevitable adjustments. After 20 years of life under government supervision, Huffman noted a lamentable trend:

> And some of these withered ones with the furrowed faces, with habiliments and dwellings neither savage or civilized, their faces tell me a sad, sad tale, for only yesterday I saw him in his ledge of skins; his robe was glossy, and upon the inside of the rude dwelling there was the odor of white clay, the pungency of willow bark and the incense of sweet grass; and he walked uprightly and proudly, and the covering upon his feet, the skin of beasts, was gayly tricked out with the quills of the porcupine, dressed and tinted by the loving hands of the women of his household; but now that indescribable something in the courage and the general tout ensemble of the red men and women that was so apparent in these people is gone and they are woefully changed.[9]

So, lest Huffman's photographs be regarded merely as pictures of people characterized by those qualities which many adopted after contact with the whites, some of these original qualities will be sketched here.

One of the traits which was outstanding among the warriors was the respect which they had for the honor of their word. Although deception in time of war was considered admirable and even praiseworthy—under the proper circumstances—it was quite another matter to lie to a friend or fellow tribesman. As Clark has pointed out, the basis for the sign for the word *lie* is two tongues or a forked tongue: and he found that "as a rule, . . . an Indian's word or promise would be kept," although it was "extremely difficult to get an Indian to make a positive promise" because they usually added some saving clause. In no phase of his life was a warrior more scrupulous of the integrity of his word than in the counting of his coups—the things which gave him prestige. One such incident needs to be told—to illustrate this point and to set down a story which should not become lost—of how an old warrior observed this code so closely that, in a white man's opinion, he leaned over backward.

Walter Campbell [10] gathered much of the material for his biography of Sitting Bull from the old chief's nephew, White Bull. A large Indian with a commanding presence and dynamic personality, White Bull was a famous warrior in his own right. Campbell, trying to solve the riddle of the battlefield of the Little

Big Horn, questioned White Bull carefully about the movements of the Indians and the troops, particularly as they concerned Custer's detachment. In describing the close of the fight on the point of the ridge where Custer fell, White Bull told Campbell that he was one of those who helped mop up this section of the field. As they overran this point, he was confronted by a big cavalryman with whom he grappled in a desperate fight. Finally he wrestled this trooper's revolver away from him and shot him through the head.

After the battle was over, White Bull pointed out the man he had killed to Bad Soup, Sitting Bull's brother-in-law. Bad Soup, who had had some contact with the soldiers in previous years, said, "That man is Custer." But White Bull never included the killing of Custer among his coups because he, *personally*, did not know the man he had killed and therefore could not—of his own knowledge—identify the trooper he had killed. Campbell, realizing that he had a great story, wanted to put the story in his manuscript but, when he pressed the proud chief for permission to use the story, he would always reply, *"They say*, I am the man who killed Custer," or he would hedge with the statement, *"If the man I killed was Custer*, then I am the man who killed Custer." Nor did he permit Campbell to use the story, and the writer kept faith with the Indian as long as the latter lived. "The man who lies is a weakling," said White Bull—and he was no weakling, even when tempted by what would have been, Indian-wise, a great honor.[11]

The Indian concept of the proper way to wage war was to do as much damage as possible with little or no loss to themselves. Pitched battles fought for an ideal without regard for losses might be proper for the white man, but Indian leaders tried to avoid such contests. So the white man called the Indian a coward. However, there were Indian warriors who measured up to the white man's code of personal bravery, and among these the Northern Cheyennes stood second to none.

Many stories have been related of the bravery of warriors in battle, but none has been told more vividly than the incident Lieutenant Clark witnessed as he rode with his Indian scouts in the charge on Dull Knife's camp.

One cold, wintry morning in the late fall of 1876, while yet the gray shadows of darkness hovered mistily over crag and gorge, some enlisted Indian scouts and regular troops charged down upon a hostile Indian village sleeping in fancied security in a canon of the Big Horn Mountains. One of these scouts, Three Bears by name, rode a horse which became crazed by excitement and unmanageable, and being wonderfully fleet, dashed with him, ahead of all others, into the very center of the hostile camp, where bullets were flying thick and fast, and where the hostiles were making a sharp resistance to protect their families. Feather-on-the-Head, another scout, seeing the trouble his friend was in, dashed after him, urging his own fast pony forward with vigorous strokes of the whip, at the same time throwing himself from side to side of his pony to avoid the shots of his enemies. Thus he followed Three Bears through the bushes and across the stream, down among the tepees, and into the very center of the village, where Three Bears' horse had fallen dead, shot through the neck. His rider scarcely touched the ground when Feather-on-the-Head, sweeping past, took him behind himself and bore him safely away out of the valley of death. Feather-on-the-Head had saved Three Bears' life at the risk of his own, and thenceforward the two were very much together, and became brothers by adoption. Feather-on-the-Head never seemed to think he had done anything very noble, and never boasted of it; but keen-eyed, brave, loyal, wiry little Three Bears deeply appreciated the service. . . .[12]

Three Bears was another of those stalwart characters whose history was never set down except for one unique note. Captain Bourke, who wrote that he was "a warrior fierce in battle and humane to the vanquished," recorded:

> I remember his coming into my tent one dismally cold night, when we lay on the Belle Fourche, on the outskirts of the Black Hills, after wiping out "Dull Knife" village. "Three Bears' " eyes were moist, and he shook his head mournfully as he said, "Cheyenne papoose heap hung'y." [13]

There are other kinds of courage besides those which come to the surface during the heat of battle. Perhaps the greatest of these involves personal integrity. Few stories can match the account of Crow Dog, a Brule Sioux Indian policeman who killed Spotted Tail without apparent good reason. Although he made a settlement with the relatives according to the Sioux customs, the government, because of the prominence of this chief, proceeded to try the Indian in the U. S. Court at Deadwood where, in March, 1882, he was convicted and sentenced to hang. Appeals for a stay of the execution dragged the matter out, and the jailer often gave the Indian the freedom of courtyard in the jail.

One evening the prisoner was missing, and the deputy sent to hunt for him found him at his home 200 miles away on the reservation. Crow Dog refused to return with the deputy, saying that he would come back when he had said farewell to his friends and his family. This he did, arriving before the officer who got drunk en route. He presented himself, dressed in his best, to be executed—but found that he had been pardoned during his absence!

A similar incident occurred on the Cheyenne reservation. In 1890 Head Chief and Young Mule, two unruly young Cheyennes, killed a young man named Hugh Boyle. The authorities demanded that the murderers be surrendered, but the Cheyennes wanted to make a property settlement. Although they bid the price in ponies and other property up to a high figure, they were finally made to understand that such an atonement was not a suitable settlement for the spilling of blood. However, they stubbornly refused to allow their young men to be tried and probably hanged. If they had to die, the young men would die as a Cheyenne should die. So the agent, James A. Cooper, was told that on an appointed day, September 13, the two young men would ride into the agency at Lame Deer with rifles in their hands, they would attack the troops, and the soldiers could kill them! There was nothing the agent could do but accept this unusual proposition.

The night before, there were solemn dances in the Indian camp; and on the fatal day the two warriors dressed and painted themselves with great care and selected their two best horses for their final ride. A troop of the First Cavalry and the Indian police were drawn up in front of the agency, and the stage was set, the Indians in the "gallery" on the surrounding hills, for the spectacular tragedy. At the appointed time the two doomed men appeared on the hill to the northeast of the agency, and, singing the traditional death song of their people, rode at full speed down toward the waiting soldiers. Sweeping past, with horses still on a dead run, they fired point-blank into the ranks. On the first pass, the Indian police

93.　"Sioux urchins, boy and girl, Jan 1879."

managed to drop one horse and its rider. The other turned and, still shooting and singing, rode deliberately past the ranks again before he and his pony were downed.[14]

They had other admirable qualities. Few there were who would steal from another in their own camp. However, another tribe or even a visiting tribe was usually not immune from surreptitious attention; but in those cases clever stealing was a desirable accomplishment rather than an underhanded means of acquisition. They were hospitable, always offering a visitor whatever food might be available, and expecting to be treated the same way in return. They were charitable toward their poor and needy in ways that provided effective relief from want. And they were generous. Clark, who ate horse and mule meat with the rest of Crook's men in 1876, observed that

I have seen white men reduced to the last "hard tack," with only tobacco enough for two smokes, and with no immediate prospect of anything better than horse-meat "straight." A portion of the hard bread was hidden away, and the smokes were taken in secret. An Indian, undemoralized by contact with the whites, under similar circumstances, would divide down to the last morsel.[15]

Not all Indians used alcohol. The Mountain Crows [16] did not tolerate liquor in camp until the late 1870's, and handled those who erred with a heavy hand. The

Cheyenne women were famous for their chastity and maintained high standards even in that age of Victorian morals. Even in other tribes whose standards of conduct were considered lax, a woman whose morals were not above question was forbidden to participate in certain religious ceremonies. Intermarriage between relatives, even distant relatives, was usually strictly forbidden; among the Cheyennes, a brother and sister did not speak directly to each other after the age of puberty; and Indian mothers-in-law did not meddle—they were forbidden to look at or speak to their sons-in-law.

Strangely enough—popular misconception to the contrary—one of their outstanding characteristics was their love of humor. Sometimes this took a form which white men thought rather grim. In 1869, in the valley of Crandall Creek on the headwaters of the Yellowstone, a band of young Crows killed two prospectors. When the bodies were found, the heads had been severed and impaled on miners' picks driven into the ground and a cup of coffee had been placed in front of each head, and a spoon in the right hand of each corpse. Years later a cowboy asked Plenty Coups, the Crow chief, about this incident. The old chief smiled out of his eyes and replied, "Long time ago, young men make joke. Put spoon so men could stir coffee." E. S. Topping, who was at Fort Pease in January, 1876, remembered another bit of gruesome horseplay. A band of Crows surprised a small party of Sioux who were watching intently the activities of some hunters from Fort Pease. The whites heard shooting but knew nothing of what had happened when the party of Crows visited the little post. When they came in "a Crow reached out a hand from under his blanket to be shaken, and when Muggins Taylor [17] (who was the man greeted) took hold of it, it was left in his clasp. It was a hand that had been cut from a dead Sioux." [18]

Although some of the humor was brutal and coarse, the Indian was capable of sly humor that was in good form in any company. W. W. Terrett, owner of the JO outfit on Beaver Creek, never tired of telling a joke on his son, Colville, which had its origin with a Cheyenne named Yellow Hair. The latter and two others were held as witnesses in the killing of Barringer's sheep herder—who had the misfortune to surprise some Indians just after they had killed a beef.[19] The Cheyennes were lodged in the jail in Miles City; and Yellow Hair,[20] not understanding the workings of the white man's law and being worried about his bride some 90 miles away, helped the others dig a hole under the wall of the jail, and then trotted back to his home. For this, the white man's court—in the name of justice—gave him a year in the state penitentiary at Deer Lodge, Montana. Fortunately this did not spoil the Indian's sense of humor. Some years later when Colville Terrett went to Deer Lodge to work in a bank, Yellow Hair inquired of the father concerning the whereabouts of his son. "He's at Deer Lodge," replied the rancher. Whereupon the Indian, knowing that the penitentiary was the dominant feature of Deer Lodge, and recognizing full well that the Terretts were law-abiding people, slyly asked, *"What for?"*

Mrs. Nannie Alderson, slight, attractive wife of an early rancher in the Rosebud Valley, always enjoyed telling of a bit of Two Moon's humor. Like many of the Indians of the time, Two Moon was "absurd and squalid-looking, with his dirty cotton shirt turned wrong side out, and his white man's pants with the seat cut out, which he wore like a pair of leggins over a breech clout"—a pathetic con-

94. "Two Young Cheyennes in War Costume, Fort Keogh, 1878."

trast to the proud man Huffman photographed in the buffalo days. But Two Moon still had a sense of humor, even if he had been reduced to begging for coffee and an occasional meal at the Alderson-Zook ranchhouse.

Two Moons' English was seemingly limited to "How," "Yes," and "No," but when he came for a meal he would always ask in signs how many horses my husband would take for me. Once when Mr. Alderson held up one finger, Two Moons laughed long and loud, so we concluded that he had a sense of humor, and that he asked the question more as flattery than with a serious view to trade. The next time he asked for my price in horses my husband began opening and shutting both hands very rapidly. Two Moons counted up to fifty or so and then said disgustedly: "God damn, too many." [21]

Although other qualities could be listed, those which have been noted indicate that these people did not merit the hard name some writers have given them. As Huffman indicated, there was considerable difference between the "wild" Indian and those of the reservation who had been contaminated by contact with the whites, and Lieutenant Clark summed up his impressions in like manner:

Unfortunately for the race, our opinions of them in many cases are based upon

95.　"Fire Wolf," an outstanding Cheyenne warrior.

the observation of the vicious habits of those who hang about the immediate presence of portions of our Western civilization, which has, by its rough and rank dissipation, demoralized the barbarian, who usually absorbs the bad and eschews the good, quickly becoming diseased mentally, morally, and physically, and in this debased condition there are few vices or crimes of which they are not capable.[22]

Although the white influence will be noted in most of Huffman's Indian portraits, many of them show the basic items of Indian dress. It must be remembered that many of these pictures show the Indians dressed in what *they* considered their best for a visit to Fort Keogh or Miles City. Naturally, they imitated their conquerors, and therefore many items are more white than Indian. Dress was not, however, a haphazard matter; and each tribe had certain characteristics in design and beadwork which were very obvious to another Indian.

In male attire, three items were considered the absolute minimum—moccasins, breechcloth or breechclout, and gee-string. To this basic ensemble might be added leggings which reached to the hip and which were also supported by the gee-string, thus providing the equivalent of a pair of pants. The torso might be protected by a shirt or coat, or, in the earlier days, by a buffalo robe. It was customary to wear the robe with the head at the right side and the wool inside, thus exposing the decorated flesh side. In the summer a sheet might replace the robe or blanket. Uniforms were sometimes worn, particularly by important men who had received them as gifts from government officials.

96. "A Shy little Cheyenne maid of six, with doll."

War bonnets such as those shown in the portraits of Two Moon, Fire Wolf, and Rain-in-the-Face were only worn by important men skilled in the ways of making war. As there are 12 large feathers in the tail of an eagle, of which only four were sometimes used, a headdress containing 60 or 70 feathers was a valuable possession. The catching of eagles required some religious preparation and much patient waiting in a covered pit on some prominent elevation; it was therefore not a simple task to acquire such a decoration.

A woman's dress consisted of moccasins, short leggings, a skirt, a shirt cut to provide freedom of movement of the arms and shoulders, and a blanket or robe. The large, capelike sleeves are noticeable in several pictures and are particularly prominent on the dress of the doll carried by one little Cheyenne girl.

Ornamentation and styles of hairdressing were two things little affected by white influence. Earrings were of a variety of shapes and sizes. The ears, however, were *slit* and not pierced; and it was not unusual for the ear to have more than one slit. In the case of the Cheyennes, the ears were usually prepared when the baby was three to six months old, and the piercing was attended by some ceremony and a substantial gift to the person conducting the ceremony. The long pendants of Dentalium shells worn by Spotted Fawn and Rain-in-the-Face's wives were common among the squaws, and bright-colored shells were particularly prized for such ornaments. High "chokers" were commonly worn, particularly by the Sioux;

97. "Sioux mother and babe, Jan 1880. Mrs Hump, 'Buffalo Humps' first wife, a very pretty woman in her youth."

and the large, circular gorgets shown in some of the pictures were usually made of abalone shell secured from the traders.

Methods of hairdressing varied with the tribe, and, to a limited extent, with the individual. The style favored by the Crow man was to cut part of the hair off squarely across the forehead, leaving a bang four to six inches long. This was then induced to stand upright by dressing it with clay, or a mixture of clay and a sticky substance prepared from certain weeds and bushes. Wrappings for the hair braids were usually strips of otterskin or red flannel. Otterskin was worn not only because it looked well and was the fashion, but also because it had the power to paralyze bad luck and strengthen good luck. Skunk skin was also used because it was supposed to possess *power*, although it was most commonly used for medicine sacks, or to tie to horses' tails in time of war.

Long straps or sashes ornamented with silver discs were sometimes worn over the shoulder or around the waist. Strings of beads varied according to the fancy of the wearer—when they did not indicate membership in some society. Rings, either bought from the trader or fashioned from wire, and arm bands were also common. And usually tucked on somewhere was a little ornament or medicine sack having peculiar significance to the wearer. The former might vary from a stuffed eaglet, as in the case of Spotted Eagle, to a small downy feather, as in the case of Red Armed Panther.

In addition to these bits of personal adornment, Sioux men often carried stone-headed war clubs, sometimes called "skull crackers," while Cheyennes

98. "Spotted Fawn, a Cheyenne girl of 13 years."

seemed to have a preference for pipe-tomahawks. The pipe bag with its supply of especially prepared tobacco [23] and stone-headed pipe with detachable stem was frequently carried and provided decoration as well as utility. Although not an ornament, men and women carried knives which served a multitude of needs from an eating utensil to a weapon. The Indian's use of a knife was unique:

> Indians in eating meat usually take a piece in the left hand, and conveying it to the mouth and grasping an end with the teeth, with a dexterity almost alarming sever the bit to be masticated from the chunk by means of a butcher-knife, one or more of which are always carried by a wild Indian in a sheath attached to his belt on the left side. These knives are only sharpened on one side, which seems to make them better for skinning, and, for some reason not well understood, to cut better and retain a fine edge longer than when sharpened on both sides, as is our custom. I have seen them cut open a deer, going right down through the backbone, cut or chop open the skull to take out the brains, and scarcely impair the edge of an ordinary knife costing about fifty cents. [24]

While the tepee is a familiar object, there are a number of things about them which may be missed in a casual study of Huffman's pictures. There was nothing haphazard about their design, manner of erection, or use, although they varied in

99.   "The Mrs Rain-in-the-Face."

size according to the wealth (in horses) of the owner. All lodges occupied an oval space on the ground with the long axis from front to rear; and they were often tilted toward the rear, thus providing greater stability in the prevailing westerly winds and bringing the opening for the smoke over the fireplace rather than the apex of the poles. The lodge door was normally placed to the east so that the lodge received the first rays of the rising sun, and, in the old days, the tripod supporting the owner's shield and medicine bundle was placed in front of it.

Within the lodge, the owner's place was at the back, the family lived on the left side, and an old woman, an essential part of the average lodge, had her place just inside the door. Good manners dictated that when moving about in the lodge one should never pass between the owner and the fire in the center—always back of the owner; and when a circle of guests were seated around the fire smoking, the pipe was never passed "across" the door.

100. "Pretty Nose, Cheyenne
girl, Ft. Keogh 1878."

Although the basic design of all tepees was the same, there were individual variations characteristic of each tribe. Huffman's photographs show Sioux and Cheyenne tepees, which used shorter poles and which were not quite as tall and beautiful as the tepees of the Crows. The Crow, Sioux, and Cheyenne tepees varied in that the smoke flaps were designed differently, and that the Sioux tilted the cone of the tepee more to the rear than the Cheyenne, and the Crows tilted least of all. However, the most striking difference was in the way the tepees were erected. The Sioux and Cheyennes used a three-pole tripod foundation, with one pole being placed so as to support the right side of the door, thus projecting slightly lower than the others at the rear. The other poles were then piled around this foundation. The Crows used a four-pole foundation, the apex of which could be easily noted below the apex of the remainder of the poles.[25] Thus it was very easy for Indians to identify the tribe occupying a particular camp, an item of considerable importance to a war party.

Aside from painting, one form of decoration was to attach a row of ornaments, made of strips of leather with the dew claws of deer attached, up either side of the junction of the covering at the front. These would rattle in the wind and, it was thought, help attract game. Being able to shoot game from his lodge door had the same degree of desirability as the white man's practice of having breakfast in bed. Imitation scalplocks are shown on the tepee of American Horse, such decorations usually being four in number for good luck. While not an orna-

101. "Sits Down Spotted. A Crow hunter in winter dress, 1879–80."

ment, the dark-colored object over the door of American Horse's tepee is his medicine bundle.

Several of these pictures show meat drying on a rack. Three days of pleasant weather was usually sufficient to dry the meat so that it would keep indefinitely. Huffman recalled:

The Indians had a way of cutting buffalo meat diagonally across the grain, in slabby pieces an inch thick and drying it without salt—salt he never bought. We were not dainty by [any] means but there were few things about a Sioux or Cheyenne tepee that one would eat with relish—, especially was this true of any mess that their women cooked,[26] but that jerked, sundried meat—if one

102. "Pretty Eyes, Cheyenne girl of 16."

could go to the pole beside the lodge and help himself—was good, nourishing "chewing."

Intestines were also dried. These were eaten fresh or dried, and sometimes were cooked with corn or Indian turnips.

Sweat lodges were an essential part of an Indian encampment, as they were used for both religious and curative purposes. Huffman's photographs show clearly the plan of such lodges and their general size and construction, with the exception of the covering of robes or blankets which was placed tightly over the top when the lodge was in use. The number of willow sticks used in the frame was often determined by the dreams of the man who constructed it; and the rocks in the center were heated outside before the lodge was occupied. Of the sweat lodges Huffman photographed, that of Brave Wolf probably represents the orthodox design and arrangement when the procedure involved more than just taking a sweat bath.

One old Cheyenne described in later days the sweat which followed his medicine fast. In this case the party, which included a medicine man, seated themselves inside the lodge and smoked while the stones were being heated. Then the pipe was placed outside with the bowl on the ground and the stem projecting upward beside the nose and eye sockets of the buffalo skull. They believed that a good spirit influence came from the nostrils of the skull along the path and into the lodge; and no worshipful Indian would cross this path, as that would stop the flow of this healing virtue. The ceremony was begun with a prayer, and then the

103.   Spotted Eagle's hostile Sioux village, winter of 1880–1881.

104. "Indian Children and Travois."

105. "Hunkpapa Sioux leather lodges near Fort Keogh, 1878."

medicine man squirted four successive mouthfuls of water on the hot stones which had been passed into the lodge, saying a prayer between each squirt. The water released from the stones the vitality and spiritual curative forces put into them by the burning wood which it, in turn, had received from the sun. Thus the steam which enveloped their bodies contained this purifying influence and as it soaked into their bodies it drove out the bad spirits which were in them, and these spirits then drowned in the sweat which dripped from their bodies.[27]

Lieutenant Clark, being curious as to what went on in a sweat bath, arranged with a Cheyenne chief and medicine man [28] to take a bath while he was stationed at Fort Keogh in August, 1881. This bath he described in detail:

I arrived before the preparations were made, and so had the benefit of witnessing all that was done. The squaws turned out to cut some wood, and soon a pile was ready near the sweat lodge, which in the meantime was covered,

106.　American Horse (Cheyenne chief) beside his tepee.

first with some untanned buffalo-skins, leaving only a small entrance, and then with canvas and blankets. This lodge was made of twelve willows, four on each side and two at each end, placed in the ground nearly in the shape of an ellipse, then bent over and fastened, so that the frame was not quite four feet high. The ground inside had been smoothed off and strewn with leaves and grass. In the center was a circular hole about eighteen inches in diameter. The squaws laid down a row of sticks a few feet outside the entrance to the lodge, and then placed a row of small stones, about six inches in diameter, on these sticks, then some more wood and then stones, till a crib about two feet high and three feet wide and four long was made, which was then set on fire.

In the meantime, I had gone into some tall weeds and thick bushes near at hand, which formed a perfect screen, and arrayed myself, by means of a borrowed strap and towel, in a breech-cloth, and stepped forth dressed for the

107. "Two Moon's Tepee, Lame Deer, 1896."

bath. My appearance created some merriment on the part of the squaws. The chief brought his pipe, tobacco, medicine-rattle, and much of his war outfit, which were placed inside first. He, with the little stick used for cleaning the Indian pipe, drew the figure of a man without arms or legs in the dirt at the bottom of the hole. A buffalo-skull, white with age, was placed just in front of the little door. We had crowded in, and were seated tailor-fashion on the ground. The chief filled his pipe, putting a little tobacco into the hole, and mixing with the tobacco some sweet-smelling dried grass. He lighted the pipe and pointed the stem to the zenith, to the figure in the hole, to the painted buffalo-skull outside, and to the four winds, at the same time muttering a prayer. After taking a few puffs, or rather inhalations, he passed the pipe to me. When we had finished smoking the stones had reached a red heat, and about this time we were joined by five other Indians, so that we were pretty closely packed in. The squaw passed in one of the stones using a forked stick, which was placed in the center of the hole and upon it the chief dropped a few bits of the sweet-smelling grass, which, as it burned, gave out a pleasant fragrance. His rattle and other trappings were then handed outside. One of the medicine-bags was then placed on the buffalo-skull, and the rest were laid on the roof of our little house. The other stones were then handed in, and when carefully piled in the hole reached about a foot above the surface of the

108.   "Young 'Plenty Bird' beside his tepee in his dancing costume."

ground. The skins and canvas were then let down over the door, and we were suddenly in total darkness. The heat became intense. There was a report like a pistol-shot, but from the sounds I knew the chief had taken some water in his mouth and spouted it out on the stones. Waves of hot air and steam passed over me, which seemed more like liquid fire than steam and air. A hand touched my right arm and was moved down to my hand, and I then felt a wooden bowl of water handed me. I supposed that it was intended that I should take a swallow, which I did, and passed it to the Indian on my left. I was sitting upright, and my head touched the roof of the little house. My hair was so hot that I could hardly touch my hand to it. I was becoming dazed and dizzy with the heat. The perspiration ran off my body in huge drops.

. . . Of course, with a slight effort I could have raised some of the skins which formed the covering to the lodge, but my pride would not let me do this. I felt that I was being physically and mentally cooked. The chief, who was also a medicine man, from time to time sang in a weird, chanting way. Suddenly the covering to the lodge was raised at the door and opposite to it, and the sunshine blazed in, and the cool air swept gratefully over me. The copper-colored forms of the Indians were all bowed, their heads near the ground at their bent knees.

This was not in worship, but merely to avoid the extreme heat of the top of the little lodge; it brought their heads nearer the hot stones, but still the heat was not nearly as intense as at the top. I also noticed that the hair of the Indians was wet. Instead of swallowing the water they had held it in their mouths for a moment, and then spouting it into the curved hands, had

109. Brave Wolf's sweat lodge.

saturated their hair with it. I at once poured some water from the bowl on my head, thoroughly saturating my hair, and it seemed to clear my brain as from a hot mist. The covering of the lodge remained up some moments, and was then closed as before. This time I held my head down, and my hair being wet, I experienced no uncomfortable sensations. A mouthful of water only was blown upon the stones as before. (Sometimes a little musk or something of the kind is held in the medicine-man's mouth, so that a pungent odor is emitted as this water is blown upon the stones.) The covering was raised and lowered four times, and then quite a quantity of water was poured on the stones, filling the little house full of hot steam. We all then went to the [Yellowstone] river and plunged in, and felt greatly refreshed. . . .

. . . .

I afterward learned that the figure in the bottom of the hole indicated what was especially wished and prayed for,—a figure of a man without limbs indicated a wish to kill an enemy; a pony track, to steal ponies. It is considered especially good luck for the medicine-man to take the bath with others, and he is master of ceremonies.[29]

The Indians got into trouble with these baths when they used them for a cure-all; for, obviously, sweat baths were definitely harmful for certain diseases. How-

110. "Cheyenne Indian Police at Lame Deer, 1892."

ever, the red men undoubtedly got much good from such baths from a curative and conditioning standpoint; and they also believed that these sweats were helpful from a religious standpoint—a point the white man is hardly in position to question.

One feature of the old-time camp life that lasted into the reservation days to the definite benefit of the white agents was the police organization. In the wild, free days all the tribes of the Northwest prairies had organizations for law enforcement. Each Crow chief had a band of dog-soldiers to enforce his orders; and the Cheyennes had six warrior societies, with the chiefs forming a seventh, which were responsible for law and order. These organizations were responsible for establishing rules of conduct within the camp, deciding how the camp was to move, conducting hunts so that the greatest number of animals could be killed, restraining the impetuous in battle, and regulating similar events. Many of these regulations, unwritten laws of long standing, were rigidly enforced, even to the extent of physical force and corporal punishment when necessary.

Among the Sioux in the Northwest, Agent McGillicuddy demonstrated, as did John Clum among the Apaches, that Indian police could keep order more effectively than soldiers. Indian police were officially sanctioned by act of Congress on May 27, 1878. "Their duties were to preserve order on the reservation, to prevent illegal liquor traffic and arrest offenders in this matter, to act as guards when rations were issued and annuities paid, to take charge of and protect at all times Government property, to restore lost or stolen property to its rightful owners, to drive out timber thieves and other trespassers, to return truant pupils to school, and to make arrests for disorderly conduct and other offenses." [30] These things the police did very well, particularly when operating with large bodies similar to the old-time camp groups.

This efficiency was due to two things. First, the Indian believed—in contrast to many white men—that orders meant what they said, and that rules were to be obeyed. Graft and leniency were actions contrary to their notions of how police should function. Second, the origin of power in the old days was with the soldier societies which possessed rituals of religious significance. To flout such power was a sacrilege. Consequently, to defy the police was, in effect, to defy the unseen powers. Such things were just not done.[31]

Huffman's pictures of the Cheyenne police show them in typical dress—a large black hat and a poorly fitting blue uniform with brass buttons on the blouse. On some reservations, boots were worn but, at the time these pictures were taken, the Cheyennes were allowed one comfortable item, their moccasins. A star, a six-shooter, and sometimes a rifle completed the equipment. The pay was a meager $10 or $15 per month, occasionally supplemented with a small house and extra rations.

Few are the intimate stories that recount the operations of these organizations, but enough have been preserved to indicate the pattern of their existence. At the "execution" of Head Chief and Young Mule, the Cheyenne police stood shoulder to shoulder with the troops and did their part of the shooting. During the Ghost Dance trouble, the Indian police stayed faithful. In the attempted arrest of Sitting Bull, 39 police and four of their relatives did not hesitate to tangle with about 165 ghost dancers. That short but deadly melee left six police dead in line of

111. "Wolf Voice and family. Wolf Voice's brother (*right*), wife and child, 1888."

duty. Although the details of their work have been largely forgotten, their duties were faithfully discharged. It is doubtful if the government has even considered the important services the Indian police rendered. Certainly it has never appreciated the quality of manhood which in those days found expression in police duty.

The most baffling feature of Indian life, to the white man, was the red man's religion. Obviously, no religion can be taken apart and explained like a piece of machinery; one believes or he does not believe. As the white man has never been much good at understanding the Indian, it is not surprising that he has found the religion of the Indian largely beyond his understanding, particularly as the medicine men, or at least some of them, were apparently capable of doing some things which did not fit into the white man's concept of what was rational or logical.

Regardless of whether some of the supernatural things credited to an Indian's medicine or to medicine men are believed or not believed, there is no doubt that many exceptional cures were effected in the case of wounds and other physical injuries. When such competent officers as Captain John G. Bourke, Captain William Philo Clark, and Colonel Homer W. Wheeler [32] record that they have seen Indians—so badly wounded that army surgeons recommended amputation of legs and arms, or pronounced them beyond hope—recover under the care of their medicine men, to the accompaniment of drum-thumping, whistle-blowing, chant-

112. "Tall Bear, Minneconjoux medicine man, in dance costume."

ing, and pipe-smoking, such cures are not myths. Undoubtedly Major Frank North, experienced leader of Pawnee scouts, meant exactly what he said when he told Clark that "he would prefer the treatment of a good Pawnee doctor for a wound to the care of an ordinary surgeon." However, not all of their treatments of wounds were successful, and treatments for contagious diseases, particularly when they involved sweat-bath treatments, were often fatal.

Some of the "supernatural" incidents also seem to be of the sort which must be accepted. Clark recorded that "Wonderful and thrilling stories are told of men who have been killed while out from camp with a war-party, and long before the party returned, or any news was heard from it, the family lodge would be entered by the spirit of the deceased." [33] Grinnell was told of a man who, in a medicine lodge ceremony, saw himself at the top of the center pole with his fingers cut and

113. "Brave Wolf and wife beside their sweat lodge, June 20, 1901."

his scalp gone. He told his wife what he had seen and, when he was killed later, his fingers were cut and he was scalped just as revealed in his vision.[34]

Closely akin to such "visions" are prophecies. Many instances have been related where good fortune or punishment have been predicted—and have come true. One of the most outstanding among these was Sitting Bull's prophecy of a victory over a force of soldiers and Indians made at the Sun Dance held 11 days before the Battle of the Little Big Horn.[35] Brave Wolf was noted, as was his father before him, for his gift of prophecy. This power was brought to him by the wolves which told him that he would die of old age, which he did though he was often on the warpath and in danger. On two occasions before going on the warpath, he prophesied accurately that he would bring back prisoners.[36] The recognition of visions, however, is about as far as a white man will go in accepting things associated with the religion of the Indian.

Visions involving animals and the messages they gave to the Indian having the vision, the meaning of various signs, and the supernatural happenings, most white people refuse to believe. These supernatural happenings even include bringing the dead to life. One incident of this kind involved They-Pass-Each-Other, brother of Mrs. William Rowland, who reportedly took his friend Little Head from a burial scaffold and brought him back to life.[37]

White Bull, or Ice, performed some of these unexplainable feats. On one occasion he bullet-proofed two warriors,[38] and, although they were hit in a battle with some Crows, the bullets are said not to have gone through their bodies. He also made the war bonnet worn by the famous warrior, Roman Nose. The wearing of this bonnet required the observance of certain other procedures; and Roman Nose, unknowingly, broke one of these when he ate meat that had been handled with a metal fork. Before he had time for a purification ceremony, he became involved in the fight with Major Forsyth's men at Beecher's Island; and the war bonnet that had provided miraculous protection on other occasions was ineffective against a bullet from a soldier's Spencer.[39]

Another incident involving White Bull is still related among the Cheyennes.[40] According to the account White Bull gave to Grinnell, this incident took place in 1867 in the valley of the Rosebud. White Bull, then 15 years old, was determined to call to him his secret helper. To accomplish this, he had a hole dug large enough for him to sit in, and then had his friends tie him securely and put him in the hole with his face to the east. The hole was then covered with a complete, specially painted buffalo robe with the head oriented to the east, and this was weighted down with a rock so large that it had to be rolled into position. A large rock was also placed on each corner of the robe. Over the rocks was placed the framework of a sweat lodge and this was covered with robes. Then a lodge, so large that three normal lodge coverings were needed to cover the framework, was set up over everything and three rows of people gathered inside the lodge to sing medicine songs.

For a time nothing happened. Then White Bull saw a little man beside him who told him to shut his eyes, slapped him on the soles of his feet, and then took him by the hair and lifted him a little. He was then told to open his eyes, and found himself standing in front of the big lodge. When the people looked inside the sweat lodge they found the rocks piled to one side of the lodge, the robe on top of them,

114.   "Cheyenne Warrior—White Bull."

115. "Catholic Sisters by Old Mission."

and on top of all the cords with which White Bull had been tied.[41]

As such accounts go, White Bull's experience was not exceptional, as other experiences related by Indians are—to the white man—equally incomprehensible. Some of the firsthand narratives of the Northwest contain interesting observations, such as those of Pierre-Antoine Tabeau who was a fur-trader among the Arikaras when Lewis and Clark came up the Missouri. Tabeau, obviously a very skeptical observer, attended a performance of "comedians, jugglers, and sorcerers" which was held in a well-lighted medicine lodge. He wrote in his journal that "I saw" a naked man show him—"nearby"—a leather garter. The Indian then rolled it in his hands and threw it on the ground changed to a "living adder." He picked up the snake and showed it to Tabeau changed back to a garter—and he repeated the performance ten times. In another act an Indian shot a gun at his companion who fell "dead" with blood gushing from the two openings made by the bullet. Yet the man was mysteriously healed after a great many "grimaces and lamentations." In like manner, he saw an elderly Indian plunge a barbed arrow into his heart, and other men pulled it completely through the man's body. For such things Tabeau had no logical explanation other than that the spectator "really believed" what he observed.[42]

Captain John G. Bourke, in addition to being a capable officer, was a competent amateur anthropologist. Soon after the end of the Sioux war of 1876, he re-

116. "Cheyenne. American Horse beside his tepee with his 2 wives, daughters, and sons, 1901."

corded the following observations at Fort Robinson where he observed a medicine man named Sorrel Horse:

He lay down on the floor, put the hot bowl of a pipe in his mouth, and alternately inhaled the smoke or caused it to issue from the stem. Pretty soon he went into a trance, and deep groans and grunts were emitted from the abdominal region. When he came to, he assured us that that was the voice of a spirit which he kept within him. He shuffled a pack of cards, and handing it to General Mackenzie, bade him take out any one he wanted and he would tell the name; Mackenzie did as he desired, and "Sorrel Horse" promptly fixed his fingers in diamond-shape and called out "Squaw," for the queen of diamonds, and similarly for the seven of clubs, and others as fast as drawn. He again lay down on the floor, and opened his shirt so that his ribs were exposed; he took a small piece of tobacco, and pretended to swallow it. To all appearances, he became deathly sick: his countenance turned an ashen hue, perspiration stood on his brow, the same lugubrious grunts issued from his stomach and throat, and

117. "Cheyenne Chief 'Two Moon' at Fort Keogh, 1879."

I was for a moment or two in alarm about his condition; but he soon recovered consciousness, if he had ever lost it, and triumphantly drew the moist leaf of tobacco from beneath his ribs.[43]

Although Huffman knew and photographed several Sioux and Cheyenne chiefs, most of his Indian manuscript material pertains to Two Moon, one of his good friends. This friendship dated back to the days at Fort Keogh when "I knew, photographed, admired—I almost said loved—the genial, young war chief." On Huffman's part, this friendly feeling arose because he "appreciated that savage, but genial, natural man chiefly and above all for the reason that he was Injun all the way through."

Evidently the admiration was mutual. Huffman treasured the memory of a day when he observed a crowd gathering to follow the old chief, then "near the close of his life" and almost blind, into a hotel in Miles City:

He went to the clerk and, not knowing that I stood close to his elbow, made the sign for the telephone by holding his right hand to his ear, and he asked the man at the desk if he could hear Patiskawpa [Cheyenne for Huffman]. . . . He made the sign with his hand in front of his face, "the man who makes the mark or thing on paper that looks like you.". . . So again we shook hands, and I was touched by the tone of his voice which I had known so well, and he was greatly pleased. Now, as I afterward learned, this was before he had eaten or rested from his sixty mile journey in a wagon.

Huffman's manuscript about Two Moon is rambling and interlarded with other information, most of which has been placed elsewhere. Part of the remainder of the manuscript follows:

Two Moon was about six feet four in his moccasins and as straight as an arrow. He walked lightly and erect and had the most remarkable voice that I remember among the many red men that I have known. The first time I heard his voice was on the day that my first picture of Two Moon in his war bonnet was taken in my old log shack at Fort Keogh while he was a prisoner at that place. After that year I did not see him for quite a long time and when I did it was for but a very brief time, but on that occasion I gave him a small copy of this picture with a written message on the back which was interpreted to him, and a short letter accompanying it, which subsequent events proved he treasured for not less than twenty years by wrapping it Indian fashion, in a little parflesh rawhide envelope, tied with a buckskin thong.

. . .   .

Quite the most thrilling thing I ever heard a white man or a red man utter, and my memory runs back to some startling and dramatic situations and speeches, was upon a day at this same agency when my good friend, Owen D. Wheeler, the historian who wrote *The Trail of Lewis and Clark* and with whom I traveled to make the illustrations for *Wonderland* and that book, was interviewing the surviving chiefs and head-men of the Cheyenne tribe on the porch of the agent's office. When we were driving to the agency, a two-day's journey from the railroad, I said to Mr. Wheeler, "When an Indian starts to answer a question or tell a story or incident of his life or of his forebears, don't stop him because if you do he will begin at the same place again, and if you stop him or make suggestions or criticisms to him a second time he will tell you nothing thereafter." The interpreter was Willis Rowland,[44] a fine man and a great interpreter of that difficult language, the Cheyenne. Mr. Wheeler did not quite get Two Moon's explanation of the opening of the battle the first time, and he asked Two Moon, "What was the first intimation you had of the approach of the white soldiers when, as you say, you and your people were mostly picking choke cherries and bathing in the Little Horn, not expecting any immediate attack—what was the first thing that called your attention to their approach?"
There was a moment of the turning of eyes of the throng of old men seated about him, and a brief silence of a minute or more when Two Moon straightened up his body, and lifted his head, and looked off toward the hills, and he said in a way that no one could imitate in that beautiful voice of his, "Ah-ha-a-a-a-a-a-a, Wa-a-ay off, papoose, squaws, boys, girls, run, run, run, and cry Nutskawehooooooooooooooooooo, Nutskawehooo, the white soldiers."

118.   "Cheyenne Chief 'Two Moon' on Custer's Hill. Twenty-fifth Anniversary of the Battle."

But, contrary to my advice, my dear friend Wheeler somehow was thinking more about the time of day that it might have been, or from what direction they came, or whether it was before or after some other event [asked a second question] so Two Moon sat silent thereafter and said no more. When one realizes as I did at that moment, knowing that man as I did, that that event was the most momentous of his life. . . .—if one can imagine the condition of mind of those young boys and girls, and those aged and withered, travel-stained mothers of those Indian children out driving the horses toward camp— can one imagine a more thrilling thing to them than their running for a mile or more in a cloud of dust with the horses and crying so that warriors could hear, "Nutskawehooo, the white soldiers—they are here!"

Although Two Moon was a respected leader and a brave man, his standing was not as high as some accounts place it. This was probably due to a combination of circumstances, and to Two Moon himself. Wooden Leg, who was somewhat younger than Two Moon, told his biographer that

Two Moon used to tell white people of his own great importance in the battle. I believe he was brave, like many others there, but he was not thought of as being very important. He was one of the nine little chiefs of the Fox warriors.[45] The only special way I heard him talked about was concerning his having a repeating rifle, the only one of such guns among the Cheyennes in this battle. When the smaller part of the Cheyenne tribe surrendered to General Miles, at Fort Keogh, Two Moon was chosen by him as their one big chief.[46]

Rufus Wallowing,[47] one of the leaders of the Cheyennes today, when questioned on this point, stated:

119. Mandan Indian graves in the hills near the Fort Berthold Indian Agency, North Dakota, 1902.

Two Moon was not considered an outstanding warrior and chief, and he took part in the Custer Battle like an ordinary warrior and he is not mentioned to have merit[ed] any honors. It was sometime after 1877 when the Cheyennes began contact with the whites, because of his personality and friendliness to the whites the body of forty chiefs made him a member of the chief,[48] with the expectation [that] he [would] gain favors from the whites for the good of the Cheyenne people. And as the Cheyennes expected, the whites spoke highly of Two Moon as a great chief and warrior.[49]

Huffman left two brief notes about Little Chief and Little Wolf. He noted that Little Chief had some trouble in adjusting himself to the difficult times in which he found himself after the surrender and before the Cheyennes were moved from Two Moon Creek [50] to the agency at Lame Deer.

Little Chief, who was discontented at that time, had left them and gone to Standing Rock, and that brave gentleman and soldier, Benteen of Custer Battle fame, was the military escort that went with Little Chief and his people on that trip, and it is related . . . that when the journey was nearly done, at Tobacco Garden Camp, Benteen called Little Chief and some of his young men to him, and said to them: "Little Chief, your men are the bravest Indians and your women the most virtuous I have ever known." And later, still discontented, Little Chief came back,[51] and when the general told him—and this was the story of the camp that day—"I can't give you rations here," the old man said: "The Great Spirit put rations on the prairie for me and my people; I don't want your rations." and so it was, I think, in his rude way, that old man knew that every privilege of this life hath its sacrifices, so at first he took sparingly of the white man's dole, and stood brooding on the wrongs of his race. . . .[52]

Although Huffman knew Little Wolf well, he wrote very little about him and

120.   An old tree burial.

his negative of this famous war chief has been lost or broken. In writing of the days at Fort Keogh, Huffman set down:

> Little Wolf was a young man then, and I think it was Clark who told me, while recounting in his presence by the help of an interpreter, many stories of that memorable raid—how, when the Cheyennes under Little Wolf were sore pressed by the army in the sand hills, and his warriors, well nigh starved and footsore, discouraged, and about to give up, Little Wolf walked way out in front, exposed to the fire of the enemy, and cried out, "They can't hit me, they can't hit me," and so gave courage to his friends, and once more they eluded the army and pressed on to the north.[53]

This retreat from Indian Territory marked Little Wolf as a great leader, and it is regrettable that, while drunk on the white man's whisky, he killed Famished Elk. This tragedy took place on Two Moon Creek in the trading store of Huffman's partner, Eugene Lamphere. Murder being an unpardonable sin among the Cheyennes, Little Wolf's people "threw him away."

It is fitting that this chapter, dealing as it does with a way of life that has gone forever, should close with a few pictures of burial places. These, too, were a part of the life in the days of skin tepees, jerked meat, and medicine visions, and they varied according to the tribe and the conditions of the moment.

The photograph of the old Mandan burials made in 1902 indicates that some of the Mandan burials were in boxes or coffins placed on a high hill; however, the

121. "Lame Deer's Tomb near [the Cheyenne] Agency."

Sioux, Cheyennes, and Crows usually buried on scaffolds, in trees, or in caves, and it is with such burials that most of these photographs deal. The body was dressed and painted as was thought fitting, and weapons, tools, or toys were wrapped with the corpse according to the sex and age of the deceased. It is said that the Mandans buried with the head toward the east, while the Crows turned the head toward the west. The Sioux usually buried on scaffolds, the Cheyennes sometimes in trees but mostly in small caves, and the Crows on a scaffold or in a tree. After the body decomposed, the Crows often buried the bones in rock crevices.

After a battle the dead were sometimes buried on the open prairie, and sometimes in a small cave to hide the body from the enemy. The burial place of Lame Deer is an example of this sort of burial after battle. Twenty-two years afterward

122.   "Old Crow woman's grave."

when Huffman visited the "blow-out" where Lame Deer's body was placed, "scarcely a relic of his burial remained, just some bits of shriveled rawhide and six brass beads." Grinnell, who visited this spot 20 years after the fight, "saw his daughter mourn for him with wailings as keen and as touching as if he had been buried only yesterday."

Some of the graves were unusual, like the grave of a Crow woman Huffman photographed and described to Neil Clark:

Sentiment ran strong in their race, and some of their ways were beautiful. There was a woman; I visited and photographed her grave. I'll not tell where it is, for it's not a place I should like to see visited for the sake of idle curiosity.

As a girl this Indian woman had been beautiful and rode a horse as gracefully as any of her people; she had lovers and a husband, became a mother, and as she grew older, was kindly and generous to a fault, and well loved. She became very fat, far too fat to ride an Indian pony any more. The only things she asked for then were a light spring wagon she could drive around, and a white woman's sewing machine so she might sew for her friends. It was work she loved, and she continued it almost to the day of her death. . . .

[When she died] they selected a spot [for her grave] on the crest of a ridge of hills, on either side of which there is a river valley. Along this divide, when alive, she used to drive to and from the homes of her friends; and in death they laid her in a sitting posture in that wagon box, protected by a tin covering, so she could, so they believed, look far out over the two valleys and feast her eyes on familiar scenes, secure against the invasion of wolves. To make her more happy and contented they left with her the things she used and loved in life, chief among them her sewing machine. There seems a beautiful sentiment in that.[54]

123.   Gall's grave at Wakpala cemetery.

Gall, that rugged warrior who stood out from among his comrades, was buried in a prosaic grave, like a white man, in the St. Francis burying ground near Wakpala, South Dakota. Only in the Sioux inscription on the tombstone is there a flavor of the old days—"*Wisaca* (man) *Owotonna* (straight) *Kin* (this) *Ohinnyan* (always or forever) *Kiksuyapi* (remember) *Kta Ce*." [55] Perhaps it would have been more fitting had he been placed on a scaffold, like the unknown warrior Huffman photographed in the buffalo days, with the sun and moon to stand guard over him, and with the wind to tug at his wrappings and whistle and murmur past the scaffold poles.

124.   "A Sioux Warrior's Grave."

EPILOGUE

There remained one other frontier for Huffman's camera to record—the frontier of the rancher. The wind and the rain had hardly blotted out the tracks of the vanished buffalo before a wave of cattle and sheep swept over this prairie land. For a little over two decades this frontier flourished and then it too withered, although it did not pass completely like the frontier of the soldier, the hide-hunter, and the bull-whacker. Huffman made a superb record of the days of the open range but, unfortunately, space does not permit its inclusion between these covers.

This has been the story of the Indian, the soldier, the hide-hunter, the freighter, and others who knew Montana's prairies when the only roads were the gently winding buffalo trails, and when life was wild and free. A few years after Huffman's coming, this life had passed and it was to live again only in the gleam in old-timers' eyes when they forgot the present and remembered the past. Huffman's picture of the solitary grave of a warrior on the wide prairie, even without the sound of the lonely, ceaseless wind, is an eloquent epitaph to these days. It must have been with poignant memories that Huffman wrote, "It was a dream and a forgetting, a chapter forever closed."

NOTES ON TEXT

PROLOGUE

1. Badger Clark, "The Old Cowman," *Sun and Saddle Leather*, p. 92.

CHAPTER 1

1. Badger Clark, "The Passing of the Trail," *Sun and Saddle Leather*, p. 171.
2. *The Helena Independent* (April 2, 1903).
3. Although Custer held the brevet rank of major general, he was reduced at the end of the Civil War to the rank of lieutenant colonel. His actual rank will be used in all references.
4. Pease was the first Crow agent; and agents were accorded the title of "major" as a mark of courtesy.
5. The best source regarding this short-lived post is E. S. Topping, *The Chronicles of the Yellowstone*. On the flyleaf of his copy Huffman wrote:

   This book came to me in 1914. . . . I knew its author well and also neighbor'd and hunted with many of the characters named in the book, both red and white. Paul McCormick and Major Pease outlived all but one of the hardy crew that built for them Fort Pease and, against such heavy odds, fought so bravely in its defense. Topping long since passed but he left a story in his "Chronicles" that will stand for all time as the truest and best. . . .

6. Grouard identified this camp as Crazy Horse's, but the Indians who were in the fight insist it was Two Moon's. John G. Bourke, *On the Border with Crook*, p. 277; Thomas B. Marquis, *A Warrior Who Fought Custer*, pp. 161–168; Stanley Vestal, interview with the authors, April 11, 1951.

7. Vestal had this experience while gathering material for his biography of Sitting Bull. Stanley Vestal, interview with the authors, April 10, 1951.

8. Robert Bruce, *The Fighting Norths and Pawnee Scouts*, p. 60.

9. This scout's name is invariably misspelled Brughier or Brughière. Larpenteur, who knew the father, used the French rendition, Bruguière, while others who knew the family spelled the name Bruguier. John Bruguier was a son of Theophile Bruguier, a well-to-do Indian trader who settled on the site now occupied by the city of Sioux City, Iowa. His mother was Anapo or Dawn, a daughter of the prominent Santee Sioux leader, War Eagle. He was killed on Poplar "Creek." Albert H. Holman and Constant R. Marks, *Pioneering in the Northwest*, pp. 104–127; Charles Larpenteur, *Forty Years a Fur Trader on the Upper Missouri*, II, 288, 297.

10. Charles M. Russell, *Trails Plowed Under*, pp. 17–21.

11. Frank Bird Linderman, "Old Trails," *Bunch-Grass and Blue-Joint*, p. 115.

CHAPTER 2

1. Huffman intended to write a book about his experiences and, when he died, left his desk stuffed with a heterogeneous assortment of notes and short manuscripts in various stages of completion. As he usually wrote with but little use of proper punctuation and capitalization, it has been necessary to do a certain amount of editing and correction of obvious misspelling. These minor changes have not been indicated.

2. John and Abraham Cuppy received land in Iowa as payment for their services against the Indians.

3. Fort Crawford, 1816–1849, was located at Prairie du Chien, Wisconsin, and Fort Atkinson, 1840–1849, in what is now the southwestern part of Winneshiek County, Iowa.

4. Probably goldenrod and the species of wild sunflower known as rosin weed.

5. These trails were in the "Neutral Ground," a 40-mile-wide strip between the territory occupied by the Sioux and that occupied by the Sauk and Fox Indians. Bruce Mahan, *Old Fort Crawford and the Frontier*, pp. 153–155.

6. The prehistoric mounds in the upper Mississippi Valley resemble those in the Ohio Valley except that, comparatively, the former are very much smaller.

7. L. A. Huffman, from the manuscript, "The Cheyenne Indians" (1900).

8. An old frontier term for ruffed grouse.

9. L. A. Huffman, fragmentary manuscript (n.d.). Hereafter, all material from manuscripts and notes which were apparently never published will not be footnoted.

10. Small clumps of trees and patches of timber which characterize the border zone between large areas of woodland and prairie soils.

11. Stirrups with leather covers—*tapaderos*.

12. Frontiersmen commonly carried their rifles across the saddle in a short leather loop (sling) attached to the pommel.

13. Frank Jay Haines secured the photography concession in the Yellowstone National Park in 1883.

14. L. A. Huffman, from the manuscript, "The Cheyenne Indians" (1900).

15. "Hi" Bickerdyke, son of "Mother" Bickerdyke, the famous Civil War nurse, became Huffman's ideal of a buffalo-hunter when the northern herd was exterminated. Bessie Huffman Felton remembered him as a tall, handsome, well-built man with a black beard who often visited her father.

16. John R. Cook, *The Border and the Buffalo*, pp. 297–311.

17. The Northern Pacific Railroad reached Bismarck on June 3, 1873, but track-laying west of the Missouri River was not started until May 31, 1879. Northern Pacific Railroad, letter to authors, November 1, 1950.

18. This freighting enterprise was the largest in Montana.
19. Apparently Northrup regarded Huffman as a fellow fugitive. Later he worked for the Diamond R as a bull-whacker.
20. This was the Tobacco Garden Station which was about halfway to Milestown. It was so named because of the wild mullen which grew in the vicinity.
21. Rough work clothes.
22. There were no major campaigns this winter. Huffman probably referred to the pursuit of a small raiding band of Sitting Bull's Sioux.
23. L. A. Huffman, from a manuscript for a newspaper article (n.d.).
24. A prominent landmark a few miles west of the present town of Jordan.
25. The Northern Pacific track-laying crew reached Miles City in September, 1881.
26. *The American Field, the Sportsmans Journal*, a sporting magazine.
27. An old name for the Shoshone River.
28. The date of this letter—September 6, 1882—is incorrect. Probably Huffman wrote September instead of October. He joined Shields' hunting party in the valley of Clark Fork on September 5.
29. His sister Ardelle.
30. A popular actor.
31. General Philip Sheridan.
32. His Kennedy rifle.
33. Reference is made to one of Joseph's fights with Colonel Sturgis' force when the former swung north on his retreat after passing through the Yellowstone National Park.
34. Crissman was an early photographer.
35. George O. Shields, *Rustlings in the Rockies*, pp. 26–49.
36. Lamphere was a nephew of Captain Frank D. Baldwin of the Fifth Infantry, then stationed at Fort Keogh. He married Comenha, a daughter of Dull Knife, the Cheyenne chief.
37. Major Guido Ilges held the rank of colonel during the Civil War.
38. Captain William Philo Clark of the Second Cavalry, and John Bruguier, the scout and interpreter.
39. This humor has a grim twist. The Indian victory at the Battle of the Little Big Horn was hardly a thing a Cheyenne would shed tears about.
40. L. A. Huffman, from the manuscript, "The Cheyenne Indians" (1900). Clark did compile an excellent dictionary of the Indian sign language—but it is not illustrated.
41. This boat was built for Leighton and Jordan, well-known trading firm in Montana. In August, 1878, Marsh set a record of 55 hours and 25 minutes with her for a run from Bismarck to Fort Buford. Joseph Mills Hanson, *The Conquest of the Missouri*, pp. 389–395.
42. Almost all the early pictures reproduced in this volume were made from one of the halves of a stereoscopic negative.
43. His oldest daughter, who was then five months old.
44. The Perry shutter was an early iris shutter having about a half-dozen leaves and perhaps a top speed of $\frac{1}{25}$ of a second. Pyro developer is still considered one of the very best developers when a quality product is desired.
45. L. A. Huffman to Perrin Cuppy Huffman, January 18, 1885.
46. L. A. Huffman to Perrin Cuppy Huffman, June 7, 1885.
47. George O. Shields, *Rustling in the Rockies*, pp. 82–86.
48. L. A. Huffman to Perrin Cuppy Huffman, September 6, 1882. See Note 28.
49. L. A. Huffman to Perrin Cuppy Huffman, November 9, 1882.
50. Cabinet photographs—photographs mounted on a stiff cardboard backing.
51. L. A. Huffman to Perrin Cuppy Huffman, April 5, 1885.
52. William Henry Jackson was the photographer with the government-sponsored expedition in 1871 to what is now the Yellowstone National Park. Dr. F. V.

Hayden was the geologist in charge of this expedition which was known as the Hayden survey. See Clarence S. Jackson, *Picture Maker of the Old West, William H. Jackson,* for pictures taken on this trip. Crissman, another photographer of note, has already been mentioned in one of P. C. Huffman's letters.

53. Dr. A. C. Peale, a geologist, who worked with Hayden on the Yellowstone expedition.

54. Apparently Huffman has confused names. As Fort Alexander was on the left bank of the Yellowstone opposite the mouth of the Rosebud, they must have visited the site of Fort Van Buren which was on the right bank near the mouth of the Tongue. Larpenteur burned Fort Van Buren in 1842 before building Fort Alexander. Charles Larpenteur, *Forty Years a Fur Trader on the Upper Missouri,* I, 170; Hiram M. Chittenden, *The History of the American Fur Trade of the Far West,* III, 965.

55. L. A. Huffman to Perrin Cuppy Huffman, August 13, 1883.

56. Huffman was probably on the headwaters of Little Dry Creek not far from the present town of Cohagen.

57. Another of Huffman's names for the "Big Open" based on its shape.

58. Kelly observed that the ankles of the forefeet are often a mass of prickly-pear thorns, the result of stamping cactus to get at the grass. Luther S. Kelly, *Yellowstone Kelly,* p. 69.

59. Member of the school board.

60. Billings County, the adjoining county in North Dakota, had similar trouble. Lincoln Lang, *Ranching with Roosevelt,* pp. 267–272.

61. A partner in the livestock commission firm of Clay, Robinson and Company.

62. L. A. Huffman, from the manuscript for a story in *The Yellowstone Journal* (July 8, 1907).

63. Thomas H. Irvine was deputy sheriff of Custer County, of which Miles City was the county seat.

64. Stuart was only 46 years old, but he was *old* on the frontier as he had been in the West since 1849 when, as a lad of 15, he accompanied his father to California.

65. Granville Stuart, *Forty Years on the Frontier,* II, 111.

66. Louis F. Grill, interview with authors, October 14, 1950.

67. John Clay, "The Passing of Conrad Kohrs," *The Breeders Gazette* (December 2, 1920), p. 1163. Kohrs was an outstanding rancher in Montana.

68. A saloon in Miles City during the frontier days.

69. The leading hotel.

70. Proprietor of a famous road ranch.

71. The brand owned by John Holt.

72. L. A. Huffman, from the manuscript for a newspaper story (1920).

73. Seventy grains of powder was the load for the .45-caliber Springfield then used by the army—a sizable charge for a cigar!

74. High Bear was a man of importance. Unfortunately, it is extremely difficult to check identities of subchiefs such as this one. Also, in this case, the situation is further complicated by the fact that there were at least five High Bears among the Sioux. (Judge Frank Zahn, letter to authors, January 4, 1953.) Huffman identified this Indian as a subchief of Spotted Eagle's band and an Oglala. He was one of Sitting Bull's lieutenants when this chief held a conference with Colonel Miles "between the lines" on October 20, 1876 (Stanley Vestal, *Sitting Bull,* p. 202); and probably he was the High Bear referred to by Cornelia Adair (later owner of the famous JA ranch in the Texas Panhandle) in her record of a council she attended with Colonel Dodge near the Sidney Barracks on the South Platte. This council was held October 8, 1874, with the chiefs of the "Cut Off" band of the Oglala, and High Bear made a speech at this council. (Cornelia Adair, *My Diary, August 30th to November 5th, 1874,* p. 95.)

75. At this time the Sioux and Cheyennes who surrendered at Fort Keogh had not

been moved to reservations. They had the status of prisoners of war, and were housed in their own camps a short distance from the post. Huffman stated in another sketch that the "big men of the camp were permitted to enter the post at certain times and frequent the trader's store, where the quartermaster employees and other citizens like myself, along with officers off duty would set in the shade along the west side of the old store and chat with them."

76. L. A. Huffman, from a manuscript for a newspaper story (n.d.).
77. Price Terrett to authors, November 19, 1950.
78. Charles M. Russell, *Trails Plowed Under*, p. 154.

CHAPTER 3

1. Charles M. Russell, *Good Medicine*, p. 37.
2. F. Geo. Heldt, "Sir George Gore's Expedition, 1854–1856," *Contributions to the Historical Society of Montana*, I, 144–148; James H. Bradley, "Affairs at Fort Benton from 1831 to 1869," *Contributions to the Historical Society of Montana*, III, 278–279; R. B. Marcy, *Thirty Years of Army Life on the Border*, pp. 401–404.
3. It has been estimated that in this year Custer County, of which Miles City was the county seat, shipped by boat and rail about 180,000 hides. Illustrated and Historical Edition of *The Yellowstone Journal* (September 27, 1900), p. 3.
4. William T. Hornaday, "The Extermination of the American Bison," *House Miscellaneous Documents, 1st Session, 50th Congress, 1887–1888*, XVIII, 444.
5. *Ibid.*, p. 446.
6. Peter Koch, "Life at Muscleshell in 1869 and 1870," *Contributions to the Historical Society of Montana*, II, 302.
7. When Huffman first became acquainted with Hornaday he was chief taxidermist of the U. S. National Museum, and when the two went on a hunting trip to Hell Creek in 1901, as related later, he was director of the New York Zoological Park.
8. Hornaday, "The Extermination of the American Bison," *House Miscellaneous Documents, 1st Session, 50th Congress, 1887–1888*, XVIII, 421.
9. *Ibid.*, pp. 421–422.
10. The testicles, also called "mountain oysters."
11. Tom Irvine, Eugene Lamphere, and "Yellowstone" Kelly. Only Irvine made the entire trip with Stuart.
12. The place at the mouth of the Big Horn River where Grant Marsh ferried Terry's troops over to Fort Pease after the Battle of the Little Big Horn.
13. Granville Stuart, *Forty Years on the Frontier*, II, 108–112, 121–125.
14. L. A. Huffman to Tom Irvine, June 14, 1916.
15. The mouth of Great Porcupine Creek is about 55 miles up the river from Miles City.
16. Stuart, *Forty Years on the Frontier*, II, 103–104.
17. Jirky [sic]. A *jerky* was an abbreviated version of the stagecoach. It was a smaller vehicle with a canvas top and sides, and a small boot fore and aft.
18. Luther S. Kelly to William R. Felton, January 28, 1912.
19. In traveling to the headwaters of Big Dry Creek, this party crossed the valleys of Beaver and Redwater creeks, both normally good buffalo ranges.
20. About 22 miles northwest of Miles City on North Sunday Creek. Here buffalo meat was once cured for market, thus giving rise to this name.
21. This process involving the use of pickling vats made of green hides was in use on the southern plains at least ten years before this date.
22. Pine with a high rosin content.
23. Theodore Roosevelt, *Ranch Life and the Hunting Trail*, p. 13.
24. In Miles City, according to one old cowboy, one could often see three or four buffalo-hunters walk up to a bar and reach inside their clothes and see who could

catch the first louse for the drinks. T. C. Abbott and Helena H. Smith, *We Pointed Them North*, p. 121.

25. John R. Cook, *The Border and the Buffalo*, p. 127.

26. O. P. Hanna, an old frontiersman in Montana and Wyoming who hunted with White in Montana.

27. Mexicans who killed buffalo with a lance from horseback.

28. Rex W. Strickland, Editor, "The Recollections of W. S. Glenn, Buffalo Hunter," *Panhandle-Plains Historical Review*, XXII (1949), 36–37, 47.

29. Huffman was coining a figure of speech in comparing the plainsmen he knew to the famous pioneers and scouts of the days of his grandfathers.

30. Hornaday, "The Extermination of the American Bison," *House Miscellaneous Documents*, *1st Session, 50th Congress, 1887–1888*, XVIII, 510. Theodore Roosevelt, *Hunting Trips of a Ranchman*, I, 47–49.

31. Philip Ashton Rollins, *The Cowboy*, p. 50.

32. There is no mention in Cook's book, *The Border and the Buffalo*, that he hunted in the north, although he was in the Indian Service at Fort Berthold. Huffman, in a note on the flyleaf of his copy of this book, definitely indicates that Cook did hunt in the north.

33. Later a sheepman with headquarters on Timber Creek.

34. H. F. Schlosser to authors, October 28, 1950.

35. Hornaday, "The Extermination of the American Bison," *House Miscellaneous Documents*, *1st Session, 50th Congress, 1887–1888*, XVIII, 467.

36. O. G. Libby, Editor, *Collections of the [North Dakota] State Historical Society*, VII (1925), 103.

37. H. F. Schlosser to authors, October 28, 1950.

38. Hornaday, "The Extermination of the American Bison," *House Miscellaneous Documents*, *1st Session, 50th Congress, 1887–1888*, XVIII, 510.

39. Quoted in Hornaday, "The Extermination of the American Bison," *House Miscellaneous Documents*, *1st Session, 50th Congress, 1887–1888*, XVIII, 503.

40. Illustrated and Historical Edition of *The Yellowstone Journal* (September 27, 1900), p. 3.

41. Probably Huffman referred to Indian tanned skins. The hide trade sometimes called a cow's skin a *robe*, and a bull's skin a *skin*.

42. Roosevelt, *Hunting Trips of a Ranchman*, II, 75–76.

43. A young bull between one and four years old and so named because of the shape and appearance of the horns, also sometimes called a "hollow horn."

44. Neil M. Clark, manuscript for the article, "He Captured the Vanishing West Before It Vanished."

45. Rollins, *The Cowboy*, p. 212.

46. Nelson A. Miles, *Personal Recollections and Observations of General Nelson A. Miles*, p. 132.

47. L. A. Huffman to Perrin Cuppy Huffman, December 3, 1882.

48. L. A. Huffman to Perrin Cuppy Huffman, October 19, 1885.

49. George O. Shields, *Rustlings in the Rockies*, p. 56.

50. Usually described as a smaller, more active animal with a finer coat than buffalo living on the plains.

51. Shields, *Rustling in the Rockies*, pp. 72–77.

52. This creek is just south of the Montana-Wyoming line. Here, in the summer of 1878, near where Shields' party camped, General Miles captured a party of Bannock Indians who had gone on the warpath a few weeks previously. Killed in this fight was Captain Andrew S. Bennett of the Fifth Infantry for whom the Creek was named.

53. See Huffman's letter dated September 6, 1883, quoted in Chapter 2.

54. Shields, *Rustling in the Rockies*, pp. 41–42.

55. *Ibid.*, pp. 43–47.

56. McNaney's wife was ill. She died the following winter.
57. Individuals locating land to file on.
58. Three-horned Dinosaur and Tyrannosaurus Rex.

CHAPTER 4

1. John Finerty, *Warpath and Bivouac*, p. 339.
2. Sergeant T. B. Glover, Troop B, Second U. S. Cavalry, was awarded a Congressional Medal of Honor for action at Mizpah Creek, Montana, on April 10, 1879, and at Pumpkin Creek, Montana, February 10, 1880. The citation reads: "while in charge of small scouting parties, fought, charged, surrounded, and captured war parties of Sioux Indians." *The Medal of Honor of the United States Army*, p. 231.
3. On March 24, 1880, a party of Sioux raided Fort Custer and stole about 50 ponies belonging to the Crow scouts. Huggins, after a difficult pursuit, fought a sharp skirmish six days later on the head of O'Fallon Creek and captured five Indians. Nelson A. Miles, *Personal Recollections and Observations of General Nelson A. Miles*, pp. 310–311.
4. *Ibid.*, p. 316.
5. *Ibid.*, p. 318. Even if the figure of 2000 included those Miles had induced to surrender three years previously, this was a sizable part of Sitting Bull's followers. In the summer of 1879 Finerty estimated that Sitting Bull had 2500 fighting men in Canada. Finerty, *Warpath and Bivouac*, p. 371.
6. *Ibid.*, p. 363.
7. Miles apparently made an effort to handle the Indians who surrendered to him in a sensible manner. The principal men were allowed to visit the trader's store on the post where Huffman, soldiers off duty, and others met them and got partly acquainted. However, they were not allowed in Milestown without an escort to assist, and to ward off contacts which might cause friction. Miles regarded the situation as being akin to a "powder keg." As a group, the Indians feared reprisals—some of them practically to the day of their death many years later—for the defeat they handed Custer; and likewise the whites never trusted the Indians. Huffman sometimes related one bit of unrecorded history: One winter Miles had a barricade built around the post—two rows of cordwood piled breast high with a space between—which he gave Huffman strict orders not to photograph!
8. Louis F. Grill, interview with authors, October 14, 1950. Irvine told the story to Grill.
9. Quoted in Elizabeth B. Custer, *Boots and Saddles*, pp. 281–284.
10. *Ibid.*, pp. 203–215.
11. Edward S. Godfrey, *General George A. Custer and the Battle of the Little Big Horn* (Reprinted from the *Century Magazine*), pp. 33–34.
12. Miles, *Personal Recollections*. p. 318.
13. Henry Romeyn (Captain), "The Capture of Chief Joseph and the Nez Pierce Indians," *Contributions to the Historical Society of Montana*, II, 284.
14. Miles, *Personal Recollections*, p. 238.
15. The Cheyenne medicine man, sometimes called Ice, is not to be confused with Sitting Bull's nephew, also named White Bull.
16. Miles, *Personal Recollections*, pp. 239–244.
17. Thomas B. Marquis, *A Warrior Who Fought Custer*, p. 297.
18. Luther S. Kelly, *Yellowstone Kelly*, p. 180.
19. Henry Keiser, interview with Louis F. Grill (n.d.); and interview with W. R. Felton (n.d.); Peter Koch, "Life at Muscleshell in 1869 and 1870," *Contributions to the Historical Society of Montana*, II, 292–303; Eleanor Banks, *Wandersong*, p. 86–104.

20. Miles, *Personal Recollections*, p. 229.
21. Kelly, *Yellowstone Kelly*, pp. xi–xii.
22. Nannie Alderson and Helena H. Smith, *A Bride Goes West*, pp. 184–185.
23. Rufus Wallowing, letter to authors, April, 1951. Mr. Wallowing heard Brave Wolf tell this story.
24. Miles, *Personal Recollections*, pp. 267–268.
25. Kelly, *Yellowstone Kelly*, pp. 193–195.
26. Miles, *Personal Recollections*, pp. 277–278.
27. The graves were marked by wooden stakes driven at the head and foot. Where the body could be identified, the name of the fallen man was written on a piece of paper, placed in an empty cartridge shell, and the shell driven into the head of the stake. Homer W. Wheeler, *The Frontier Trail*, p. 210.
28. These pictures were probably taken by S. J. Morrow, an early photographer who accompanied this detail. The negatives have long been a part of the Huffman collection.
29. These were held out when the bulk of the arms were surrendered. In later years one woman told how she carried a rifle hanging down her back under her blanket. Other arms were dismantled and some of the pieces worn as ornaments until they were reassembled and hidden under the floor.
30. W. P. Clark, *Indian Sign Language*, p. 80.
31. Finerty, *Warpath and Bivouac*, pp. 344–346.
32. The Cheyenne chief, Two Moon.
33. Finerty, *Warpath and Bivouac*, pp. 327–328.
34. Stanley Vestal, *Sitting Bull*, pp. 225–228.
35. Marquis, *A Warrior Who Fought Custer*, p. 381; Vestal, *Sitting Bull*, p. 171; Stanley Vestal, interview with the authors, April 10, 1951.
36. It was the practice of these Indians to carry a lariat looped over one shoulder—a very useful bit of equipment for a warrior on foot who hoped to go home on someone else's horse.
37. Poor Elk, sometimes called Famished Elk, was killed by Little Wolf while the latter was drunk.
38. Clark, *Indian Sign Language*, pp. 381–382.
39. Thomas B. Marquis, *Memoirs of a White Crow Indian*, pp. 306–310.
40. Granville Stuart, *Forty Years on the Frontier*, II, 216–223.
41. A former trapping partner of "Yellowstone" Kelly who was somewhat of a character around Miles City, where he was often called "Catfish Sandy" because he sometimes fished for a living.
42. John G. Bourke, *On the Border with Crook*, p. 414.
43. Alice Blackwood Baldwin, *Memoirs of the Late Frank D. Baldwin, Major General, USA*, pp. 18–19.
44. Alderson and Smith, *A Bride Goes West*, pp. 215–218.
45. Robert H. Lowie, *The Crow Indians*, p. 238.
46. Not to be confused with the Cheyenne chief with the same name.
47. Joe De Barthe, *Life and Adventures of Frank Grouard*, pp. 231–232.
48. Lowie, *The Crow Indians*, p. xvii.
49. G. I. Powers, letter to authors, December 15, 1950. This information was furnished by Crow informants. Deaf Bull died in 1905, aged 59 years.
50. Frederic Remington, *Pony Tracks*, p. 5.
51. James Mooney, "The Ghost-Dance Religion and the Sioux Outbreak of 1890," *Fourteenth Annual Report of the Bureau of Ethnology*, Part 2, pp. 829–842.
52. *Ibid.*, pp. 816–893.
53. According to Remington, the Cheyennes' name for themselves.
54. Wolf Voice, who also served under Lieutenant Clark years before, is now known as Old Wolf Voice.
55. It was probably Remington's portly appearance that amused the scouts. His

weight sometimes approached the 250-pound mark.

56. Remington, *Pony Tracks*, pp. 22–23.
57. Miles, *Personal Recollections*, pp. 332–333.
58. *Ibid.*, pp. 294–301.
59. Baldwin, *Memoirs of the Late Frank D. Baldwin*, pp. 14–18.
60. *Ibid.*, pp. 191–193.

CHAPTER 5

1. Johnny Ritch, "Shorty's Saloon," *Horse Feathers*, p. 8.
2. Granville Stuart, *Forty Years on the Frontier*, II, 102. This boothill cemetery is preserved today.
3. Located on the north bank of the Yellowstone River opposite the present town of Custer. The site has now been entirely washed away. This was the Frenchman's Ford named in Andy Adams, *Log of a Cowboy*.
4. Sam Gordon, *Recollections of Old Milestown*, p. 3.
5. Those civilians who drifted to the post for protection from hostile Indians, and who, even though they were undesirable to have around, could not be turned out to face the dangers of the hostile land.
6. Major Pease, interview with W. R. Felton, n.d.
7. Stuart, *Forty Years on the Frontier*, II, 105.
8. Gordon, *Recollections of Old Milestown*, pp. 18–19.
9. Illustrated and Historical Edition of *The Yellowstone Journal* (September 27, 1900), pp. 1–2.
10. "Blue Hen" Tomatoes was a brand sold on the frontier for many years.
11. Stuart, *Forty Years on the Frontier*, II, 104.
12. Gordon, *Recollections of Old Milestown*, pp. 27–28.
13. Illustrated and Historical Edition of *The Yellowstone Journal* (September 27, 1900), p. 18.
14. I recall when President McKinley was assassinated, the mayor put out a proclamation requesting all business houses and saloons to close during the funeral hour. There was great consternation among the saloon proprietors. They could find no keys. Actually there were no keys, never had been. However, they nailed a board across the front door and remained closed for an hour. —William Lakin to authors, January 18, 1950.
15. *Ibid.*
16. One of the two earliest recollections of Huffman's daughter Bessie was of the yelling and shooting associated with the cowboys' visits to town. (The other was the howling of the coyotes on the badland bluffs just north of Miles City— a nightly serenade in the wintertime which started with the lighting of the lights in the evening.)
17. Quoted in the *Miles City Daily Star* (May 24, 1934), Sec. II, pp. 9, 16.
18. *Ibid.*, Sec. III, p. 16.
19. Gordon, *Recollections of Old Milestown*, p. 5.
20. Illustrated and Historical Edition of *The Yellowstone Journal* (September 27, 1900), pp. 18–19.
21. Nannie T. Alderson and Helena H. Smith, *A Bride Goes West*, p. 22.
22. *Ibid.*, p. 21.
23. Gordon, *Recollections of Old Milestown*, p. 4.
24. E. C. Abbott and Helena H. Smith, *We Pointed Them North*, p. 128.
25. Gamblers.
26. Lakin to authors, January 18, 1950.
27. Equivalent of a burlesque show or low-grade vaudeville.
28. Abbott and Smith, *We Pointed Them North*, p. 126.
29. Alderson and Smith, *A Bride Goes West*, pp. 114–117.

30. Badger Clark to authors, December 28, 1950. Mr. Clark's father preached Calamity Jane's funeral sermon.
31. Estelline Bennett, *Old Deadwood Days*, pp. 220–221.
32. John G. Bourke, *On the Border with Crook*, pp. 299–300.
33. *Miles City Daily Star* (May 24, 1934), Sec. III, p. 7.
34. Younger sons of titled families who came to the West and who were supported, to varying degrees, by remittances from home.
35. An anvil was "shot" by turning it upside down and filling the small hole in the center of the base with powder and then laying a train to the outside edge. A second anvil was then set on top and the train lighted. The ensuing explosion would toss the upper anvil off and made considerable noise.
36. Huffman was president of a social club of bachelors.
37. Theodore Roosevelt, *Ranch Life and the Hunting Trail*, p. 7.
38. Stella W. Brummitt, *Brother Van*, pp. 33–35.
39. Psalm singers—ministers.
40. Charles M. Russell to Rev. W. W. Van Orsdel, March 20, 1918. Quoted in *Miles City Daily Star* (May 24, 1934), Sec. V, p. 19; Charles M. Russell, *Good Medicine*, p. 98.
41. Prominent merchant of the firm Leighton, Jordan and Company.
42. Gordon, *Recollections of Old Milestown*, pp. 4–5.
43. Price Terrett to authors, November 3, 1950.
44. Neil M. Clark, "He Captured the Vanishing West Before It Vanished," *The American Magazine* (February, 1927), pp. 12, 74.
45. Price Terrett to authors, November 3, 1950. Geddes actually got 99 years at the first trial. The verdict was appealed and nothing more came of the matter. Eventually Geddes drifted out of the country.
46. *Ibid.*
47. Abbott and Smith, *We Pointed Them North*, pp. 122–124; Charles M. Russell, *Trails Plowed Under*, p. 151.
48. Neil M. Clark, draft manuscript for "He Captured the Vanishing West Before It Vanished."
49. *The Medal of Honor of the United States Army*, p. 226.
50. Just east of the present town of Terry.
51. One of Parrott's lieutenants.
52. This account credits Wilson with being in the famous Adobe Walls fight, June 27, 1874. He may have been in the vicinity but his name is not listed by Billy Dixon. Olive Dixon, *Life of Billy Dixon*, p. 160.
53. Clark, draft manuscript for "He Captured the Vanishing West Before It Vanished."
54. Agnes Wright Spring, *The Cheyenne and Black Hills Stage and Express Routes*, pp. 200, 252, 254, 285, 287; *The Yellowstone Journal* (July 17, 1880; July 31, 1880); *Avant-Courier* (February 20, 1879); *The Park County News* (Wyoming) (July 9, 1934); *Judith Basin County Press* (March 6, 1933); Frank Conley letter to Ray Stilth, December 19, 1933.
55. Gordon, *Recollections of Old Milestown*, p. 38.
56. One friend of Huffman's commented that he strongly suspected that the photographer was one of this "3-7-77" committee but he was never able to confirm the suspicion.
57. Illustrated and Historical Edition of *The Yellowstone Journal* (September 27, 1900), p. 6.
58. *Ibid.*
59. *Ibid.*
60. Gordon, *Recollections of Old Milestown*, pp. 41–42.
61. *Miles City Daily Star* (May 24, 1934), Sec. II, p. 2.
62. Quoted in an unidentified newspaper clipping.

63. A. D. McAusland, interview with W. R. Felton (n.d.).

CHAPTER 6

1. Joseph Mills Hanson, *The Conquest of the Missouri*, pp. 174–185.
2. Illustrated and Historical Edition of *The Yellowstone Journal* (September 27, 1900), p. 1.
3. W. A. Clark, "Centennial Address" etc., *Contributions to the Historical Society of Montana*, II, 58.
4. Robert Vaughn, *Then and Now*, p. 242.
5. John K. Rollinson, *Pony Trails in Wyoming*, p. 266.
6. Illustrated and Historical Edition of *The Yellowstone Journal* (September 27, 1900), p. 1.
7. Paul McCormick was associated with Major Pease in the ill-fated attempt to establish a trading post at the mouth of the Big Horn in 1875–1876. M. Carroll was Matthew "Matt" Carroll, the partner in the Diamond R freighting company who personally supervised the train supplying Gibbon's troops in 1876 and who remained at Fort Keogh until 1878.
8. Document in the library of the Historical Society of Montana.
9. From a copy of the original document, courtesy of Historical Society of Montana.
10. Corrine, Utah, the point on the Union Pacific Railroad to which freight was delivered for pickup by freighters from central Montana.
11. Alexander Toponce, *Reminiscences of Alexander Toponce*, pp. 91–92.
12. Matthew Carroll, "Diary of Matthew Carroll," *Contributions to the Historical Society of Montana*, II, 229–234.
13. Vaughn, *Then and Now*, pp. 113–114.
14. The animals hooked together as a unit were called a *team* regardless of whether they numbered two or 20.
15. Luther S. Kelly, *Yellowstone Kelly*, p. 104.
16. Sam Gordon, *Recollections of Old Milestown*, pp. 20–21.
17. Lewis F. Crawford, *Rekindling Campfires*, p. 101; Toponce, *Reminiscences*, p. 114. The term "galvanized" referred to a very thin coating of loyalty to the Union covering a man who was at heart an unreconstructed Rebel.
18. Gordon, *Recollections of Old Milestown*, p. 20.
19. *Ibid.*, pp. 20–21.
20. A merchant in Helena.
21. From an original contract dated "July 10 & 11, 1874" in the library of the Historical Society of Montana.
22. *The Helena Independent* (March 1, 1937).
23. Hiram M. Chittenden, *History of Early Steamboat Navigation on the Missouri River*, II, 330.
24. The R in the trademark stands for Roe who apparently used this mark as a trademark before the freighting company was formed.
25. Chittenden, *History of Early Steamboat Navigation*, II, 325–330.
26. *Ibid.*, II, 329.
27. Toponce, *Reminiscences*, pp. 89–90.
28. *The Helena Independent* (March 1, 1937).
29. *The Helena Weekly Herald* (June 25, 1868).
30. A form contract used by the contracting office in St. Louis and dated 1874 contained the following stipulations regarding shipments. In view of the settlement the founders of the Diamond R forced on La Barge, that provision specifying that cost of the shipment *at point of origin* should govern in event of any claims is extremely interesting.

Received from _____ the following packages, contents unknown, in apparent good order, dangers of river navigation excepted: Marked and Numbered as per margin, to be transported from ST. LOUIS to their said place of ultimate destination. The packages aforesaid must pass through the custody of several carriers; it is understood as a part of the consideration on which said packages are received, that the exceptions from the liability made by such carriers as a part of the consideration on which the said packages are received, that the exceptions from the liability made by such carriers respectively, shall operate in the carriage by them respectively of such packages, as though herein inserted in length; and especially that neither said carriers, or either or any of them shall be liable for leakage of any kinds of liquids, or for losses by the bursting of Casks or Barrels of Liquids, arising from expansion or other unavoidable causes; breakage of any kind of Glass, Carboys of Acids, or articles packed in Glass; Stoves and Stove Furniture, Castings, Machinery, Carriages, Furniture, Musical Instruments of any kind, packages of Eggs; or for loss or damage on Hay, Hemp, Cotton, or the evaporation or leakage of Alcohol; or leakage of Oil of any description, or for damage to perishable property of any kind, occasioned by delays from any cause or change of weather, or for loss or damage by fire, or for loss or damage on the sea or rivers. And it is further especially understood, that for all loss or damage occurring in the transit of said packages, the legal remedy shall be against the particular carrier only, in whose custody the said packages may actually be at the time of the happening thereof. All goods carried by this company are charged at actual gross weight, excepting such articles as are provided in our General Tariff.

All property will be subject to necessary cooperage, and the freight to be paid on the actual gross weight, as ascertained by the Company's scales. Claims for damage must be reported by the consignee to delivering line within thirty-six hours after the arrival of the freight at the point of delivery indicated above. In the event of the loss of property under the provisions of this agreement, the value or cost at the point of shipment shall govern the settlement of the same.

No liability will be assumed for wrong carriage or wrong delivery of goods that are marked with initials, numbered or imperfectly marked.

No liability will be assumed for any losses that may occur in the transportation of Merchandise, &c. by the Missouri River from Bismarck to Carroll.

NOTICE.—In accepting this contract, the shipper or other agent of the owner of the property expressly agrees to all its stipulations, exceptions and conditions.

31. Vaughn, *Then and Now*, p. 240. Broadwater may have been a partner from the start, *Montana Post* (June 19, 1868).
32. The Illustrated and Historical Edition of *The Yellowstone Journal* (September 27, 1900), p. 1.
33. George O. Shields, *Rustlings in the Rockies*, p. 153.
34. Arnold O. Goplen, *The Career of Marquis de Mores in the Badlands of North Dakota*, pp. 33–37.
35. John Clay, *My Life on the Range*, pp. 86–87.
36. Granville Stuart, *Forty Years on the Frontier*, II, 100–101.
37. The "last spike" was driven at Gold Creek, Montana, on September 8, 1883. Either Huffman is in error about the extent of old Nig's service or this horse worked on some branch lines in Idaho.
38. Shields, *Rustlings in the Rockies*, pp. 136–137.
39. Nannie T. Alderson and Helena H. Smith, *A Bride Goes West*, p. 25.
40. *Ibid.*, pp. 24–25.

CHAPTER 7

1. Charles M. Russell, *Good Medicine*, p. 27.
2. Struthers Burt, *Powder River*, p. 198.

3. George F. Kennan, "America and the Russian Future," *Foreign Affairs*, 29 (April, 1951), 356.

4. A grain or gunny sack used as a substitute for a trunk.

5. Huffman, "The Cheyenne Indians," Illustrated and Historical Edition of *The Yellowstone Journal* (September 27, 1900), p. 14.

6. Outstanding among these were Captain John G. Bourke, General Crook's aide, and Huffman's friend, Lieutenant (later Captain) William Philo Clark, whom the Indians called "White Hat."

7. Granville Stuart, *Forty Years on the Frontier*, II, 51.

8. Quoted in Homer W. Wheeler, *The Frontier Trail*, p. 303.

9. Huffman, manuscript for "The Cheyenne Indians" (1900).

10. Campbell is "Stanley Vestal."

11. Campbell, interview with author, April 10, 1951.

12. W. P. Clark, *Indian Sign Language*, p. 82.

13. John G. Bourke, *On the Border with Crook*, p. 407. Bourke identified Three Bears and Feather-on-the-Head as Sioux.

14. John McLaughin, *My Friend the Indian*, pp. 303–306.

15. Clark, *Indian Sign Language*, p. 186.

16. These people ranged south of the Yellowstone. The Cheyennes and Arapahoes forced some Crows north of the Missouri. These allied themselves with the Gros Ventres of the Prairie and were known as the River Crows. Clark, *Indian Sign Language*, p. 134; Frederic Webb Hodge (ed.), *Handbook of American Indians North of Mexico*, I, 368–369.

17. Taylor was a scout with Gibbons' troops during the campaign against the Sioux; Terry sent him with dispatches to Fort Ellis after Custer's defeat.

18. E. S. Topping, *Chronicles of the Yellowstone*, p. 163.

19. This killing in 1897 caused a little flurry of apprehension among the settlers.

20. Yellow Hair and his wife, Teressa, had the first Christian marriage ceremony among the Cheyennes.

21. Nannie T. Alderson and Helena H. Smith, *A Bride Goes West*, pp. 47–48.

22. Clark, *Indian Sign Language*, p. 148.

23. There are various recipes. Usually it was half plug tobacco shaved thin and half dried inner bark of red willow or the bark of "kinnikinic," commonly known as "larb."

24. Clark, *Indian Sign Language*, pp. 230–231.

25. Walter Campbell, "The Tipis of the Crow Indians," *American Anthropologist* (January–March, 1927), pp. 87–104.

26. Clark made the general observation that

> Indians, as a rule, are more careful in regard to the cleanliness of their cooking utensils than their usually dirty and sometimes filthy personal conditions would indicate. . . . Indians now use large iron camp-kettles issued by the agent and sold by the traders, and nearly every article of food is cooked by boiling. Meat is seldom fried. Should they desire a change, or when away from their camps, hunting, etc., the meat is roasted by hanging on a stick near the fire. In this way it retains its juices, and is wonderfully good.

Clark, *Indian Sign Language*, p. 123.

27. Thomas B. Marquis, *A Warrior Who Fought Custer*, pp. 135–137.

28. Probably the noted medicine man, White Bull, or perhaps Brave Wolf.

29. Clark, *Indian Sign Language*, pp. 365–368.

30. Hodge, *Handbook of American Indians North of Mexico*, I, 23.

31. Clark Wissler, *Indian Cavalcade*, pp. 119, 132.

32. Bourke, *On the Border with Crook*, p. 343; Clark, *Indian Sign Language*, pp. 252–253; Wheeler, *The Frontier Trail*, pp. 182–184, 246–300.

33. Clark, *Indian Sign Language*, p. 186.

34. George Bird Grinnell, *The Cheyenne Indians*, I, 84.
35. Vestal, *Sitting Bull*, pp. 152–153.
36. Grinnell, *The Cheyenne Indians*, II, 112–113.
37. *Ibid.*, II, 152–153.
38. Vestal, *Warpath*, p. 132.
39. Grinnell, *The Fighting Cheyennes*, pp. 276–277. Roman Nose was killed September 17, 1868.
40. Rufus Wallowing letter to authors, April, 1951. The present version is that White Bull died while the Cheyennes were camped in the vicinity of the present Busby School. He was buried, and a stone which it took ten men to lift was placed on the grave. The next morning he was alive and walked into his tepee. The heavy stone was found laid to one side.
41. Grinnell, *The Cheyenne Indians*, II, 115–117.
42. Anne Heloise Abel (ed.), *Tabeau's Narrative of Loisel's Expedition to the Upper Missouri*, pp. 187–189.
43. Bourke, *On the Border with Crook*, pp. 407–408.
44. Half-breed son of William Rowland.
45. A Cheyenne warrior society.
46. Marquis, *A Warrior Who Fought Custer*, p. 381. Wooden Leg also related that, on one occasion when in Washington with a delegation, Two Moon spun a long story about the Battle of the Little Big Horn and his own importance. "None of us said anything in dispute to him at the meeting, but when we got away to ourselves Black Wolf said to him: 'You are the biggest liar in the whole Cheyenne tribe.' Two Moon laughed and replied: 'I think it is not wrong to tell lies to white people'" (p. 360).
47. President of the Northern Cheyenne Tribal Council.
48. One of the seven warrior societies, whose membership was composed of the principal chiefs. Grinnell refers to this group as the "Chief Soldiers."
49. Rufus Wallowing to authors, April, 1951.
50. A small creek just west of Fort Keogh now called Moon Creek.
51. As Little Chief was involved in the Ghost Dance trouble this was probably after 1890.
52. Huffman, "The Cheyenne Indians," Illustrated and Historical Edition of *The Yellowstone Journal* (September 27, 1900), p. 14.
53. *Ibid.*, p. 13.
54. Neil M. Clark, draft manuscript for "He Captured the Vanishing West Before It Vanished."
55. This is Huffman's translation.

NOTES ON PHOTOGRAPHS

2. "This is a very distant shot of the open country. The long line of cottonwoods across the background indicates where the river finds its way down the valley. The foreground shows the camp and cavvy corral, likewise down the river is another camp the same—and the dust across the river indicates a third. These range dwellers needed lots of room and they had it." L.A.H.

3. This picture was taken in November, 1902, on the Fort Berthold Indian reservation while accompanying Olin D. Wheeler. This author observed, "In my visit to the reservation in the fall of 1902 I saw two of these lodges and obtained photographs of them. If there were any differences between these and those of one hundred years ago, except the substitution of wooden for skin doors, they were so slight as not to be noticeable offhand. . . . Those I saw were forty feet in diameter, perhaps, and the first had nine sides and the second eleven." (O. D. Wheeler, *The Trail of Lewis and Clark 1804–1904*, I, 219–220.)

4. O. D. Wheeler interviewing Two Chiefs and his daughter, Mrs. Baker. In checking on the effects of the terrible scourge of smallpox on the once-powerful Mandan tribe, Wheeler asked Two Chiefs "how many full blood, pure Mandans" he thought still remained. The old man, 72 years of age, stood in deep thought for several moments, and then replied, "Not more than ten families; all the others are mixed blood." (Wheeler, *op. cit.*, I, 242.) This Indian and Leggins (*Picture no. 5*) were small children when the tribe was practically wiped out. This photograph was taken near Elbow Woods, North Dakota.

5. Wheeler, in commenting on the dignity and character ascribed to Meto-Tope' and other early Mandan leaders by Maximilian, Catlin, and others in the pre-smallpox days, noted that, "Two Chiefs and Leggins . . . must also have been men of dignity and character." (Wheeler, *op. cit.*, I, 240.)

8. Huffman referred to this Indian, Scorched Lightning, as a member of Spotted Eagle's band.

9. "The Spotted Eagle Village was the last great leather lodge village seen on the Yellowstone. These lodges were pitched in the fall of 1880 near Fort Keogh when the Spotted Eagle band numbering nearly 2500 people of the Sioux nation surrendered to General Miles. This is the village where Rain-in-the-Face was also a prisoner of war. General Miles said, to the author of this picture, only a few years before he passed away, 'This was the last place, so far as I know, where the Indian still used buffalo meat for his food, tanned the skins for his leather lodge, and the robes for his blanket.' " L.A.H.

10. "This picture shows the main street looking west from near the center, before there were any cross streets. Also toward the ferry crossing of Tongue River on the road leading to . . . Fort Keogh. . . . The old road wound in and out around the mud holes. The buildings, mostly log covered with the earliest shingles brought into the country by steamboat and whipsawed cottonwood boards of the native cottonwood trees. The buildings were occupied by dealers in red alcohol, later known as whiskey and used as dance halls where proprietors had both white, and under some roofs saddle-colored black women as partners for their male patrons. On the right side of the street are shown the "Diamond R" and other large merchandising establishments that bought buffalo hides and other peltries from the Buffalo hunters and carried extensive stocks of general merchandise. Some of these firms, at a later date and prior to the coming of the Northern Pacific Railroad, added to their stocks merchandise suitable to the use of the Trail drivers and cattle men then about to make their first appearance lured by the abundance of free grass on what was soon to be the outlet, the grazing ground for vast numbers of cattle from the south and south western breeding grounds of trail cattle." L.A.H.

11. This was the studio at Fort Keogh. The type of construction was similar to that used in the cantonment except that many of the roofs at the first post were flat. Note the double window at the right and the skylight.

12. Huffman left a partial identification as follows: (seated on chairs, *left to right*) "Stager, Yates, Phil Sheridan, Mc Cullough," unidentified; (on ground, *left to right*) unidentified, unidentified, "Mike Sheridan," unidentified, "Philo Clark." William Philo Clark was the officer of the Second Cavalry whose name occurs frequently in Chapters 4 and 7 as a close student of Indian life.

14. "Some of the buildings of the Indian Agency are shown in the distant center of the picture. It was just a little to the left of this group of distant buildings that I built my first home in Montana in 1880. After discussing the proposition with Granville Stuart and Tom Irvine I turned loose the first HL cattle, and they were the first range cattle, as far as I know, in this section of the country. This afterward became the Agency for 'Two Moon' and his Northern Cheyennes." L.A.H.

15. Huffman identified this man, Spotted Bear, as a Sioux although he put in his notes that he lived among the Cheyennes.

17. "This typical scene of Old Powder River Days is at the mouth of 10 mile creek on Powder River, just below the old '44' crossing. See the blazed faced stocking legged, cutting horse at work turning the white steer. You can almost smell the sage brush and the dust, while in the back along the creek, the peaceful roundup camp shows plainly, with the grazing cavvy on the hillside beyond." L.A.H.

19. On Custer's last battlefield. These are horse bones. Note the detopped cavalryman's boot hung on the top of a grave stake, and the white tents of the camp of the burial detail at the foot of the slope.

21. "Fifteen wild buffalo (count them) quietly grazing on the prairies of Northern

Montana. This photograph was taken in the country between the Yellowstone and Missouri Rivers during the last stages of the great tragedy—the extermination of the American bison on this continent." L.A.H.

22. Huffman identified High Bear as a "sub chief of Spotted Eagle's band." There were several prominent Indians with this name.

23. "In the eighties it was still possible to see herds of six hundred to one thousand buffalo in many of the smaller valleys or on the high plateaus between the Yellowstone and Missouri Rivers. This picture is thought by the author to be the most typical and portrays best what he saw from between his horse's ears in this then savage land." L.A.H.

25. "I knew when this old camp, a relic of the buffalo days, was built in the late seventies. The hill at the back of it was the hunter's lookout, from which he located the migrating herds of buffalo and planned his day's work. The spring had failed years before. Thrifty young pines and cedars grew in the path the hide hunters had made so long ago." L.A.H.

26. "This picture shows the killing of nine cows and spikes and my old flaxey saddle horse and the 45 by 120 Reliable Sharps gun. The original negative was taken in the Smoky Butte country in 1882, near the end of the great tragedy, the extermination of the American bison by red men and white, which was then nearing its culmination, between the Missouri and the Yellowstone. . . . Nine animals are shown. The killing was scattered over a mile of rough breaks, and numbered a total of forty cows and young bulls in all. What an AWFUL waste it was!" L.A.H.

   This is photograph "No. 188" referred to in the letter dated March 19, 1882. The ninth buffalo—Huffman to the contrary—was never shown in this group of pictures. Apparently it lay nearby as its head, cut off for a skinning wedge, shows in another photograph.

28. "The picture shows a couple of bulls and the skinning wedge. First off once a killing was down, a head was taken from a medium sized bull, the horns, not too large, served as handles. They were roughened by hacking with skinning knives or hatchet, so that the handles would not slip thru the greasy, bloody hands when it was being carried or dragged from one carcass to another by a lariat attached to the horn of the saddle. The reason this wedge was used was because it was the only thing available, the country being treeless and the rocks frozen down. It was used to slip under the half skinned carcass so that it would be easier to get the heavy bull hide from under [the carcass]." L.A.H.

29. "This was taken in rougher country [than the other series] and shows our saddle horses and the skinners at work on a monster bull when weather was extremely cold and the carcasses scattered in difficult situations." L.A.H.

   In contrast to the cow shown in another photograph, the hide has been cut around the neck and the head left entirely unskinned. This picture shows the skinning wedge in use with the nose placed outward, perhaps to hide the unsightly severed end. One Texas hunter wrote, "Another way of skinning was . . . [to] take the head off at the neck and place the nose under the buffalo with the horns on the ground turning the buffalo up against it."

30. The head of the skinned animal shows the customary practice of skinning out all of the head on cows and spikes except for a small area around the horns. Note the butcher's steel, for touching up the skinning knife, lying on the skinned carcass.

31. This is the camp to which Huffman referred in the letter to his father: "The camp where you see the two grindstones is where we divided up." The grind-

stones are on either side of the door. Note the mountain sheep's head, buffalo fetus, and the large scabbard containing skinning knives and a butcher's steel on the belt of the nearer hunter.

35. This photograph indicates the popular hunting arms of this date. Seated on the left is Ed Forest, a settler on Clark Fork, with an 1873 Winchester. This long-popular arm was a .44–40 caliber, carried 15 cartridges in the magazine, and, in the octagon barrel, weighed nine pounds. Just behind Forest is Shields with his .40–75 Sharps-Borchardt. The very fast hammerless action, coupled with the traditional Sharps accuracy, made this rifle one of the best single-shot rifles. William Allen, with an 1873 single-action Colt, has a .45–70 "Centennial" model Winchester, which drew its name from the year of its manufacture —1876. This rifle weighed nine and a half pounds and carried 12 cartridges. Allen's son, Willie, has a Stevens "Premier" rifle with a "tip-up" action, probably in a .32 caliber. Mike Weise, standing, also had a .45–70 1876 Winchester, and R. J. Sawyer holds a .50–95 1876 Winchester which, in this caliber, was known as the "Winchester Express." Huffman's Kennedy is not shown.

38. "A professional wolfer's 'roost' in the Hell Creek Breaks of Northern Montana. Wolfers lead a lonely life. Some of them are educated men and tidy housekeepers. A wolfer destroys wolves for the bounty paid by the state, the pelts sold to fur dealers, and ofttimes for an additional fee from nearby cattlemen." L.A.H. (Sieber's Cabin)

40. "This picture shows a portion of Spotted Eagle's village beside the old freight road that led from Fort Abraham Lincoln, where the city of Mandan, N. D. is now situated near the Missouri River, to Bozeman and Virginia City, Montana by way of Fort Keogh, Coulson and Livingston. This road was trodden by the 'Diamond R' bull trains and hundreds of six mule army wagons carrying goods for these outlying posts in the late seventies." L.A.H.

44. The wives of Chief Hump were obviously sisters, sisters being more desirable for plural wives than nonrelatives because they quarreled less.

45. Little Chief, a wise and able leader, was respected among his people for his sincerity and dignity. An old photograph reproduced in John M. Cook, *Fifty Years on the Old Frontier*, shows Little Chief wearing this cross ornament when he surrendered his Sharps carbine to John Cook at the end of the Ghost Dance trouble, January 15, 1891. He was also known to his people by the names Red Nose and Cross Necklace. He died in 1905 and was buried in the vicinity of Busby, Montana.

47. Huffman referred to this warrior, Red Armed Panther, as "a good scout, a good shot and a royal good hunting companion . . ." After scouting for Miles, he became an Indian policeman at Lame Deer, and was killed when lightning struck the head of his couch as he slept.

48. Major Guido Ilges, a genial Bavarian who held the rank of colonel during the Civil War, was stationed at Fort Benton during the Nez Perce trouble, and took the surrender of Gall and his followers at Poplar River in January, 1881. Lieutenant Frederick W. Sibley was in charge of the party of 25 soldiers and three civilians who played a desperate game of hide and seek in the Big Horn Mountains with the Sioux after the Battle of the Rosebud. W. D. Knight was editor of *The Yellowstone Journal* in Miles City. Joe Culbertson, scout, was the son of Alexander Culbertson and Medicine Snake Woman, daughter of a Blood (Blackfoot) chief. Lieutenants Defrees and Aris and Huffman (Nibbs) completed the party.

50. Note the expressive "sign" for the shooting of a rifle. This sign was followed, when describing a battle, by a very rapid clapping of the hands to imitate rifle fire.

51. The "sign" is easy to read and very expressive. Lieutenant Clark describes it thus:
   "Exterminate. Conception: Wiped out. Hold left hand in front of the body, palm up, fingers extended, touching, pointing to front and right; bring palm of extended right hand just over left wrist, fingers extended, touching, and pointing to left and front; move the right hand outwards and to right, pressing palms together. . . ."
   The white man is Olin D. Wheeler, publicity man for the Northern Pacific Railroad.

52. Huffman identified this group as, "Hump, war chief of Minneconjoux Sioux, with head men—Tall Bear, Wht [White] Magpie, Wolf Voice, Big Road, & Wolf Robe." Properly interpreted, Big Road becomes Broad Trail. Tall Bear, a medicine man, is seated in the center holding a staff wrapped with otter skin with one hand and a bunch of sacred sage with the other.

53. *Captain Keogh's* bones were removed from the battlefield (along with those of several other officers) and were buried at Auburn, N. Y., on October 25, 1877. The officer in the foreground was Lieutenant Henry J. Nowlan.

54. Stakes mark the locations of the bones buried by the detail. The bones in the foreground are, obviously, horse bones. Note the cavalryman's boot from which some Indian cut the top.

55. The bones used to fill the center of the first monument on the Custer battlefield were horse bones.

57. One day in 1877 Dull Knife and his family lunched with General Crook and his staff at Fort Robinson. Bourke observed: ". . . his three daughters. . . . were fairly good looking—the Cheyennes will compare favorably in appearance with any people I've seen—and were quite young; one of nine or ten, one of twelve, and the oldest not yet twenty—a young widow who, with the coquettishness of the sex, wore her skirts no lower than the knees to let the world see that in her grief for her husband, killed in our fight of November 25th, she had gashed and cut her limbs in accordance with the severest requirements of Cheyenne etiquette."

58. Lariats were often worn in the old days (as shown) when the men went out to the horse herds in the morning. It was the carrying of this piece of equipment by horse thieves slipping stealthily across the country on foot that gave rise to the term "lariat Indians."

60. Huffman's title, "Good Eye, Fierce old Crow buck," is in error as to the name but not as to the Indian's nature.

61. These scouts undoubtedly date back to the late 1870's.

62. Sweetmedicine was one of the first Cheyennes to accept the Christian faith. He died in June, 1932.

63. If this warrior was an important individual, it is strange that his name does not appear in the histories of these days. One lifelong student of the Plains Indians has suggested this may be a case of multiple names. If Huffman's notes are correct, this man may be Big Foot whose band was practically wiped out at Wounded Knee.

76. "T. H. Irvine . . . was one of the old time sheriffs of Montana. The man at his right got his early education man-hunting with the Texas Rangers. . . . At this writing only one of the five has passed in his checks. These men could write interesting stories, but are not built that way, they were men of action. . . . Taken at Milestown in the early eighties." L.A.H.
   Left to right: Billy Smith (later a stock inspector), Jack Hawkins (ex-Texas Ranger), Tom Irvine (Huffman's good friend), Louis King (a saloon keeper), and "Eph" Davis (a frontiersman).

78. Corner of Fifth and Main—also known as the Diamond R Corner. Looking west: Broadwater, Hubbell & Co., Chinnick's Saloon (next), and Borchardt's Store (then the post office) at the further corner.

79. "A Cheyenne Scout In the Old Stockade. Scaffold, Noose, keg that was to be kicked, coffin and white shroud all had been provided but he fixt it that only the last two—coffin and shroud—were needed. Now the site is covered by a bank block." L.A.H.

83. "This is a characteristic jerk line team of twelve horses on the old toll road [on the north bank of the Yellowstone] between Billings and Miles City. The jerk line held by the driver who rides the near wheel horse is passed over the hame of each horse on its way to the bit of the trained lead horse, as shown. One hard pull or jerk . . . was the signal for him to bear left, two steady pulls or jerks meant the opposite, and in this way the team was guided." L.A.H.

93. Captain Bourke observed that he thought Indian children were probably the happiest in the world.

94. *Left*—Little Eagle; *right*—Young Bear.

99. Rain-in-the-Face is said to have "had seven wives, few of whom lived long or happily with him; the last wife was found in his tipi with her throat cut."

101. "I made this picture at Fort Keogh, Montana in 1879 or 1880 when a large band of Crows were hunting, trading, racing horses and bartering buffalo skins and their women with the white hunters and rivermen wintering near Fort Keogh. Sits Down Spotted shows the old time Crow pompadour, so characteristic of that time. His necklace and hair ornaments, and his old Hudson Bay blanket coat make up an ensemble very much not in evidence among Agency Indians." L.A.H.

There is some question whether the name given is correct. The Sharps is believed to have been Huffman's.

102. The knife and sheath have apparently been arranged for pictorial effect. Normally it would be carried on a belt around the waist.

103. The buffalo hide on the frame is probably in the last or softening stage of the tanning process, and the long gray object nearby is a travois basket with a hide covering.

104. The wicker cage is called a travois basket, a very comfortable conveyance to ride in. The hut almost hidden in the background is of considerable interest as it is the type used by the Chippewa in the upper Mississippi River country. As the Cheyennes are thought to have migrated westward from this region in the dim past, this hut would appear to be a remnant of a culture dating back many, many years.

105. "These Indians, like the Spotted Eagle Indians, were very poor, and the picture shows how the hungry dogs at night would chew holes in the lodges to get the sinews with which the tepees were sown together. Such holes had to be mended with Indian cloth." L.A.H.

The tepee just beyond the twisted tree illustrates well the characteristic Sioux slope to the rear and the three-pole foundation with the front pole projecting well below the others. In a tinted picture Huffman indicated that these patches were bright green and red in color.

106. Note the medicine bundle over the entrance to the tepee, and the manner of stacking the poles.

108. " 'Plenty Bird' was a friend, a good sign talker. Had a tidy Cheyenne wife, easy to look at." L.A.H.

110. Beginning on the left, these men are: Woman Leggins, John Strange Owl,

Zac. Rowland, Charles Little Sun, John Crazy Mule, Miles Seminole, Frank Stump Horn, Dick Bull Head, Sponge, Young Bear, Hubert Hollow Breast, White Shield, Weasel Bear, Charles Spotted Elk, William Red Bird, Crane, Robert Ridge Walker, Arthur Ghost Bull, Charles Teeth, John Black Wolf, William Wolf Name, Red Fox, and Jacob Tall Bull. Of these, Miles Seminole and Hubert Hollow Breast were living in 1951.

111. Wolf Voice is shown in his uniform as an Indian policeman. His brother, William Yellow Robe, was living in 1951.

112. The wrapping on the staff that Tall Bear is holding appears to be otter skin, and the material in the left hand is a bundle of sacred sage.

113. "Brave Wolf was a trusted scout, and a friend of Lieut. Hunter Liggett (now Brig. General Liggett, retired). Lt. Liggett and Brave Wolf were frequent visitors at my log shack at Fort Keogh, M.T." L.A.H.

   Brave Wolf was a brave, intelligent man who was highly respected by all who have written about him. War correspondent Finerty noted that he "was as graceful as a courtier, and had a face of remarkable refinement." His wife's name was Hokŏtă, or Corn Woman. Note that Huffman, for pictorial effect, has moved the buffalo skull from its proper position in relation to the sweat lodge; also that respectable Indian women sit gracefully with their feet both on the same side, never cross-legged.

114. White Bull, also called Ice, was a famous Cheyenne medicine man, and the first warrior to enlist as a scout under General Miles in 1877.

115. Shown are the original buildings of the Saint Labre Indian Mission founded in 1885 near Ashland, Montana. Huffman took this picture about 1898 at which time he posed the staff at the school beside the then-abandoned original buildings. Shown (*left to right*) are Sisters Gertrude, Barbara, and Monica, Mother Mary of the Angels (Superior), Sisters Thecla and Hildegarde, and Father Vermaat.

   The founders were Father Eilers, a Jesuit priest, and Mother Ignatius, Mother Joseph, Sister Angefa, and Sister Mary Gertrude, members of the Ursuline order. The founders were succeeded by the staff shown.

116. "American Horse, his two wives, two daughters and son beside the camp in which he spent his last days in peace and quiet. His life had been a stormy one. In spite of his domestic relations being openly contrary to our ethics, these wives, children, sons-in-law, and some aged ones all seemed to love and respect American Horse. Hospitable he was, with a quiet voice and manner." L.A.H.

   Shown (*right to left*) are American Horse, Walter, Ma-ove-sa, Mo-no-ne, Maheone-ho-ne, and Ta-ta-amha. The decorations on the tepee are imitation scalplocks, said to be symbols of good luck.

117. " 'Two Moon,' whose name in Sioux as We-no-pa, . . . is shown in his war bonnet in my old log shack at Fort Keogh. His Cheyenne name seldom used, except by his own people, never by myself, was Isha-O-Nishus." L.A.H.

118. "This picture of chief 'Two Moon' is the most classic one of the many that were made of him in his lifetime. Two Moon, at my suggestion, stood six feet in front of the monument on Custer's Hill and took off his old straw hat with the feather in it, lifted his hand while I told him that he would never see it again. Thereafter he was almost blind for seven years. How it chanced that he did see it again for a time before his death is another story." L.A.H.

124. "Taken in January 1879 when we were buffalo hunting near the present site of Jordan, Montana. The grave was new, its occupant having been killed but a few days. The site overlooked a vast plain, checkered with trails and dotted with moving herds of buffalo." L.A.H.

BIBLIOGRAPHY

A. MANUSCRIPTS, etc.

Huffman, L. A.
    Miscellaneous manuscripts, letters, and notes.
Historical Society of Montana
    Miscellaneous papers.

B. NEWSPAPERS, MAGAZINES, etc.

The American Anthropologist.
The American Field.
The American Magazine.
The Awk.
The Billings Gazette.
The Black Hills Engineer.
The Breeders Gazette.
Evening Montanan.
The Fergus County Argus.
Foreign Affairs.
The Frazier Journal.
Helena Independent.
The Judith Gap Journal.
Miles City American.
Miles City Daily Star.
The Mississippi Valley Historical Review.
The Montana Magazine of History.
The National Geographic Magazine.
North Dakota History.
Panhandle-Plains Historical Review.
Popular Mechanics.
The Saturday Evening Post.
The Square Butte Tribune.
The Yellowstone Journal.

C. BOOKS, PAMPHLETS, etc.

Abbott, E. C., and Smith, Helena Huntington. *We Pointed Them North.* New York, 1939.

Adair, Cornelia. *My Diary: August 30th to November 5th, 1874.* Bath (England), 1918.

Aikman, Duncan. *Calamity Jane and the Lady Wildcats.* New York, 1927.

Alderson, Nannie T., and Smith, Helena Huntington. *A Bride Goes West.* New York, 1942.

Allen, William A. *Adventures with Indians and Game.* Chicago, 1903.

Alter, J. Cecil. *James Bridger.* Salt Lake City, 1925.

Baldwin, Alice Blackwood. *Memoirs of the Late Frank D. Baldwin, Major General, USA.* Los Angeles, 1929.

Banks, Eleanor. *Wandersong.* Caldwell, 1950.

Bennett, Estelline. *Old Deadwood Days.* New York, 1935.

Benton, T. H., and Gray, A. L. *Soil Survey of Clayton County, Iowa.* Washington, 1925.

Birney, Hoffman. *Vigilante.* New York, 1929.

Bourke, John G. *On the Border with Crook.* New York, 1902.

Bradley, Lieutenant James H. "Journal." (See *Contributions to the Historical Society of Montana.* Vols II, III, VIII, and IX.)

Brininstool, E. A. *Crazy Horse.* Los Angeles, 1949.
————. *A Trooper with Custer.* Columbus, 1925.

Bronson, Edgar Beecher. *Cowboy Life on the Western Plains.* New York, n.d.

Bruce, Robert. *The Fighting Norths and Pawnee Scouts.* Lincoln, 1932.

Brummitt, Stella W. *Brother Van.* New York, 1919.

Burdick, Usher L. *Life and Exploits of John Goodall. The McKenzie County Farmer.* Watford City, 1931.

Burt, Struthers. *Powder River, Let'er Buck.* New York, 1938.

Byrne, P. E. *Soldiers of the Plains.* New York, 1926.

Chittenden, Hiram Martin. *The American Fur*

Trade of the Far West. 3 vols. New York, 1902.

———. *History of Early Steamboat Navigation on the Missouri.* 2 vols. New York, 1903.

Chittenden, Hiram Martin, and Richardson, Alfred Talbot. *Life, Letters and Travels of Father Pierre-Jean De Smet, S.J. 1801–1873.* 4 vols. New York, 1905.

Clark, Badger. *Sun and Saddle Leather.* Boston, 1922.

Clark, William Philo. *Indian Sign Language.* Philadelphia, 1885.

Clay, John. *My Life on the Range.* Chicago, 1924.

Cody, William F. *Life and Adventures of Buffalo Bill.* Chicago, 1917.

Cook, James H. *Fifty Years on the Old Frontier.* New Haven, 1925.

Cook, John R. *The Border and the Buffalo.* Topeka, 1905.

Coues, Elliott (ed.). *History of the Expedition Under the Command of Lewis and Clark.* 4 vols. New York, 1893.

Crawford, Lewis F. *Rekindling Campfires.* Bismarck, 1926.

Custer, Elizabeth. *Boots and Saddles.* New York, n.d.

De Barthe, Joe. *Life and Adventures of Frank Grouard.* Buffalo, n.d.

Dick, Everett. *Vanguards of the Frontier.* New York, 1941.

Dimsdale, Thomas J. *The Vigilantes of Montana.* Virginia City, 1921.

Dixon, Olive K. *Life of "Billy" Dixon.* Dallas, 1927.

Dodge, Theodore Ayrault. *Riders of Many Lands.* New York, 1894.

Fee, Chester Anders. *Chief Joseph.* New York, 1936.

Finerty, John F. *Warpath and Bivouac.* Chicago, 1890.

Fougers, Katherine G. *With Custer's Cavalry.* Caldwell, 1942.

Freeman, Lewis R. *Down the Yellowstone.* New York, 1922.

Garretson, Martin S. *The American Bison.* New York, 1938.

Godfrey, Edward S. *General George A. Custer and the Battle of the Little Big Horn.* New York, 1908. Reprint from *Century Magazine.*

Goplen, Arnold O. *The Career of the Marquis De Mores in the Badlands of North Dakota.* Reprint from *North Dakota History,* Vol. XIII, Nos. 1 and 2 (January–April, 1946).

Gordon, Sam. *Recollections of Old Milestown.* Miles City, 1918.

Graham, W. A. *The Story of the Little Big Horn.* New York, 1926.

Grinnell, George Bird. *Beyond the Old Frontier.* New York, 1928.

———. *The Cheyenne Indians.* 2 vols. New Haven, 1923.

———. *The Fighting Cheyennes.* New York, 1915.

———. *Two Great Scouts and Their Pawnee Battalion.* Cleveland, 1928.

———. *The Story of the Indian.* New York, 1937.

Hanson, Joseph Mills. *The Conquest of the Missouri.* Chicago, 1909.

Hodge, Frederick Webb (ed.). *Handbook of American Indians.* 2 vols. From *Bureau of American Ethnology Bulletin 30.* Washington, 1907.

Holman, Albert M., and Marks, Constant R. *Pioneering in the Northwest.* Sioux City, 1924.

Hornaday, William T. "The Extermination of the American Bison." In *Miscellaneous Documents of the House of Representatives,* Vol. 18, Part 2, Washington, 1889.

Hyde, George E. *Red Cloud's Folk.* Norman, 1937.

Jackson, Clarence S. *Picture Maker of the Old West, William Henry Jackson.* New York, 1947.

Jackson, William Henry. *Time Exposure.* New York, 1940.

Kelly, Luther S. *"Yellowstone" Kelly.* New Haven, 1926.

King, Charles. *Campaigning with Crook and Stories of Army Life.* New York, 1890.

Kuhlman, Charles. *Legend Into History.* Harrisburg, 1952.

Lang, Lincoln A. *Ranching with Roosevelt.* Philadelphia, 1926.

Langford, Nathaniel Pitt. *Vigilante Days and Ways.* Chicago, 1923.

Larpenteur, Charles. *Forty Years a Fur Trader on the Upper Missouri.* 2 vols. New York, 1898.

Linderman, Frank Bird. *Bunch-Grass and Blue-Joint.* New York, 1921.

Lowie, Robert H. *The Crow Indians.* New York, 1935.

Luce, Edward S. *Keogh, Comanche and Custer.* 1939.

Mahan, Bruce E. *Old Fort Crawford and the Frontier.* Iowa City, 1926.

McLaughlin, James. *My Friend the Indian.* Boston, 1910.

McWhorter, Lucullus Virgil. *Yellow Wolf: His Own Story.* Caldwell, 1940.

Marcy, R. B. *Thirty Years of Army Life on the Border.* New York, 1866.

Marquis, Thomas B. *Memoirs of a White Crow Indian.* New York, 1928.

———. *A Warrior Who Fought Custer.* Minneapolis, 1931.

Meredith, Grace E. *Girl Captives of the Cheyennes.* Los Angeles, 1927.

Miles, Nelson A. *Personal Recollections and Observations of General Nelson A. Miles.* Chicago, 1897.

(Montana). *Contributions to the Historical Society of Montana*. Vols. I–X. Helena, 1876–1940.

Mooney, James. "The Ghost Dance Religion and the Sioux Outbreak of 1890." In *Fourteenth Annual Report of the Bureau of Ethnology*, Part 2. Washington, 1896.

(North Dakota). *Collections of the State Historical Society*. Vol. V. Grand Forks, 1923, Vol. VII, 1925.

(Northern Pacific Railway) *Wonderland*. St. Paul, 1905.

Raine, William MacLeod, and Barnes, Will C. *Cattle*. Garden City, 1930.

Remington, Frederic. *Pony Tracks*. New York, n.d.

Ritch, Johnny. *Horse Feathers*. Helena, 1940.

Rollins, Philip Ashton. *The Cowboy*. New York, 1924.

Rollinson, John K. *Pony Trails in Wyoming*. Caldwell, 1946.

Roosevelt, Theodore. *Hunting Trips of a Ranchman*. New York, n.d.

———. *Ranch Life and Hunting Trail*. New York, 1920.

———. *The Wilderness Hunter*. 2 vols. New York, 1907.

Russell, Charles M. *Good Medicine*. Garden City, 1930.

———. *Trails Plowed Under*. Garden City, 1927.

Russell, Charles M., and Stuart, Granville. *Studies of Western Life*. Spokane, n.d.

Russell, Charles M. (illustrator). *Back-Trailing on the Old Frontier*. Great Falls, 1922.

Sabin, Edwin L. *Kit Carson Days*. Chicago, 1914.

Schmitt, Martin F. *General Crook. His Autobiography*. Norman, 1946.

Shields, George O. *Rustlings in the Rockies*. Chicago, 1883.

Spring, Agnes Wright. *The Cheyenne and Black Hills Stage and Express Routes*, Glendale, 1949.

Strayhorn, Carrie Adell. *Fifteen Thousand Miles by Stage*. New York, 1915.

Stuart, Granville. *Forty Years on the Frontier*. 2 vols. Cleveland, 1925.

Tabeau, P. A. *Tabeau's Narrative of Loisel's Expedition to the Upper Missouri*. Norman, 1939.

Taft, Robert. *Photography and the American Scene*. New York, 1938.

Taylor, Joseph Henry. *Kaleidoscopic Lives*. Washburn, 1902.

———. *Sketches of Frontier and Indian Life*. Bismarck, 1887.

Toponce, Alexander. *Reminiscences of Alexander Toponce*. Salt Lake City, 1923.

Topping, E. S. *The Chronicles of the Yellowstone*. St. Paul, 1883.

(U. S. Army). *The Medal of Honor of the United States Army*. Washington, 1948.

———. *The Official Record of the Reno Court of Inquiry* (Colonel W. A. Graham, ed.). Pacific Palisades, 1951.

Van de Water, Frederic F. *Glory Hunter*. Indianapolis, 1934.

Vaughn, Robert. *Then and Now: or Thirty-Six Years in the Rockies*. Minneapolis, 1900.

Vestal, Stanley. *The Missouri*. New York, 1945.

———. *New Sources of Indian History*. Norman, 1934.

———. *Sitting Bull*. Boston, 1932.

———. *Warpath*. Boston, 1934.

Wellman, Paul I. *Death on the Prairie*. New York, 1934.

Wheeler, Homer W. *Buffalo Days*. Indianapolis, 1925.

———. *The Frontier Trail*. Los Angeles, 1923.

Wheeler, Olin D. *The Trail of Lewis and Clark, 1804–1904*. 2 vols. New York, 1926.

Wissler, Clark. *Indian Cavalcade*. New York, 1938.

ACKNOWLEDGMENTS

For the writer, this book started 40 years ago when, as a boy, he read with breathless interest the first of James Willard Schultz's incomparable stories in *The Youth's Companion*. Since that time he has hoarded like a pack rat every bit of information he could find about everyday life on the frontier. For the co-author, this volume had its inception when he read in *Rustlings in the Rockies*, George Shields' accounts of his hunting trips in Montana. Years later, on a cold April day in 1906, he arrived in Miles City as a location engineer for the Chicago, Milwaukee, and Saint Paul Railroad, then building lines in Montana. That evening in a drugstore he noted some postcards with pictures identical to some of the illustrations in Shields' book. He promptly hied himself to the Huffman residence where the photographer entertained him royally with stories of the frontier. The pictures fascinated him, as did one of Huffman's daughters, and he returned again and again to absorb like a sponge the details about the photographs—and to acquire for himself a wife. Twenty years ago the authors met, and the bond which cemented the friendship formed at that time was, again, a mutual interest in these splendid pictures.

Although the authors started with a substantial stock of information, it immediately became evident that extensive research was necessary. The magnitude and difficulty of that task, however, only became apparent when the manuscript was completed and the pile of correspondence and notes was appraised. The writers are grateful for this opportunity to express their appreciation for the assistance others have provided.

It would have been impossible to compile the material for this book without the kind coöperation of Ruth Huffman Scott of Miles City, Montana, who owns the Huffman negatives.* Bessie Huffman Felton provided the file of her father's letters and also supplied many details about various individuals and events of the times. Thanks are likewise due to Vernon L. Scott who, in addition to supplying helpful information, handled details pertaining to the reproduction of prints from the negatives.

The Indian photographs posed the most difficult task as notes on many of the portraits were either scanty or missing completely, and a few were found to

* With very few exceptions, the photographs reproduced in this volume were new prints from these old glass plates. Photographs from these negatives are still available to collectors.

be in error. Suitable printed records being almost nonexistent, a check had to be made with old Indians who might have known the persons in question. Among the Northern Cheyennes, Rufus Wallowing and Reverend Milton Whiteman, both of Lame Deer, Montana, were extremely helpful in checking and securing checks on identities, supplying names, and providing supplementary data. Robert Yellowtail of Lodge Grass, Montana, and Gordon I. Powers of Crow Agency, Montana, were equally cooperative in supplying information involving Crow Indians. Others who assisted in this problem were Ben Chief, Pine Ridge, South Dakota; Frank B. Farr, Mrs. Rudolphe Petter, and John S. Timber, all of Lame Deer, Montana; and Judge Frank Zahn, Fort Yates, North Dakota. Reverend S. Winterroth of Ashland, Montana, supplied information concerning the Saint Labre Indian Mission.

Among those who have been particularly helpful in supplying information of various sorts are William C. Almquist of Miles City, Montana; Badger Clark of Custer, South Dakota; Margaret Daily of Billings, Montana; Lee M. Ford of Great Falls, Montana; Louis F. Grill of Miles City, Montana; Sam Hotchkiss of Stacey, Montana; Wallis Huidekoper of Big Timber, Montana; William Lakin of Miles City, Montana; Alvin C. Leighton of Central Point, Oregon; Historical Society of Montana, Helena, Montana—with a special bow to Anne McDonnell, assistant librarian, for her fine service; Harry F. Schlosser of Miles City, Montana; William Stone of Miles City, Montana; Colville and Zola Terrett of Billings, Montana; Julian Terrett of Brandenburg, Montana; R. Price Terrett of Paso Robles, California; John Wilson of Lewistown, Montana; Ben Woodcock of Miles City, Montana; and Major General James Ulio, USA, Retired, of Washington, D. C.

In addition to those who supplied data, there have been others who helped in various ways. Western artists Harold Bugbee and Ross Santee "believed in" the project from the start and lent their support in several ways. Professor Walter Campbell (Stanley Vestal) of the University of Oklahoma advised on the plans for the manuscript and, later, went over the entire collection of prints with the writer and supplied many helpful comments from his storehouse of knowledge pertaining to the frontier. Dr. Raymond Estep of Montgomery, Alabama, read the manuscript with meticulous care and offered many valuable criticisms both general and specific. Charles B. Dull of Bellevue, Nebraska, also read the manuscript and supplied many helpful suggestions. Jack Coffrin of Miles City, Montana, toiled patiently over the old negatives to make the best possible prints: and General Alfred F. Kalberer, USAF, was helpful in several ways.

Others who lent a helping hand are Bessie Haynes Arnold of Honolulu, Hawaii; S. B. Bean of Savage, Montana; Bernard Blum of the Engineering Department of the Northern Pacific Railroad, Saint Paul, Minnesota; A. Bond of Brockway, Montana; Barnum Brown of the American Museum of Natural History, New York, New York; M. P. Browne of Lambert, Montana; Harry R. Chamberlain of Ekalaka, Montana; Charles R. Cutts of Billings, Montana; M. H. Duffy of Paxton, Montana; Patty Alderson Eaton of Wolf, Wyoming; W. R. Felton, Jr. of Sioux City, Iowa; Edith H. Franz of the New York Zoological Park, New York, New York; J. E. Haynes of Bozeman, Montana; V. G. Hooker of Glendive, Montana; Claude Ivers of Omaha, Nebraska; J. H. Lemmon of Lemmon, South Dakota; Mrs. J. Locke of the British Embassy, Washington,

D. C.; Whitman Longley of Forsyth, Montana; Dr. J. D. Lutton of Sioux City, Iowa; Jack Milburn of Grass Range, Montana; Jessie L. Mullin of Lame Deer, Montana; Ruby Niehaus of Waukon, Iowa; David Pease of Crow Agency, Montana; Anna Polk of Miles City, Montana; J. K. Ralston of Billings, Montana; L. F. Sheffy of the Panhandle-Plains Historical Society, Canyon, Texas; Ethel Cato Tarbutton of Kyle, Texas; I. E. Thomas of Terry, Montana; Jean Todd of the Parmly Billings Memorial Library, Billings, Montana; and Lillian Wheat of Mill Iron, Montana.

The following authors, authors' agents, and publishers have kindly given their permission to use material from:

"He Captured the Vanishing West Before It Vanished" by Neil M. Clark. Copyright, 1927, by American Magazine. Reprinted by permission of the author and American Magazine.

Horse Feathers by Johnny Ritch. Copyright, 1940, by John B. Ritch. Reprinted by permission of Minnie R. Ritch.

A Warrior Who Fought Custer by Thomas B. Marquis. Copyright, 1931, by Midwest Company. Reprinted by permission of Minnie-Ellen Marquis Hastings.

Good Medicine by Charles M. Russell. Copyright, 1929, by Nancy C. Russell. Reprinted by permission of Estate of Nancy C. Russell.

My Life on the Range by John Clay. Copyright, 1924, by John Clay. Reprinted by permission of John Clay, Jr.

The Memoirs of the Late Frank D. Baldwin, Major General, U.S.A. by Alice Blackwood Baldwin. Copyright, 1929, by Wetzel Publishing Company, Los Angeles, California. Reprinted by permission of the publishers.

Forty Years on the Frontier by Granville Stuart. Copyright, 1925, by The Arthur H. Clark Company. Reprinted by permission of the publishers.

Sun and Saddle Leather by Badger Clark. Copyright, 1917, by Richard G. Badger. Copyright, 1942, by Chapman and Grimes, Inc. Reprinted by permission of the publishers.

A Bride Goes West by Nannie T. Alderson and Helena Huntington Smith; Farrar and Rinehart, Inc.

We Pointed Them North by E. C. Abbott and Helena Huntington Smith; Farrar and Rinehart, Inc.

Powder River by Struthers Burt; Farrar and Rinehart, Inc.

Yellowstone Kelly by Luther S. Kelly; Yale University Press.

Trails Plowed Under by Charles M. Russell; Doubleday, Page and Company.

Bunch-Grass and Blue Joint by Frank B. Linderman; Charles Scribner's Sons.

Hunting Trips of a Ranchman by Theodore Roosevelt; Charles Scribner's Sons.

Last, but not least, thanks are due to the writer's wife and children who, for months on end, patiently allowed him to pound his noisy typewriter in the living room—a procedure which more often than not extended into the small hours of the morning. Had this not been a work of love, he probably would not have been allowed to disrupt the family life for such an extended period.

Mark H. Brown

Alta, Iowa
September, 1955

INDEX

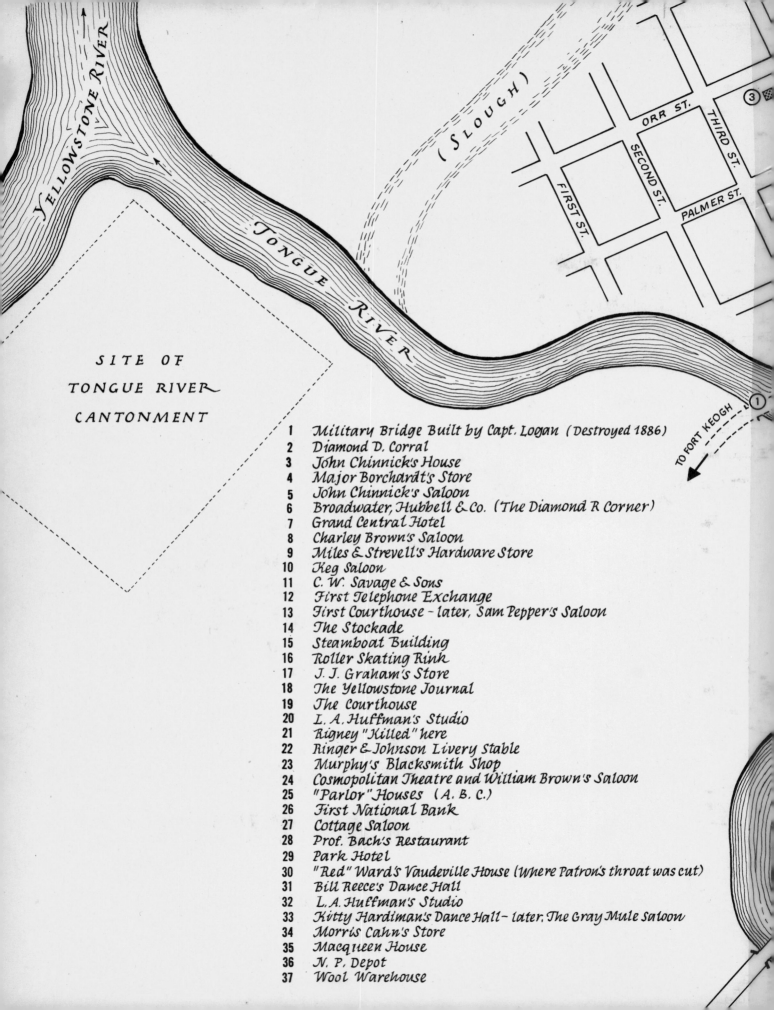

YELLOWSTONE RIVER

(SLOUGH)

TONGUE RIVER

ORR ST.

SECOND ST.

FIRST ST.

THIRD ST.

PALMER ST.

③

①

SITE OF
TONGUE RIVER
CANTONMENT

TO FORT KEOGH

1   Military Bridge Built by Capt. Logan (Destroyed 1886)
2   Diamond D. Corral
3   John Chinnick's House
4   Major Borchardt's Store
5   John Chinnick's Saloon
6   Broadwater, Hubbell & Co. (The Diamond R Corner)
7   Grand Central Hotel
8   Charley Brown's Saloon
9   Miles & Strevell's Hardware Store
10   Keg Saloon
11   C. W. Savage & Sons
12   First Telephone Exchange
13   First Courthouse - later, Sam Pepper's Saloon
14   The Stockade
15   Steamboat Building
16   Roller Skating Rink
17   J. J. Graham's Store
18   The Yellowstone Journal
19   The Courthouse
20   L. A. Huffman's Studio
21   Rigney "Killed" here
22   Ringer & Johnson Livery Stable
23   Murphy's Blacksmith Shop
24   Cosmopolitan Theatre and William Brown's Saloon
25   "Parlor" Houses (A. B. C.)
26   First National Bank
27   Cottage Saloon
28   Prof. Bach's Restaurant
29   Park Hotel
30   "Red" Ward's Vaudeville House (Where Patron's throat was cut)
31   Bill Reece's Dance Hall
32   L. A. Huffman's Studio
33   Kitty Hardiman's Dance Hall - later, The Gray Mule Saloon
34   Morris Cahn's Store
35   Macqueen House
36   N. P. Depot
37   Wool Warehouse